Captive Insurance for Medical Professionals and Hospitals

Inga Ivsan,
J.D. *cum laude*, LL.M. (Estate Planning)

Ivsan Law Press
Weston, Florida

CONTENTS

ABOUT THE AUTHOR

INGA IVSAN, J.D. *cum laude*, LL.M. (Estate Planning)

Inga Ivsan is a member of the Board of Managers of the Lighthouse Group of companies, a Swiss-headquartered group of trust, insurance, and financial services companies. For many years, Ms. Ivsan was based with Lighthouse in Switzerland to provide expert advice and support to captive insurance space clients around the globe. In the United States, Ms. Ivsan is currently responsible for supervising administrative support services for Lighthouse Captive Management.

Ms. Ivsan obtained a combined Juris Doctor *cum laude* and Master of Laws in Estate Planning from the University of Miami School of Law, where she was the recipient of the prestigious Heckerling Scholarship. She clerked at the nationally-recognized law firm of Black, Srebnick, Kornspan & Stumpf, P.A., working alongside famed criminal attorney Roy Black.

A frequent writer on matters concerning asset protection, captive insurance, and wealth management planning, Ms. Ivsan's research and analysis on insurance taxation law contributed toward the landmark U.S. Tax Court decision recognizing insurance for complex financial products in R.V.I. Guaranty Co. Ltd. v. Commissioner. Among Ms. Ivsan's published articles are "Emerging Challenges in Asset Protection Planning," 2 U. Miami Bus. L. Rev. (2015), and "The Judge is Supposed to be an Independent Arbiter; Allowing Boundless Judicial Discretion

Violates the Sixth Amendment Under Hurst v. Florida," U. Miami L. Rev. Insights (2016).

In 2015, Ms. Ivsan served on a committee of leading attorneys responsible for drafting the 2015 amendments to the Nevis International Exempt Trust Ordinance, regarded as one of the most formidable examples of asset protection trust legislation anywhere in the world. She also assisted with revisions to LLC legislation in Nevis, and she has consulted on changes to LLC laws in the State of Wyoming and the Cayman Islands.

ACKNOWLEDGEMENTS

I wish to acknowledge the support and contributions of several individuals, without whom this book would not be possible.

Reda Noreike and Telbert Glasgow are the directors of Lighthouse Captive Management, headquartered in the Caribbean island of Nevis and with service offices in Switzerland and Florida. Reda and Telbert have provided fantastic support, guiding me in my research and offering their insight into the day-to-day operations of a captive insurance company.

Martin Eveleigh is the past chairman of the North Carolina Captive Insurance Association. Martin been helpful in familiarizing me with the State of North Carolina as a friendly jurisdiction in which to operate a licensed captive insurance carrier. Under Martin's leadership, the NCCIA took a proactive role in testimony before Congress concerning the benefits of § 831(b) microcaptives. I have no doubt that Congress would not have extended the exemption amount under § 831(b) without the guidance of the NCCIA.

Finally, my husband, John, is a tax lawyer and captive insurance expert who trained under one of the first captive insurance lawyers to have worked with Fred Reiss, the founding father of captive insurance. Since that time, John has educated an entire generation of lawyers in captive insurance, including yours truly. John's approach to training – looking to source materials on which much IRS guidance is based – is what inspired me to take on the IRS distinction between "insurance risks" and "investment risks." The analytical approach which I developed was reviewed and ultimately adopted by the U.S. Tax Court in <u>RVI Guaranty Co. Ltd. v. Commissioner</u>, 145 T.C. No. 9 (2015), and is now the governing legal principle on insuring investment risks.

FOREWORD: THE MEDICAL CAPTIVE REVOLUTION

REDA NOREIKE

DIRECTOR, LIGHTHOUSE CAPTIVE MANAGEMENT LTD.

Today's physician lives in a golden age for risk mitigation. Yet, many doctors are completely unaware of the benefits of captive insurance.

Too often, doctors feel constrained by a false set of choices: Either to pay exorbitant premiums for malpractice coverage (particularly in high risk fields such as obstetrics) or to "go bare" and not have any insurance whatsoever. Neither choice is a perfect solution.

Traditional insurance is overpriced and rewards the bad doctor at the expense of the good doctor. Most policies are riddled with exclusions, leaving doctors to question whether they have the coverage that they need. Even if a doctor is covered for professional liability, his medical practice is left exposed to significant uninsured risks.

Will traditional insurance cover the loss in income when the nurse practitioner is injured and cannot work for three months? Who will pay to extricate the medical practice from a lawsuit if hackers tap into the credit card processing terminal at the front desk? In most cases, traditional insurance is no narrowly tailored as to exclude coverage in all but the most egregious cases, and then coverage is limited to out-of-pocket expenses. Meanwhile, the loss of patients and the damage to your reputation go uncovered.

On the other hand, going without insurance is really not a solution and is the worst possible choice a physician could make for his business and his family, much less his patient. The uninsured doctor pays a higher effective tax rate by self-insuring. Moreover, all fifty states in the USA have laws allowing patients to pursue the assets of the doctor and his family members if an uninsured claim goes unpaid. Spouses and children can find themselves liable to court judgments, regardless of their level of knowledge or intent.

There is a better way to protect physicians, secure affordable coverage, and protect family wealth: Captive insurance. By owning your own captive insurance company, you decide the level of protection you want for your business. Tailoring a captive insurance program to the specific needs of your business means that you get to decide what is covered and by how much, helping you save on the cost of traditional malpractice insurance.

Most importantly, insuring through a captive enables you to profit from your own efforts to control your liabilities. Instead of seeing insurance premiums "wasted" year after year, the careful physician is rewarded with a handsome stream of underwriting profits. Tax incentives for small captives may boost the value of those underwriting profits. Best of all, gaining access to this heretofore untapped revenue stream enables you to plan with your family for a brighter financial future in an asset-protective environment.

I am pleased to have worked with Inga Ivsan on captive insurance planning for many years now. I laud Ms. Ivsan for her valuable efforts to better educate clients on the merits of captive insurance planning. Engaging in a captive insurance plan is a serious commitment of time and financial resources. Ms. Ivsan has carefully explained the extent of that commitment in this book. I therefore encourage you to read this book first before making any decision. If you are like any of our other clients, this book will introduce you to a whole new universe of exciting planning opportunities.

INTRODUCTION

Back when I first started working with clients in captive insurance, there was no single reference book that any lawyer could recommend to his client. That did not seem right to me; something had to change.

Now, with the benefit of hindsight, I have the distinct opportunity to share the knowledge and wisdom I have gained from representing clients in captive insurance. In sitting down to write this book, I determined that I wanted something legible and comprehensible to the medical professional with little to no exposure to complex legal subjects. Yet, I knew that the book would need to have enough information so as to provide a clear picture for the reader.

Some readers may find portions of these materials to be difficult to digest, while other readers will undoubtedly crave to learn more than can be compressed into the pages of this book. Whatever your appetite may be, please take your time to read and enjoy the book. If you still have questions after perusing these pages, please give me a call. I welcome your questions.

-Inga Ivsan, J.D. *cum laude*, LL.M. (Estate Planning)

CHAPTER 1.

WHAT IS "CAPTIVE INSURANCE"?

Introduction

Every year, throughout the United States, medical professionals suffer losses in their businesses that are not covered by insurance. An interruption in business due to an outside cause such as a hurricane or significant regulatory change can inflict costly damage to your practice. Just as well, you may stand to lose substantial revenue due to malfunctioning equipment or an action taken by a government agency against your practice. Doctors everywhere have to worry about the ever-increasing costs of litigation defense arising from the explosion of tort litigation and runaway juries handing out verdicts in malpractice cases as if money grows on trees.

Fortunately, there is insurance available to cover most of these cases. Unfortunately, the cost of insurance can be very expensive or practically unattainable for doctors in many states. Even those who can afford the insurance often find that it does not protect them or their business from many common forms of business losses.

Some doctors choose to combat the high cost of liability insurance by reducing coverage or "going bare" and not purchasing any insurance at all. By doing so, these physicians are knowingly taking on increased risk to their financial well-being.

Perhaps they believe that they will not be sued, and that they are very good at managing their liabilities.

The Secret Behind Insurance Company Profits

Surprisingly enough, a growing trend amongst physicians is to simply chose not to insure themselves. As absurd as that may seem to some of us, there is some method to this madness. Insurance statistics prove this out: Approximately 80% of all insurance claims are made by fewer than 20% of all insureds. In other words, most doctors never have a claim, but they are paying for the claims of others by purchasing insurance.

Those doctors who are not buying insurance have, in many cases, simply figured out the dirty little secret of insurance. If everything goes well, and there is no claim at the end of the year, the entire premium paid to the insurance company for that year becomes pure profit for the insurance company. Of course, the insurance company will incur a number of losses from other doctors, but the insurance company is not in this game to provide a public service; it is here to make a profit.

By offering liability insurance to doctors, the insurance company is publicly advertising that it thinks it can make a profit on such insurance. This is because, on the whole, the majority of doctors will not have any claims, and the insurance company actuaries have figured this out.

Turning Insurance Company Profits to Your Advantage

When you buy liability insurance from the insurance company, the insurance company is making an investment in *you*. The insurance company is betting its own money that you will not have a claim, and that those valuable premium dollars you paid to buy the policy will become pure profit for the insurance company.

In this book, we will cover an increasingly popular planning solution that allows you to capture these insurance profits for yourself. By setting up and using your very own captive insurance company, you can turn insurance company profits to your advantage.

In order to capture these profits for yourself, you should best understand how likely it is that you will incur a loss in your own business. Are you the type of physician who carefully manages his risk exposure and liabilities? If you can answer "yes" to this question, then captive insurance may allow you to capture those insurance company profits for yourself.

"Captive Insurance" Defined

Captive insurance is insurance that your purchase for your business from an insurance company that you own. The term "captive" refers to the fact that you directly or indirectly own and control the insurance company. If the captive insurance company makes a profit, it is your profit.

By utilizing a captive insurance company, you make an investment in yourself and your business. You bet your own money that, hopefully, you will not incur a loss in your business. In return, the premium dollars that your business pays to your very own captive insurance company become profits for you and your captive.

How Captive Insurance Works

Captive insurance is a simple concept. Working with a lawyer experienced in captive insurance and a captive management services provider, you incorporate your very own insurance company. We refer to this insurance company as a "captive" because it is owned and controlled by you. Also, unlike insurance companies that sell insurance to the general public, your captive only sells insurance to you and businesses that are affiliated with you.

Your business pays premiums to your captive in return for insurance covering the potential liabilities and risks of your business. If all goes well, and there are no claims at the end of the year, your captive gets to recognize those premiums as pure profit.

In the next few chapters, I will discuss how this works in detail. I will also explain what happens when you actually incur a loss in your business and seek reimbursement from your captive.

Why Should I Care About Captive Insurance?

I titled this book "Captive Insurance for Medical Professionals and Hospitals" to reflect the fact that a growing number of doctors throughout the United States are implementing captive insurance as an integral part of their business and estate plans. As more and more doctors are getting burned by the high cost of liability insurance, and are seeing premium dollars wasted when no claims are made, an increasing percentage of these same doctors are choosing to instead insure themselves through their own captives, keeping those profits for themselves.

The focus of the next chapter is on the benefits to your business from captive insurance. In addition to learning how your very own captive insurance company enables you to capture insurance premium dollars as profits, I will also walk you through the many ways your own captive insurance company can help you to better protect your business.

It is extremely important to note that the insurance we are discussing is real insurance. Moreover, the type of company that we refer to as a "captive" insurance company is, in fact, a licensed insurance company owned by you (and, hence, "captive"). Your captive is licensed, regulated, managed, and maintained just like any other insurance company out there. Probably the only difference between your captive and every other insurance company out there is this: Since you are the shareholder, you profit from the captive's performance.

The benefits gleaned from captive insurance begin and end with the availability of completely customized insurance coverage for your business. I will outline many common forms of business risk that could catastrophically harm your business but for which, if you are like most doctors, you probably have no current insurance. Together, we will consider how running your very own captive insurance company allows you to obtain comprehensive insurance coverage protecting your business against these types of risks.

Later in this book, I will show you how captive insurance

also helps protect your family. Every year, thousands of doctors are named as defendants in litigation, ranging from professional liability and malpractice claims to personal tort lawsuits, divorce proceedings, and business disputes.

If you are like most doctors, the money you earn in your business goes into a bank or brokerage account titled in your own name, or in the name of a conventional trust set up by a neighborhood estate planning lawyer. Unfortunately, as many doctors can painfully attest, that money is unprotected and can be taken from you by plaintiffs' lawyers.

If your money instead flows into a captive insurance company, you stand a better chance of protecting your wealth. *I will introduce you to a cutting edge technique, developed by some of the best known asset protection attorneys in the United States, that uses your own captive insurance company to shield your wealth from unanticipated creditors and unwanted litigation.*

Throughout this book, we will also touch on some of the important financial and tax aspects of captive insurance. Tax benefits do not, in and of themselves, justify the use of captive insurance. Nevertheless, a properly structured and valid captive insurance arrangement offers some useful tax benefits, including the ability to exempt up to $1.2 million of business income from federal income tax every year.

Captive insurance, however, is not a tax panacea. The tax benefits must be weighed against the tax cost of liquidating the captive or taking out periodic dividends. Depending on your time horizon, a captive insurance plan may not offer tax benefits. However, with careful planning, one can accumulate significant tax-mitigated wealth through the use of a captive insurance company.

About Our Case Studies

I wrote this book specifically at the request of many of my clients who are medical professionals. Many of my clients are surprised to see a busy lawyer taking his time to write a book tailored to their specific needs.

I see this as a valuable opportunity to draw from client experiences and help simplify what may at first be considered a complex subject. I have sifted through a number of files files and spoken with clients and colleagues to develop a representative set of typical cases. I have also worked with underwriters and actuaries in the field to elicit their insight and gain their contributions to a comprehensive set of case studies that are contained in the following chapters.

Many of my own clients have offered their own suggestions. As you will probably gather from reading these case studies, many clients are so pleased with the results of their captive insurance plan that they frequently enlist their colleagues and business partners to partake in captive insurance as well.

My objective here is to demonstrate, in a manner that is easy to understand, that captive insurance offers tremendously valuable benefits to just about any medical professional and his or her practice. There is a revolution going on in the medical field using captive insurance, and I intend to show you how you can prosper from it.

If You Have Questions and Want More Information

I wrote this book purposefully as a non-technical explanation of captive insurance for physicians. Some readers will have more curiosity than others about certain technical aspects of captive insurance: Insurance laws and regulations, tax rules, and policy design, just to name a few. If, after reading this book you still have questions, please give me a call and allow me the opportunity to provide you the answers you seek.

CHAPTER 2.

PROTECTING YOUR BUSINESS WITH CAPTIVE INSURANCE

Introduction

Dr. Michael Weiss[1] is a successful dental surgeon in Southern California. His story is a typical model of success for a small surgical practice. After completing his studies in 1982, Michael went to work for a practice consisting of three experienced surgeons working out of a single location in a suburban Orange County location. Michael paid his dues, worked long hours, and gained enough experience to know that he was a very good dental surgeon but that he would never make as much money working for others as he would if he worked for himself.

In the early 1990s, Michael struck out on his own and opened his own practice. In the beginning, he had a skeletal staff to keep a lid on overhead costs, and he did not take a salary out of the practice for the first year of his business. Moreover, he took a gamble on a new location in a part of Orange County that was sparsely populated and had no dental surgeons in the immediate vicinity.

By the mid-2000s, Michael's business had proven to be a clear success. He had four full-time nurse practitioners working under his tutelage, and his billings on each practitioner ran over $1 million per year. In a good year, his business would gross almost $6 million.

A few years ago, Michael decided that he needed to begin preparing his business to accommodate another dental surgeon. Michael was not ready to take on a business partner just yet, so he hired a recent graduate, David, and began training him in the business. Shortly after hiring David, Michael determined that David would be a viable successor: He has a good work ethic and functions well as a member of a much larger team of working professionals.

With determination and a bit of luck, Michael hopes to be able to retire soon. In order for his plan to succeed, however, he needs to be able to rely on his surgeon employee and his nurse practitioners to generate revenue and preserve the going-concern value of the business.

Fortunately or unfortunately, most of Michael's net worth is tied up in his business: A series of real estate investments with some local business partners did not go so well when the real estate meltdown hit Southern California in late 2007. While the partnership continues to experience positive cash flow, the partners do not expect to be able to sell any of their properties without incurring substantial losses. Therefore, Michael needs to be able to rely on his medical practice to support his retirement lifestyle.

In analyzing the business insurance needs of Dr. Weiss, we should consider a number of factors:

- What financial risks does the business face in its daily activities?

- What forms of insurance are available to protect against those risks?

- Which types of insurance may be better suited to purchasing through a captive rather than through a retail insurance company?

What are the real financial risks of a medical practice?
Malpractice Liability

Every medical professional faces the risk of malpractice liability in his or her business. How one deals with malpractice liability varies from state to state, hospital to hospital, and individual to individual. Some states, such as Colorado, Massachusetts, and Pennsylvania mandate that a doctor carry malpractice insurance of a minimum amount. Hospitals in many states, Florida being one of them, require a physician to have a minimum amount of malpractice liability insurance in order to be able to treat patients in their facility.

Each year, malpractice insurance premiums go up, and there is no end in sight to the long-term trend of increasing premiums. Some doctors have responded to this alarming trend by electing to not carry malpractice liability insurance, also referred to as "going bare." Later on in this discussion, I will explain to you why I think that going bare is a really bad decision from many different viewpoints: Financially, professionally, and personally.

Legal Expenses

Related to malpractice liability insurance is a category of business expense that I will call "legal expenses." I chose to treat this as a separate category because I want to focus on legal expenses that arise in business generally, and not just medical malpractice litigation.

If you are sued for malpractice, most likely your malpractice insurance carrier will assign a lawyer to help defend against the claim. You may also have your own private attorney defending you against malpractice liability claims; sometimes your lawyer may even sue the insurance company, such as when the insurance company refuses to honor a claim. Malpractice insurance may sometimes cover these legal expenses, but sometimes these policies do not.

If someone slips and falls in the lobby of your office building, your property and casualty insurance may provide coverage. Just as with malpractice liability, the insurance carrier may assign a lawyer to the case, and sometimes you may hire your own attorney just to ensure that your interests are adequately protected. Again, just like with malpractice insurance, property and casualty insurance may or may not reimburse you for your legal expenses.

Most business owners incur legal expenses in one form or another when dealing with employees who leave or are terminated. The issue becomes particularly acute with medical practices, when sometimes a handful of physicians leave one practice in order to form another practice. In the ensuing fallout, you may find yourself confronted with legal bills incurred dealing with aggrieved employees and upset business partners.

Legal expenses may arise if your business is subject to a regulatory action (discussed below), or if your business is made the subject of a tax audit. If you are one of the unlucky few business owners subject to a state or federal tax audit, the expenses of hiring lawyers and accountants to extricate you from an assessment can be significant.

Damage to Property

Equipment costs represent a substantial investment for most physicians. Medical equipment includes not only the latest and greatest laser to conduct precision surgery, but the Windows- and Mac-based computers, servers, and internal systems used to schedule appointments and store patient records electronically. In addition, an increasing number of practices incorporate offsite storage and backup, as well as the technology to restore systems in the event of a catastrophic failure.

In the era of modern medicine, most medical professionals would be unable to conduct their practices without the proper equipment. Some medical equipment costs more than the building used to house the equipment along with the entire medical practice.

With the intersection of computers and medical equipment, we are seeing increasing amounts of patient data and treatment histories electronically recorded. Therefore, a loss of equipment may result in the loss of valuable business and patient data at the same time.

Careful thought needs to be given not only to the forms of tangible and intangible property that can be lost or damaged, but to the type of event that gives rise to the loss. For example, most property and casualty policies do not provide any form of coverage for losses attributable to a flood. Businesses in hurricane-prone areas require specific coverage to protect against hurricane damage.

Loss of Valuable Employees

In Dr. Weiss' practice, his nurse practitioners are individually responsible for over $1 million a year each in patient billings. When I first began working with Michael, I asked him what the loss of a single nurse practitioner would mean to his business. "Catastrophic," he replied. "For me to recruit and train someone to replace any one of my nurses, I would have to start all over again, and meanwhile I would be out $1 million, or at least a significant amount of revenue until a new nurse practitioner could be properly trained to fill her predecessor's shoes."

In fact, a short time after I began working with Dr. Weiss, one of his nurse practitioners became pregnant and had to take a leave of absence from work. Her absence was brief and she returned to the practice a few months later. However, Michael lost out on approximately $80,000 worth of billings each month that she was absent, and he was unable to hire anyone to take up the slack. Many of those billings ended up going to competitors that have moved into his neighborhood.

Regulatory Actions

When I first started working as a lawyer, a colleague of mine had an office that was located a few blocks from a prestigious medical practice operating in conjunction with a leading regional hospital. I remember that all of the lawyers in town scrambled to try and land work with this particular medical practice, as it was one of the largest practices in the region.

Within a year, the practice was gone. It had been completely wiped off the face of the map by a Medicare fraud investigation. I am not a Medicare expert by any stretch of the imagination, but my understanding is that the government did not like how the medical practice was billing Medicare patients for certain procedures.

Perhaps the government felt that these particular doctors were billing Medicare too much. Whatever the reason, we will never know: The mere threat of a fraud investigation was enough to bring down the whole business. The doctors all left, a receiver stepped in, and the business disappeared practically overnight.

I understand that many physicians choose not to accept Medicare patients. However, Medicare is only one government program, and there are dozens of federal and state programs that doctors and their patients frequently participate in. For that matter, accepting any client with health insurance exposes your practice to regulatory risk, and that risk can arise from any number of sources: A patient aggrieved over a medical bill, an insurance adjuster looking to pad his Christmas bonus by making an example out of you, or a terminated employee who seeks to harm your business and your professional reputation by making false allegations.

Other Financial Risks

The preceding paragraphs provide several examples of the types of financial risks that you may encounter in your medical practice from day to day. The foregoing is certainly not intended to be an exhaustive list of all the forms of risk that are out there. Rather, this is a simplification intended to help you consider the leading risk types that can affect the value of your business and the amount of income you can be expected to derive from that business. Furthermore, you may be aware of other categories of financial risks that have not been discussed in the preceding materials.Please keep these risks in mind, both the risks that I have summarized as well as any others that you can think of and which are not mentioned already. We will discuss in the following pages how a captive insurance company helps you to address many of these types of risks.

How does business insurance protect against those risks?

The purpose of business insurance is to shield you and your business from the risks that you encounter in your daily business activities. In fact, all of the sample risks that I outlined above are eligible for coverage under commercial insurance policies that you can purchase in most states. By paying premiums to an insurance company, your business shifts the liabilities associated with the foregoing risks to the insurance company and away from your business.

There's just one problem: At the beginning of this book, we discussed that 20% of business insurance clients are responsible for all of the claims that are made. Another way of saying this is that 80% of business insurance clients never have claims, and yet they still purchase insurance year after year knowing full well that the premiums they pay constitute pure profit for the insurance companies.

Why do businesses pay for insurance when, on the surface, it appears to be a waste of money? Certainly there must be some rational explanation for what appears to be highly irrational behavior. Well, if you ask my client, Dr. Weiss, he will tell you that the only reason he carries retail business insurance is to protect himself and his business from *catastrophic claims.*

In fact, before Michael started up his first captive, when it came to minor things, Michael was more inclined to handle the matter himself and not involve his insurance carrier. For example, if a patient complained about a procedure, Michael figured that it was just easier on everybody if he looked at the patient himself and corrected any problems on his own. Even though Michael was losing valuable time spent attending to a patient complaint, solving the problem on his own meant that he was sparing his insurance company an expense it would otherwise have to pay.

On the other hand, if you were to ask Michael if he would be willing to "go bare" and not carry business insurance, he would dismiss the idea as crazy. His primary worry is a large malpractice claim that could take down his business in the absence of liability insurance coverage. If a patient suffered a traumatic injury arising from a surgery gone wrong, or a slip and fall in the lobby, Michael would expect his retail commercial insurance carrier to step in and pick up the tab.

In summary, the purpose of business insurance is to protect you and your business from many types of financial risks that may arise in the day-to-day pursuit of your professional activities. However, on a practical level, most businesses do not look to their insurance carriers to reimburse them on minor claims. Rather, most insureds – the 80% of businesses that never file claims – treat business insurance as a remedy to be called upon only when a catastrophic claim presents itself. This attitude best explains why it is that so few insured businesses submit claims to their insurance companies, and why insurance is so wildly profitable with respect to the vast majority of business insurance customers who never file claims.

Should I "go bare" and not carry insurance?

Absolutely not!!!

Permit me to explain why it is that "going bare" is such a horrible idea by referring to a news article reported in the Associated Press regarding a doctor in West Palm Beach, Florida, who practices without malpractice liability insurance because of the high cost of coverage.[2] The doctor boasts in the article that he has no assets in his name, everything having been titled in his wife's name.

<u>Problem #1: Fraudulent Transfer Law</u>

Debtor-creditor laws in every state require that you carry sufficient assets or insurance in your name if you are engaged in a business or profession. If you pursue a business activity with insufficient resources to pay your reasonably anticipated creditors (for example, your patients), a court may find that you engaged in a "fraudulent transfer" by titling assets in your spouse's name. The same principle applies if you transfer assets into a trust or make gifts to children or close friends and business partners.

The type of "fraud" referred to here is not fraud in the criminal sense, but civil fraud. If you transfer assets "fraudulently" so as to deny your creditors the ability to obtain relief, your creditors can go to court and get a judgment against the transferee of your assets. The judgment allows the creditor to go after your transferee much in the same way that your creditor can go after you.

In the example cited in the Associated Press article, in a poorly conceived strategy, this doctor has unnecessarily exposed his wife to untold liabilities. If a patient were to ever sue this doctor for malpractice, you better believe that this doctor's spouse would face enormous personal liabilities under fraudulent transfer law.

Importantly, fraudulent transfer laws make the transferee liable for the full amount of the transfer, even if the transferee no longer has the assets. If the doctor in this news article had transferred a stock portfolio worth $1 million to his wife, and the portfolio subsequently became worthless, the doctor's wife may still be on the hook for the full $1 million.

Problem #2: Uncompensated Risk

The Associated Press article reports that this particular doctor's insurance would cost $95,000 per year for $250,000 of coverage. Understandably, the doctor has balked at paying such a huge premium for such a small amount of coverage. By "going bare," the doctor has instead chosen to hold sufficient assets in his name to meet the $250,000 net worth requirement of Florida law for uninsured physicians.

What is the value of exposing $250,000 of your personal net worth to potential malpractice insurance claims? According to the article, retail malpractice insurance costs this particular doctor $95,000. In other words, if the doctor pays $95,000 to the retail insurer, the doctor is able to deduct $95,000 from the taxable income of his practice. Yet, this doctor gets no deduction because he has not paid any insurance premium; he has chosen to "go bare."

Please do not misunderstand me; self-insurance is a rational financial strategy in the sense that, by not paying premium to an insurance company, this doctor probably believes that he saves himself $95,000 in insurance expense. However, this is a very bad idea in the context of a doctor "going bare" and forgoing malpractice liability insurance altogether. The doctor incurs $95,000 of risk every year by exposing his personal net worth to potential malpractice claims and gets no tax deduction for having taken on such a substantial amount of risk.

There is a better way, and it is called captive insurance.

What are the shortcomings of retail insurance?

Retail insurance hosts a number of potential pitfalls. The following paragraphs summarize some of these deficiencies. When we then turn our discussion to captive insurance, I will explain how captive insurance may help minimize some of these deficiencies.

Risk of Non-Payment

There is no such thing as iron-clad insurance coverage. In particular, if you incur a catastrophic liability in your business, you can expect your insurance carrier to fight vociferously to avoid paying out on the claim, even if you are stuck with the liability to pay from your personal assets. This is why many insureds often have to hire their own lawyers to make sure that the insurance company does not attempt to avoid paying on the claim.

Insurance companies can deny a claim for any number of reasons. Perhaps your secretary forgot to mail in the last premium payment. If you suffer a claim, most policies require you to file a claim within an allotted period of time; a late claim may be denied altogether. Other policies only cover you as long as they remain in force; if you cancel a policy or switch carriers to save a little money, you may find that your past coverage has disappeared and your new carrier will not cover you.

Standard business policies are riddled with exclusions drafted by their lawyers for the sole purpose of avoiding liability for certain types of claims which you may very will think are covered. Even if a claim is covered, many times you will find that the insurance company has tasked an adjustor with the sole purpose of trying to reduce the insurance company's liability. Periodically, this leads to a bad faith claim against the insurance carrier, and insurance companies face litigation every year on bad faith claims.

If you thought just pinning down the terms of the policy was enough, you also need to consider the creditworthiness of your carrier. In the last recession, a number of insurance companies collapsed or, in the case of AIG (one of the largest insurance carriers in the United States), received a bailout from the government. Insurance companies do fail from time to time.

One-Size-Fits-All Coverage

As a retail product, business insurance policies are regulated by state insurance commissioners and have to conform to certain specifications. As well intentioned as some state regulation may be, the consequence is that your insurance agent is often limited in the type and extent of insurance coverage that can be provided to your business.

Perhaps your insurance carrier does not offer coverage for the loss of key employees, or maybe your insurer has not yet developed the type of policy that specifically covers that new surgical procedure that you offer. Some carriers may require you to pay an extraordinary deductible on every claim in order to keep your insurance costs within reason, meaning that you are taking on all the risk on modest-sized claims.

Just as every business is unique, gaps will exist in the type and extent of insurance that covers your business. While the market demands that insurance companies tailor their coverage to your business, most carriers have business and regulatory barriers that prevent them from serving this need.

Expensive Coverage Leads to No Coverage

The high cost of insurance puts many doctors to a difficult question: Should you just grin and bear the expense, or should you save the money and not purchase the insurance? Earlier in this chapter, we covered the many pitfalls of "going bare," i.e., not purchasing medical malpractice liability insurance. In my opinion, "going bare" is an unwise decision that needlessly exposes your family and your assets to enormous liabilities, while failing to factor in the financial "cost" of incurring that risk without compensation.

As we have previously discussed, malpractice coverage is not the only instance in which you may be uninsured for substantial risks in your business. The risks that we covered earlier in this chapter are risks for which standard retail insurance is readily available in most states. Some of these coverages are extremely expensive, and many doctors choose to forego coverage rather than incur the high cost of premiums for these types of policies.

My point here is that the high cost of retail insurance causes many doctors to not carry appropriate insurance to protect their businesses against these key categories of risk. Many doctors do not insure against the loss of a valuable nurse practitioner, even though that employee's absence may incur a dramatic loss in revenue and patients. Other doctors have no insurance to help them if Medicare conducts an audit of their practice, or if the state licensing board imposes sweeping new regulations that drive up the cost of compliance.

In reality, by not purchasing insurance to protect your business from these substantial forms of risk, you are self-insuring your business. Unfortunately, when you self-insure out of your own pocket, you get no financial credit for the fact that you are exposing your family and your assets to potential liability through your business. You cannot deduct an insurance premium against the taxable income of your business if you never actually pay that premium to someone. The only person who ends up paying is you, and you reap no financial benefit from absorbing that risk yourself.

How does captive insurance improve upon retail insurance?

Compared with retail insurance, captive insurance offers a number of distinct advantages. In fact, when you add up all the benefits and weigh them against the cost of implementing a captive insurance plan, most likely you will agree with me that captive insurance deserves careful consideration as part of any medical practice.

Tailored Coverage

With captive insurance, you get to decide which insurable risks in the business you want to have covered by your captive. You also get to determine just how much risk you want to shift to your captive.

Take again the example of my client, Dr. Weiss. His primary concern is that his malpractice liability carrier be there to protect him in case he gets hit with a multi-million-dollar malpractice claim. He is good at controlling his day-to-day risks and really only needs help with catastrophic risks that would bring down his entire business.

Dr. Weiss meets a team of insurance underwriters who have been asked to examine Dr. Weiss' medical practice up close and in detail. They monitor the company's revenue-generating activities, examine his medical equipment and office premises, and focused on his work processes. Dr. Weiss provides the underwriters with a complete history of past insurance claims as well as claims that were never filed for reimbursement. The underwriters also review the existing insurance policies purchased by the business, examining their scope and checking for gaps in coverage.

The underwriters make the following recommendations for insurance for Dr. Weiss' medical practice. Several of the lines of coverage they recommend are unique to medical practices, while others are applicable to most types of businesses. The following are examples of the types of risks that captives may cover:

- <u>Deductible Reimbursements</u>: With this form of coverage, the captive reimburses Dr. Weiss for deductibles that Dr. Weiss may have to pay another insurance carrier for coverage under an existing policy (e.g., malpractice liability).

• Reputational Damage: If Dr. Weiss' practice is the subject of adverse publicity on television, in the newspapers, or – increasingly common these days – over the internet, this type of policy reimburses the practice for lost revenue as well as the expenses of overcoming the adverse publicity.

• Administrative Actions: This type of coverage reimburses the medical practice for expenses associated with any regulatory proceedings, agency actions, and even private arbitrations. Coverage may even include fines and assessments imposed by a hospital or regulatory entity.

• Environmental Damage: In the event of environmental damage or pollution that requires a specialized clean-up, this type of policy reimburses the medical practice for its expenses incurred to resolve the damage.

• Data Restoration: Most medical practices depend on their computer systems to perform critical functions and provide valuable client data. A data restoration policy enables the captive to reimburse the medical practice for its expenses incurred in repairing and restoring computer systems. Coverage can also provide reimbursement for lost income attributable to loss of data.

• Uncollected Receivables: Dr. Weiss uses an outside bill collector to chase up his aged receivables, taking a substantial cut of any amounts collected. With this type of coverage, the captive reimburses Dr. Weiss for expenses incurred in using a bill collector.

• Work Stoppage: Dr. Weiss' medical practice resides in an earthquake prone area. Earthquake insurance covers property damage, but not lost revenue from being unable to operate a medical practice following an earthquake.

Now, the captive stands ready to reimburse the medical practice for revenue lost and mitigation expenses incurred if a a natural disaster, power outage, or similar incident prevents Dr. Weiss and his staff from operating the business.

• Legal Expenses: This type of coverage protects the medical practice from the high cost of attorneys' fees, court costs, settlement costs, expert witness costs, and fines and penalties incurred, whether the allegations are civil or criminal in nature.

• Audit Defense: Medical practices typically incur a higher tax audit rate than many other types of businesses. After all, tax agencies are drawn to money, and physicians tend to make more than the average taxpayer. With this type of coverage, the captive reimburses the medical practice for legal and accounting expenses incurred in response to a tax audit.

• Wrongful Acts: Coverage for negligence, errors and omissions, and similar acts may include reimbursement for expenses incurred in trying to minimize the loss associated with the wrongful act, as well as for income lost as a result of the wrongful act.

• Loss of Key Employee: If any of Dr. Weiss's physician assistants or nurse practitioners is unable to work due to disability, illness, or similar reasons, Dr. Weiss's captive reimburses the medical practice for the lost income. Coverage may extend to include an impairment in the value of the company due to the permanent loss of services of a key employee.

For Dr. Weiss, a tailored plan means keeping his existing malpractice liability insurance in place, but increasing the deductible from $20,000 per claim to $250,000 per claim. His captive insurance company then writes a policy to cover the first $250,000 "layer" of risk. This way, if he gets sued for a small claim, he can resolve it on his own and seek reimbursement from his captive insurance company. At the same time, if he gets sued for anything north of $250,000, he knows that he can count on his retail malpractice liability carrier to protect him from a catastrophic claim.

Dr. Weiss also insures the potential loss of key employees in his business. Given the sizable losses that may arise from the absence of any one of his nurse practitioners, the captive underwrites the risk. Dr. Weiss is able to determine with the underwriters for his captive each employee to be covered and how much in benefits a given insurance policy will pay out from his captive. If he manages a low claims history with his captive, those profits will belong to Dr. Weiss's captive and not to a retail insurance carrier.

Better Control of Risks

We have just seen that using a captive insurance company enables you to design insurance coverage for your business that matches your needs. You can determine how much and what kind of risks you want to shift to your captive, how much you may want to keep with a retail insurance carrier (to protect against catastrophic losses, for example), and which risks you would rather not insure at all.

A captive enables you to design your insurance coverage to conform to the requirements of your business. A captive also helps you to manage risks in a way that cannot be achieved with retail insurance.

With your very own captive, you get to determine who will manage the cash and investments inside your captive. If you happen to think that your captive is better off investing in conservative bonds and gold, you can cause your captive to invest in a conservative manner. A captive gives you the comfort of knowing that the funds held by your captive are available to help pay your claims, rather than to be used by a retail insurance company to speculate in the local real estate market.

If you are faced with a claim, an experienced captive manager will work with you to help determine liability under the claim and administer its resolution. Rather than fighting with a retail insurance company over the best legal strategy, you get to determine with your captive manager how your captive insurance company should best handle the claim. Retail insurance carriers pay their adjustors to deny the payment of claims, even if it means you get stuck with liability; your captive manager is much more likely to work with you to see that a proper claim gets paid.

Profit Potential

Perhaps the most valuable aspect of a captive insurance company for any medical professional is the ability to profit from a low claims history. At the beginning of this book, I said that your retail insurance carrier – by issuing you a commercial liability policy – makes a bet on you. Your retail insurer is betting that, in all likelihood, you will not have a claim and that the premium you pay will turn into pure profit for the insurance company.

If you are such a careful doctor, why would you let the insurance company make all this profit off of you? A captive enables you to capture some of this profit for yourself. Granted, by venturing into the business of insurance, you are taking on increased risk that your captive, rather than the retail insurer, may have to pay out on a claim. Yet, if you are successful at managing your claims, your captive enables you to capture these insurance profits for yourself.

As with my client, Dr. Weiss, you probably will not want to shift all of your risks to your captive. Most likely, you could stand to keep a deep-pocketed retail insurer around to cover your business against any catastrophic loss. Some risks are better suffered with other people's money. A thorough analysis of the insurable risks in your business, and your existing retail coverages, with the assistance of experienced underwriters and legal counsel will help you best determine which risks are appropriate for a captive.

Profit Potential Leads to Complete Coverage

One of the shortcomings of retail insurance, which we discussed earlier in this chapter, is that the high cost of retail insurance causes many doctors to go without appropriate coverage in their businesses. Perhaps you are carrying critically needed malpractice liability insurance, but you have chosen not to purchase loss of key employee insurance because the cost is too high. However, by not carrying this insurance, you are essentially insuring yourself: If you suffer a loss that is not covered by insurance, you have to pay for that loss out of your own pocket.

The profit potential with captive insurance affords doctors a compelling incentive to consider broader insurance coverage. Risks that previously went uninsured may be well suited for insurance through your captive. After all, if you are going to have to pay out of your own pocket for certain types of losses in your business, you might as well get some credit for having self-insured those losses by having the risk of those losses underwritten by your very own captive insurance company.

Captive insurance permits you to choose between paying retail insurance premiums and premiums to your captive, allowing you to focus on gaining complete coverage for your business rather than having to economize on insurance expenses. To the extent that you choose to insure risks through your captive, your business may be able to deduct the premiums paid to your captive against the taxable income of the business. By comparison, no such deduction exists if you choose to forego insurance coverage and self-insure the risks of your business out of your own pocket.

Conclusion

I wish to provide a brief summary of the important points covered in this chapter:

- Medical professionals face all forms of substantial risks in their practices every day. These risks extend beyond malpractice liability and property damage to include things like loss of key employees, interruption of business from bad weather or administrative actions, changes in regulations, loss or damage to specialty medical equipment, and loss or damage to computer equipment or patient data. A serious loss from any of these events can substantially harm your business or drive you out of your practice.

- Retail business insurance is designed to protect you from many of these risk categories. However, retail insurance is expensive. Moreover, most doctors never incur claims, meaning that the premiums they have paid are a complete loss for them and pure profit for the insurance company.

- Thinking of saving on insurance by cutting back on coverage or "going bare" by not carrying malpractice liability insurance? Think again! Not carrying insurance is one of the worst financial and business decisions you could make. Not only do your jeopardize your professional reputation by "going bare," you needlessly expose your family and your assets to enormous liabilities arising from your business. You cannot deduct against the taxable income of your business the financial risks that you and your family incur from self-insuring the liabilities of your business.

- As expensive as it is, retail insurance is full of pitfalls. You may find that your claims are denied, or the insurance company may go out of business. The one-size-fits-all approach of retail insurance leaves a lot to be desired, resulting in gaps in coverage for your business. The high cost of retail insurance leads many doctors to go with no protection, or inadequate protection, against many common forms of substantial business risk.

- Captive insurance provides an ideal solution to the shortcomings and high cost of retail insurance. You can tailor coverage to best meet the needs of your business and the risks you face from day to day. You can still keep your retail policy to protect against certain catastrophic liabilities, while shifting other risks to your very own captive insurance company.

- By owning a captive insurance company, you gain enormous control over how your premium dollars are invested to provide for your business in a time of need. You effectively mitigate the risk that your insurance carrier will go out of business or make risky investments.

- When retail insurers issue insurance to your business, they are making a bet that your business will not incur a claim and that the premiums you pay will turn into pure profit for the insurance company. Captive insurance enables you to make that same bet on yourself and, by enjoying a low claims experience, to capture those profits for your own benefit.

1 All client names have been changed to protect their privacy.
2 "Doctors Going Without Malpractice Insurance," Associated Press (June 18, 2004).

CHAPTER 3.

PROTECTING YOUR FAMILY WITH CAPTIVE INSURANCE

Introduction

In Chapter Two, we discussed the many ways in which you incur risk every day in your medical practice. The risks we analyzed in Chapter Two are risks that vary from practice to practice, and physician to physician, but each of these risks have the potential to damage or destroy your business.

While you can protect your business from some of these risks through retail insurance, such insurance is expensive and presents a number of potential pitfalls. By contrast, captive insurance allows you to better protect your business and secure yourself against these risks. Moreover, captive insurance enables you to profit from your own careful claims management, allowing you to accumulate significant wealth, often in a tax-advantaged manner.

The fact that captive insurance permits you to accumulate wealth, many times at reduced income tax rates, opens the door to a number of estate planning opportunities. Many years ago, a number of bright estate planning attorneys figured out how to translate the benefits of captive insurance into estate planning opportunities. In this chapter, I intend to expand upon the discussion and explain how captive insurance enhances your personal net worth and the well being of your family.

We will begin this chapter with a foray into the income tax aspects of captive insurance. You will learn that captive insurance may permit you to shift taxable income from your business into insurance premiums that enjoy an exemption from income tax. We will then analyze how, by accumulating tax-mitigated wealth inside your captive, we can also minimize the impact of estate taxes. Finally, we will evaluate how a captive protects your wealth from unanticipated creditors, conferring valuable asset protection benefits for you and your family.

Income Tax Aspects of Captive Insurance

In order to understand how captive insurance permits you to accumulate wealth, oftentimes in a tax-mitigated manner, I would like to briefly cover some of the more important income tax aspects of captive insurance.

Deducting Insurance Premiums

When your business pays premiums to an insurance company for a policy covering potential losses arising in the business, those premiums are normally deductible against the taxable income of your business. I say "normally" because there are some practical limits under income tax law.

The general rule of thumb is that your business can only deduct those expenses that are "reasonable and necessary" to the business. There are lengthy regulations and a litany of court cases governing the meaning of the phrase "reasonable and necessary." Rather than spending hundreds of pages on this one subject alone, I suggest that you discuss this issue with a qualified tax advisor if you decide to embark on a captive insurance plan.

Properly calculated, the amount your business pays in insurance premiums – whether to a retail insurance company or to your very own captive insurance company (or both) – may be deducted against the taxable earnings of your business. This means that your business taxable income may be reduced dollar for dollar by the amount spent on insurance premiums.

831(b) Captives – The $2.2 Million Exemption

While the premium paid to your captive insurance company is

deducted against the taxable income of your business, in certain circumstances that premium is exempt from taxable income in the hands of your captive insurance company. Under IRC Section 831(b),[3] for tax years beginning on or after January 1, 2017, an insurance company with premium income of no more than $2.2 million per year may elect to be <u>exempt</u> from corporate income tax on its premium income.

This exemption is annual, meaning that your captive may be able to exempt up to $2.2 million each and every year. As a result of recent legislation,[4] this exemption is even indexed for inflation, increasing in $50,000 increments. For tax years prior to 2017, the exemption is not as generous, but nevertheless respectable at $1.2 million per year.

Many small captive insurance companies can easily qualify for this exemption. Even foreign insurance companies that elect[5] to be taxed as domestic insurance companies can enjoy this exemption.

Normally, a tax election that produces a financial benefit involves some form of trade-off. However, Section 831(b) is one of those few provisions in the Code that, in my opinion, has no downside. If your captive insurance company does not bring in more than $2.2 million in premium income per year, then serious consideration should be given to making the 831(b) election.

Taxation of Insurance Companies – Dividends, Interest, and Capital Gains

I just mentioned that, in my opinion, Section 831(b) of the Code does not appear to have any downside; there is no trade-off whereby making the election makes you worse off in any manner. Rather, if there is a trade-off, it is in the taxation of the captive insurance company itself.

A captive insurance company is taxable as a "C corporation" under the Code. This means that your captive files tax returns and pays taxes as if the captive were an individual, but with slightly different rates and rules applicable to C corporations. For one, a small insurance company electing under Section

831(b) does not pay any income tax on its premium income (as long as its premium income does not exceed $1.2 million per year through 2016, or $2.2 million per year beginning in 2017). For another, C corporations have two tax brackets: 15% and 35%, and the 15% bracket is surpassed at a very small amount of income.

C corporations do not enjoy a lower capital gains like individuals do; C corporations pay ordinary income tax rates on their capital gains. However, a C corporation does get to deduct at least 70% of its dividend income (and may be able to deduct 100% of dividend income from certain wholly-owned corporate subsidiaries).

Practically speaking, this means that your captive insurance company pays less in taxes than you do on dividend income, about the same on interest income, and definitely more in taxes on capital gain income. If you sit down with your tax advisor and your investment advisor simultaneously to discuss this issue, most likely they would agree that the investment portfolio inside your captive insurance company would look quite different from the composition of your personal investment portfolio. Growth stocks and other long-term capital gains-producing investments would be eschewed in favor of stocks that consistently pay good dividends.

The important point here is that captive insurance companies are not bad tax-wise; they are just different. Your tax advisor and your investment advisor should appreciate the subtle differences between how you are taxed and how your captive insurance company is taxed. With the right amount of planning, you should find that a captive insurance company enables you to pursue dividend-yielding investment strategies that are surprisingly tax efficient. Meanwhile, you can leave the growth stocks to your personal portfolio outside of your captive.

Estate Planning Opportunities
Vesting Ownership in Succeeding Generations
According to the old adage, "You can't take it with you when

you die." As you succeed in your medical profession, most likely you will need to consider the impact of estate taxes when you die. Estate taxes are generally imposed on the size of your estate at the time you pass away. While the precise tax rates are subject to change, the combined incidence of federal and state estate taxes can be in excess of 50% of your estate.

Even if you don't have a lot of money in the bank, the value of your business is includible in your taxable estate. At your death, your heirs may be compelled to sell assets at "fire sale" prices just to come up with enough cash to settle your estate tax debt. After decades invested building up your business, your heirs could be forced to dispose of everything you have worked for.

One of the most frequent solutions to estate tax problems is for people to give away their assets before they die. Whether you can make sufficiently sizeable, timely gifts to your heirs depends on a number of factors, and many states will not permit you to transfer your ownership in a licensed medical practice before you die. Even as you attempt to minimize potential estate taxes, you may incur gift taxes that are no less confiscatory. Meanwhile, you have to make sure that the assets you retain are sufficient to support you in your anticipated lifestyle for as long as you live. This is no easy task.

Implementing a captive insurance plan enables you to shift tremendous sums of wealth to your family free of gift and estate taxes. If your heirs own shares of stock in your captive insurance company, then they share in the ownership and profits of the captive alongside you. Premiums paid from your business to the captive may result in a continuing stream of profits accumulating inside the captive. Those premiums are not gifts. Instead, they are payments made in order to purchase insurance coverage for your business. When you die, the captive is not considered part of your taxable estate. You only incur estate taxes on the shares that you own.

New 831(b) Diversification Requirement
Shifting wealth through a captive to escape estate taxes is a

fantastic planning idea. Unfortunately, sometimes the best laid estate plans come under fire from the Internal Revenue Service. In 2015, the IRS decided that using a captive to (i) enjoy the 831(b) income tax exemption and (ii) escape estate and gift taxes was too much of a good thing, and they lobbied Congress to change the rules.

Fortunately, members of our team were there to carefully explain the merits of this particular strategy to members of the U.S. Senate Committee on Finance. The resulting legislation still permits family members to shift wealth through a captive. However, there is now a new "diversification requirement" that limits the extent to which this can be done.

In order to enjoy the benefits of the $2.2 million exemption, the new diversification requirement must be satisfied in one of two ways. This first way to meet this diversification requirement is if no more than 20% of new written premiums of the captive are attributable to any one policyholder.[6] This requirement would be satisfied if, for example, you own a captive along with nine other people, each of whom owns his or her own business, and the captive issues policies of relatively equal value among all ten businesses. In other words, captives with a diverse pool of policyholders automatically meet the new diversification requirement.

The second alternative way in which to meet this new diversification requirement is to demonstrate consistency in ownership levels between those family members who own the captive and those family members who own the insured business.[7] The objective of this particular provision is to preclude use of the 831(b) election if a spouse or lineal descendant owns a disparately larger interest in the captive than they do the insured business. The Joint Committee on Taxation explains this particular rule by way of example:

> [A]ssume that in 2017, a captive insurance company does not meet the requirement that no more than 20 percent of its net (or direct) written premiums

personally while going about your daily activities. We will then examine how captive insurance enables you to protect your personal net worth from these types of liabilities

Examining Personal Liability: The Example of Auto Insurance

Every time you get behind the wheel of your car, you assume the risk that you won't cause an accident. Unfortunately, auto accidents are a normal risk attendant with driving automobiles. For this reason, most of us have auto liability coverage that protects us in case we injure someone or damage property with a car.

Let us assume for a moment that, on your way home from work tomorrow, you wind up in a collision that causes serious injury to someone. The police at the scene determine that you are at fault for the accident. Like most people, you inform your insurance carrier, and they conduct their own investigation. Absent unusual circumstances, you can expect your insurance company to cover your liabilities arising from the accident to the extent of your policy limit.

Most likely, you will then be contacted by a personal injury lawyer representing the victim in the accident. Personal injury lawyers in most states work on a contingent fee basis. This means that they typically represent their clients without charging an up-front fee, instead taking a share of whatever money they recover for their clients. In many states, the lawyer's share of the recovery may be as much as 50% of the value of the claim.

Have you ever considered the policy limits on your automobile insurance? In many states, auto insurance carriers cannot over more than perhaps $300,000. Most auto insurance policies actually provide what is called "split-limit liability" coverage in which there are two types of limits: a limit on the amount paid for each injured person in an accident, and a separate overall limit on the amount that can be claimed in any one accident. The majority of auto policies limit claims per injured person to only $100,000.

Contrast the amount of coverage your auto policy provides with the average jury verdict for personal injuries in an auto accident. The median jury verdict nationally for a foot injury alone is just under $100,000.[9] The average wrongful death verdict is over $4 million![10]

Most likely, you do not have $4 million worth of personal liability coverage available under your auto insurance policy. Even if you ask for maximum coverage, in most states it will be capped at $300,000 or $500,000. In other words, every time you drive, you run the risk of ruinous personal liability far in excess of your available auto insurance coverage.

A Word About Umbrella Insurance

You can purchase personal excess liability coverage (often referred to as an "umbrella" policy) to help protect against extraordinary liability in cases such as auto accidents and someone being injured on your property. However, many umbrella policies have very strict requirements before they will pay out. If your primary insurance carrier goes bankrupt, or refuses to pay under the terms of your policy, your umbrella insurance carrier will likewise deny your claim. Umbrella policies often do not cover any liabilities arising in your business or from conducting your medical practice.

I always recommend that my clients purchase umbrella coverage, but I also warn them to read the fine print and not assume that they will be covered. Also, you should keep in mind that even umbrella policies have their limits. Umbrella policies are sold in $1 million increments by most insurance carriers, and many people only purchase the first $1 million of coverage. Going back to my example of a wrongful death claim, where the average jury verdict is over $4 million, this means that the typical $1 million umbrella insurance policy holder still faces personal liability of as much as $3 million after insurance.

Shielding Your Assets from Liabilities – Asset Protection Planning

In the face of potential personal liabilities that may not be covered by insurance, it is good to know how captive insurance can help you and your family to protect your personal wealth from unanticipated creditors. When we discuss planning techniques that help shield your assets from creditors, we engage in the pursuit of what is commonly referred to as "asset protection."

Insurance is a form of asset protection. The objective with insurance in many cases is to provide a source of liquidity to pay an unanticipated creditor, such as an injured patient, so that you do not have to use your personal net worth to resolve those claims.

There are limits to the amount of insurance that you can afford to carry to protect yourself from personal liability. For this reason, asset protection planning considers the many techniques that can be used to further shield your assets from unanticipated creditors beyond mere insurance.

A key principle of asset protection planning is that your creditor cannot take from you what you do not own. If you periodically make substantial gifts to family members, it is unlikely that an unanticipated creditor would ever be able to reach that amount of wealth which you transfer to your family. Likewise, one of the most prevalent asset protection planning techniques in use today involves establishing a special type of trust known as the "asset protection trust" and funding the trust with gifts that deplete your estate of assets that might otherwise attract creditors.

Deducting Premiums from a Liability-Generating Business

Captive insurance offers a dimension of asset protection planning that is quite formidable. By purchasing insurance coverage from your very own captive insurance company, your business takes money that might otherwise be profit and applies it toward insurance premiums.

If a creditor later comes along and sues your business, most likely the creditor will not be able to reach the assets of your captive insurance company. Your captive is an independent business acting at arm's length when it provides insurance coverage to your business. Once those premium dollars are paid out of your business, they are no longer available to a creditor of your business.

You may recall from earlier in this chapter that, with captive insurance, you may deduct premiums paid by your medical practice to your very own captive insurance company. This helps reduce the taxable income inside your medical practice, saving you taxes.

In a similar way, paying premiums from your medical practice to your very own captive insurance company helps shield those premium dollars from unanticipated creditors. Gifts and other forms of gratuitous transfers are normally subject to attack by creditors, but an arm's-length payment of insurance premiums from your medical practice to an insurance company – including a captive – normally cannot be set aside by a creditor. This is true even if your family members are shareholders in the captive, sharing in the profits from insuring your medical practice.

Of course, there are always some exceptions to this rule, such as if your business files for bankruptcy. The key principle to understand is that your captive insurance company may be used to accumulate substantial wealth, through premium profits, that might otherwise be left on your company's balance sheet and exposed to its creditors.

Domestic versus Offshore Captives

Relevant to the discussion of asset protection is that you can form a captive insurance company outside of the United States. In the captive insurance industry, we refer to this type of entity as an "offshore" captive.

Utilizing an offshore captive provides a level of asset protection that far exceeds what is typically available from using a domestic captive insurance company established under state law. If your creditor has to go offshore to pursue your investment in a captive insurance company, your creditor is likely to think twice before committing the added expenses to hire new lawyers and pursue a claim in a foreign legal system.

In many jurisdictions that are popular for captive insurance, the legal systems are hostile to unanticipated creditors, and the courts there will not recognize ridiculously high jury awards arising out of a U.S. court. Some types of judgments that are normally enforceable in the U.S., including fines, penalties, and treble damage awards, are not enforceable at all in an offshore jurisdiction. Even if your creditor has a recognizable claim, a foreign legal system is likely to require your creditor to post a bond with the court and will make the creditor pay your legal fees if the creditor's case is unsuccessful.

Believe it or not, captive insurance companies are far easier – and more cost-effective – to establish offshore than in the United States. This is because a number of offshore jurisdictions seek to host captive insurance business, as it provides a source of employment for their residents and enables their governments to collect revenue from registration fees.

While a thorough discussion of the tax aspects of an offshore captive exceeds the scope of this book, an offshore captive is fairly easy to maintain for U.S. tax purposes. Under IRC Section 953(d), you can even elect to have your offshore captive taxed as if it was formed in the United States (and an electing offshore captive can make an IRC Section 831(b) election to avail itself of the annual $1.2 million exemption on premium income). The practical effect of this is to enable you to choose the jurisdiction for your captive based on practical considerations such as costs and fees, and regulatory and legal climate, and not be concerned with any differences in tax outcome.

Using a Trust to Own Your Captive Insurance Company

As you may have figured out from the preceding paragraphs, one asset protection concern to consider with a captive insurance company is whether your creditor may attempt to seize your ownership interest in your captive. After all, if you own a captive insurance company, your ownership interest is a personal asset that may be reached by your creditors.

In some jurisdictions, particularly offshore, creditors face regulatory and legal restrictions preventing them from seizing a membership interest in your captive. While this may help to keep your creditor at bay, it does not prevent your creditor from waiting until you receive dividends, or redeem your captive shares, and collect against those proceeds.

A far more practical solution is to use an asset protection trust to own your captive shares. As previously discussed, an asset protection trust is a type of trust which you establish and fund with gifts. Once those gifts transferred to the trust, they are no longer part of your personal net worth and may not be reached by unanticipated creditors.[11]

Over the years, your captive insurance company may accumulate significant wealth from profitable insurance activities. The accumulated wealth inside your captive may serve as a rich target for creditors who happen to see your appreciated ownership interest reflected on your personal net worth statement. Transferring your ownership interest to an asset protection trust provides an added layer of protection and, when conducted properly, prevents any unanticipated creditor from ever reaching the value of your ownership interest.

Asset protection is not a panacea. As much as your creditor cannot collect from you what you do not own, neither can you! If you transfer assets, including your ownership in a captive insurance company, to an asset protection trust, you most likely will need to work with the trustee of your asset protection trust in order to receive distributions from the trust.

As cumbersome as this may seem, the trade-off is a substantial increase in safety for your assets, particularly against those claims that are not adequately dealt with through insurance. In my experience, most of my clients do not mind working with a trustee (even offshore) who administers their assets, including their ownership interests in captive insurance companies.

Conclusion

We have covered quite a bit of material in this chapter, spanning taxation, insurance, personal liabilities, and asset protection. Therefore, a summary of the key points is in order.

- "Reasonable and necessary" insurance premiums paid by your business to your captive may be deductible against the taxable income of your business.

- A captive insurance company is taxed as a "C corporation"; while it does not enjoy a preferential tax rate on capital gains, your captive pays a rate of tax on dividends that is much lower than for individuals, making dividend-paying stocks a tax-efficient form of investment inside your captive.

- Small captive insurance companies can elect under IRC Section 831(b) to exempt up to $1.2 million of premium income annually. This means that premiums deducted against taxable income in your business remain free of income tax inside your captive insurance company.

- A captive insurance plan may enable you to shift significant wealth to your family free of estate and gift taxes. Family members may directly own shares of stock in your captive insurance company. Alternatively, you may consider using a special type of trust to hold those shares for your family and outside of your taxable estate.

- You need to concern yourself with personal liability, arising from both day-to-day activities (e.g., driving a car) and from your medical practice. While umbrella insurance helps to supplement existing coverage, umbrella insurance is not airtight and still may not be enough.

- "Asset protection" involves shielding your assets from unanticipated creditors, most often by transferring those assets to family members. You can also use a special type of trust known as an "asset protection trust" to protect your personal net worth from unanticipated creditors.

- Captive insurance enables you to transfer wealth, in the form of insurance premiums, from your business to your captive insurance company. Not only may you enjoy valuable tax deductions for premiums paid to your captive, but creditors are may not be able to reach premiums paid to your captive for actual insurance coverage.

- Given that a captive can be used to accumulate significant tax-mitigated wealth, you should consider how to protect your ownership interest in your captive. Consider transferring your ownership interest in your captive to an asset protection trust.

- Forming your captive "offshore" (i.e., outside the United States) makes it less likely that a creditor will pursue your ownership interest in a foreign jurisdiction. Not only is it usually cheaper and easier to form your captive offshore, but there are no practical tax differences between a domestic and offshore captive insurance company.

3 Section 831(b) of the Internal Revenue Code of 1986, as amended (the "Code").

4 The $2.2 million exemption and index for inflation was set by amendment to Code Section 831(b) pursuant to Section 333(b) of the the Protect Americans from Tax Hikes (PATH) Act of 2015.

5 See Code Section 953(d).

6 Code Section 831(b)(2).

7 Code Section 831(b)(2)(B).

8 Code Section 831(b)(2)(C) (invoking attribution rules of Code Sections 267(b), 707(b), and 1563).

9 Ronald V. Miller, Jr., "The Value of Foot Injury Cases: Median National Jury Verdicts," http://www.marylandlawyerblog.com/2008/01/the_value_of_foot_injury_cases.html (January 2, 2008).

10 Ronald V. Miller, Jr., "Average Wrongful Death Verdict,"

http://www.marylandmedicalmalpracticeattorneyblog.com/
2010/05/average-wrongful-death-verdict.html (May 11, 2010).
11 In several instances throughout this discussion, I make a
distinction as to "unanticipated creditors" who may be unable to
reach the assets of an asset protection trust. This distinction is
intentional; you cannot use an asset protection trust to avoid a
known creditor to who you owe money. If you attempt to
transfer assets to someone else, particularly an asset protection
trust, in an effort to avoid a known creditor, the recipient may
be liable to your creditor as a "fraudulent transferee."

CHAPTER 4.

CASE STUDY #1: THE SURGEON

Client Background

Matthew Walker is a neurosurgeon specializing in complex spine and minimally invasive spinal procedures. He is a member of a regional practice in St. Louis, Missouri, where he is the managing partner. However, Dr. Walker's practice is effectively a business within a business, as he has his own medical staff and accounting department.

Dr. Walker has enjoyed consistently growing revenues in his medical practice. In just the last three years alone, his gross revenues have grown from $3 million to over $5 million annually. His projections for the next year are to continue steady, albeit slightly slower, growth.

The activities of Dr. Walker's practice consist of patient visits at his office and surgeries scheduled at three regional hospitals. Dr. Walker also enjoys a favorable public profile and is widely regarded as a leader in his field. Accordingly, he periodically serves as an expert witness at medical board hearings and in malpractice cases. In addition to his medical practice, Dr. Walker also purchases and leases radiology equipment to one of the regional hospitals where he also performs surgeries.

The medical practice employs one nurse practitioner and two medical assistants. The nurse practitioner, Jessica, has proven to be a gold mine for Dr. Walker. Not only does she contribute directly to the practice's revenue base, but she also helps relieve Dr. Walker of his workload, freeing him up to pursue higher-profile procedures and realize even higher revenue from the same set of working hours.

Underwriting Analysis

Early on in my analysis, I sent a team of insurance underwriters to St. Louis to take a look at Dr. Walker's medical practice, interview him and his staff, and evaluate his privileges with area hospitals. Our immediate impression was that Dr. Walker's medical practice lacked adequate insurance coverage in handful of key risk areas. The underwriters believe that Dr. Walker was leaving his practice woefully exposed to substantial financial harm from a distinct set of well-defined risks that are increasingly impacting individual medical practices in the State of Missouri.

We also found that Dr. Walker was paying a very high premium every year for medical malpractice liability insurance. He was incurring this higher cost in order to keep the deductible on his policy affordable. Yet, when we looked at his history of insurance claims, he never once had been sued for malpractice. Every year, he was paying tens of thousands of dollars in malpractice insurance premiums for a low-deductible policy on which, in all likelihood, he would never need to make a claim.

The following paragraphs summarize the recommendations made by the insurance underwriters for insurance coverage designed and offered by Dr. Walker's captive insurance company. Some of these lines of coverage may be familiar to you, and others you may not have ever heard (but are available in the public insurance market). You should consider whether any of these risks may also be present in your business:

Administrative Actions

The underwriters believe that Dr. Walker would benefit from a policy designed to shield his practice from action taken by a government agency, medical licensing board, or hospital against his practice. A typical policy of this type covers regulatory risks arising from a medical practice in three ways: First, the policy reimburses the practice for all costs associated with defending the practice against a regulatory action. This reimbursement extends to lost earnings as a result of personnel being tasked to defense matters and away from revenue-producing activities.

Second, a policy shielding against administrative actions provides a form of reimbursement for any fines or assessments that are imposed on the medical practice by the regulating entity. Third, a comprehensive policy reimburses the medical practice for income lost as the result of a regulatory action that prevents the business from carrying on, such as a suspension of a physician's medical license.

Inability to Practice/Loss of Key Employee

The underwriters recommend a policy that would compensate the practice if Dr. Walker were unable to continue practicing medicine, whether as a temporary matter or as the result of a permanent condition.

This type of policy is intended to be supplemental to a disability or life insurance policy. For example, events covered by this type of policy would include significant travel delay, kidnap, jury service, imprisonment etc. It would also cover loss of the services of the nurse practitioner from similar causes.

One advantage with this type of policy is that the underwriters can work with Dr. Walker to develop a list of key employees and the benefits payable if one of those employees is unable to work. In their analysis, the underwriters developed the following list of employees and the monthly payment that would be made available under the policy:

	Monthly Benefit	Aggregate Limit
Dr. Walker	$50,000	$300,000
Jessica (Nurse Practitioner)	$30,000	$200,000

Work Stoppage (Business Interruption)

This covers the risk of events that do not damage the premises of the medical practice but which nonetheless result in business interruption. Natural disasters might include windstorms, tornados, or floods. Other possible covered risks would include power outages or the unavailability of staff due to illness, such as a virus outbreak.

Dr. Walker relies on access to his the offices of his private practice at three separate locations. If one of those locations were inaccessible due to a natural disaster, Dr. Walker would have to scale back the number of procedures performed significantly. This would directly impact the bottom line of the medical practice.

Legal Expenses

All medical practices incur legal expenses, but few medical practices actually carry insurance coverage to protect against high legal bills. The underwriters have proposed a form of coverage that would be extremely broad and cover legal expenses incurred both in defending lawsuits as well as initiating certain forms of litigation to protect the medical practice.

We noticed with the underwriters that legal expenses for the medical practice have, fortunately, been modest in the past. For this reason, the underwriters suggest that Dr. Walker carry a reasonably low aggregate annual deductible of $5,000. Once the medical practice's legal bills exceed $5,000 in any one year, the captive's policy would kick in to reimburse the remaining expenses for the medical practice.

Tax Audit Expenses

Dr. Walker's medical practice produces a lot of revenue and incurs significant expenses. He uses a top-flight accounting firm to stay on top of the company's books and produce reliably accurate tax returns. Nevertheless, the IRS and state tax authorities are always looking for new sources of revenue, and they tend to focus their efforts on high income earners (going "where the money is").

The underwriters propose that Dr. Walker purchase a policy that reimburses him for the expenses incurred undergoing a tax audit. Whether the examining agency is federal or state, the medical practice would be able to seek reimbursement from the captive subject to a modest deductible, regardless of whether the tax agency would actually impose an assessment.

Wrongful Acts

As mentioned in Chapter Two, one advantage of owning your own captive insurance company is that insurance coverage can be tailored to fill in the gaps left exposed by inadequate retail insurance coverage. One area of increasing exposure for businesses and, in particular, medical practices is employment practices liability. It is frequently common in business to incur litigation on the basis of a discrimination claim, and the claimed discrimination may be based on sex, race, sexual orientation, age, physical or mental disability, or other factors.

Coverage for wrongful acts can be design to cover these gaps in insurance coverage. In the case of Dr. Walker, the underwriters found that his medical practice did not have comprehensive coverage. Furthermore, the coverage that he had contained was riddled with exclusions that could be used to deny a claim for reimbursement.

The underwriters designed a comprehensive policy covering all forms of negligence, errors and omissions, and similar acts, including employment practices liability. This was not intended to replace any existing retail coverage that Dr. Walker had, but to instead supplement that coverage and provide comprehensive protection from anything that might be excluded from coverage under a traditional retail policy.

In addition to reimbursement for expenses incurred in trying to minimize the loss associated with the wrongful act, the underwriters recommended that the captive reimburse the medical practice for income lost as a result of the wrongful act. Therefore, they not only closed a gap in coverage, but they expanded the existing coverage to include lost income attributable to a wrongful act claim.

Loss of Income Due to Reputational Damage

All doctors run the risk that a hit to one's reputation may lead directly to a loss of income. In fact, damage to one's reputation or brand identity is now the fourth most identified business insurance risk according to Aon's annual Global Risk Management Ranking.[12]

Dr. Walker's risk is particularly pronounced. He enjoys a high public profile and is well known at the hospitals where he conducts surgeries. In addition to practicing medicine, his equipment leasing business relies on his favorable relationship with one of the hospitals he works at. For these reasons, the underwriters consider Dr. Walker to be facing an elevated risk of reputational damage.

Deductible Reimbursement (Medical Malpractice)

Dr. Walker's medical practice purchases medical malpractice coverage from a large commercial carrier. The retail policy contains a maximum reimbursement of $1 million per claim of $1 million and $3 million in the aggregate. His deductibles are $10,000 per claim and $30,000 in the aggregate.

By increasing his deductibles to $25,000 per claim and $75,000 in the aggregate, Dr. Walker can reduce the premium on his retail policy from $30,000 per year to $23,000 per year, a 23% reduction in costs. However, taking the lower premium means that, in the event of a claim, Dr. Walker's medical practice needs to pay a substantially higher deductible, a risk that makes him understandably nervous.

The underwriters have recommended that his captive offer a deductible reimbursement policy for claims made on his malpractice liability insurance. Under this type of policy, his captive would not be insuring his practice for medical malpractice liability. Rather, if his practice filed a claim with the malpractice liability carrier, the practice would be able to seek a reimbursement of the deductible it pays by submitting a claim to the captive insurance company.

This gives Dr. Walker the confidence that his practice will not be out of pocket $75,000 in the event of a series of catastrophic malpractice claims brought against his practice. Instead, he will be able to look to his own captive insurance company as a source of liquidity.

Actuarial Analysis

Once the underwriters had completed their review of the possible insurance coverages to be offered by the captive insurance company, we then turned to the actuaries to tell us how much such coverage would cost in the retail insurance market. The actuaries rated the proposed insurance program to illustrate the projected losses that might be incurred.

The underwriters proposed the following coverages, which the actuaries then priced out:

	Limit
Administrative Actions	$500,000
Inability to Practice/Loss of Key Employee	$500,000
Work Stoppage (Business Interruption)	$500,000
Legal Expenses	$500,000
Tax Audit Expenses	$250,000
Wrongful Acts	$500,000
Reputational Damage/Loss of Income	$250,000
Deductible Reimbursement (Medical Malpractice)	$50,000
Total (8 lines of coverage)	*$3,300,000*

The actuaries considered a number of risk factors in their analysis, including whether the Dr. Walker's medical practice would continue to perform as projected, the fact that projections could only be made annually and would have to be adjusted with time, and the fact that loss rates and cost factors would be projected based on claim frequency and severity statistics. They were careful to point out that actual losses would almost certainly deviate from expected losses.

As a result of their analysis, the actuaries priced the coverage out at $331,710 per year. Specifically, they calculated the aggregate premium amount by pricing each line of coverage as follows:

	Annual Premium
Administrative Actions	$66,408
Inability to Practice/Loss of Key Employee	$49,710
Work Stoppage (Business Interruption)	$62,811
Legal Expenses	$12,917
Tax Audit Expenses	$25,522
Wrongful Acts	$64,429
Reputational Damage/Loss of Income	$21,219
Deductible Reimbursement (Medical Malpractice)	$28,694
Total (8 lines of coverage)	*$331,710*

Captive Analysis

Our firm then proceeded to analyze the establishment and maintenance of a captive insurance company for Dr. Walker. Critical to the performance of the captive program is to ensure that you have a good partner in the form of a captive management company. The captive manager takes primary responsibility for helping to license and operate the captive, to correspond with the regulator, accountants and auditors on the captive's activities, and to provide reports to the shareholder and counsel on the captive's performance.

In this case, we selected a Cayman Islands Segregated Portfolio Company (SPC) to function as the client's captive insurance company. A SPC is a type of company in which a host parent company sponsors multiple SPCs, and each SPC serves a separate entity with its own distinct assets and liabilities. The advantage with an SPC is that it is generally easier to establish and maintain, as it relies on its host entity to comply with all corporate formalities and requirements of local law.

We formed Walker Insurance as Dr. Walker's captive insurance company with a special type of trust as its shareholder: A Belize asset protection trust. Under the laws of Belize, Dr. Walker can rest easy knowing that creditors cannot reach his ownership of the captive insurance company. Two layers of protection shield premiums that flow from his medical practice into the captive: The offshore trust and the offshore captive. At the same time, Dr. Walker retains significant control over his trust and captive insurance company, accessing cash when desired and with minimal effort.

Tax and Financial Analysis

Dr. Walker's medical practice deducted the premium ($331,710) it paid to his captive insurance company. According to his accountants, this saved Dr. Walker approximately 41% in combined federal and state income taxes: $136,001.

Had Dr. Walker not purchased insurance coverage through his captive, he would have received net income from his medical practice of $195,709 after taxes. Instead, Dr. Walker paid $331,710 into his captive insurance company, which paid no income taxes. In addition to saving $136,001 in taxes, Dr. Walker now has an extra $136,001 to invest through his captive insurance company.

Over four years, Dr. Walker was able to accumulate approximately $1 million in his captive insurance company. Last year, his captive paid out over $100,000 in litigation expense claims submitted by Dr. Walker's practice after the city attempted to zone some land neighboring Dr. Walker's office for a multistory office building. The building would have blocked any view of Dr. Walker's practice from the adjoining street, as well as block the line of sight from Dr. Walker's offices. Also, the building would have eliminated a valuable parking area and made the entire office complex too congested for patients to enjoy convenient parking.

Most of the money is deployed into stock and bond portfolios that help strengthen the reserves of the captive insurance company and enable it to continue offering value insurance coverage to Dr. Walker's medical practice. In consultation with his tax advisor and an SEC-registered investment advisor overseeing his captive's investment portfolio, Dr. Walker's captive is invested primarily in high dividend-yielding stocks. Due to the captive's status as a C corporation, Walker Insurance can claim a dividends-received deduction equal to 70% of the dividends it receives. This means that the captive pays an effective corporate tax rate of 10.5% on its dividend income. Last year, for example, Walker Insurance generated $78,000 in dividends on which it paid federal income taxes of $8,190.

We projected out what would have happened to Dr. Walker had he instead not utilized a captive and had invested the net income on his own. Instead of $1.2 million in his captive, Dr. Walker would have had approximately $700,000 in net after-tax proceeds. Rather than $78,000 in dividend income, his financial advisor calculates that Dr. Walker would have earned only $46,020 in dividends, on which he would have incurred taxes of $18,868. This means that he would have net after-tax dividend income of $27,152, instead of close to $70,000 inside his captive.

At first glance, it is amazing to consider that Dr. Walker has almost twice as much in assets in his captive insurance company as he would have in an after-tax bank account in his own name. What I consider more dramatic is that the after-tax dividend income in his captive is two and half times the after-tax income he would realize in his personal portfolio. In other words, Dr. Walker is able to accumulate more wealth in the tax-mitigated environment of his captive insurance company.

It should be noted that Dr. Walker would incur a tax cost in liquidating his captive insurance company during his life. In the liquidation of his captive after the first year, he would realize a long-term capital gain to the extent the liquidation proceeds exceed his initial investment in the captive. This is true even though Dr. Walker's medical practice would have claimed ordinary income tax deductions on the premiums paid into his captive. Better yet, if he dies with the captive in his estate, his heirs may liquidate the captive at a stepped-up basis and, one would anticipate, income tax-free.

12 Wojcik, Joanne, "Reputation Damage Becoming Greater Risk Management Concern," Business Insurance (September 12, 2012).

CHAPTER 5.

CASE #2: THE DENTIST

Client Background

Carl Dennison is a dentist in Boston, Massachusetts. He is the only physician in his practice, but he has plenty of company. His wife, Veronica, who is a skilled accountant, keeps the books for the business. Veronica also generally supervises the staff, which consists of eleven part-time employees. Veronica likes to ensure that her husband can concentrate on his work and reserve plenty of time to pursue his hobby of flying.

I should warn you that Dr. Dennison is no ordinary pilot. Dr. Dennison is an accomplished telemetry pilot, tracking wildlife movements from high up in the sky. Carl began his flying career with the U.S. Army Aviation Division before he went to medical school. He now volunteers his time for the Massachusetts Division of Fisheries and Wildlife and other conservation organizations. Most weekends, Carl flies an aircraft outfitted with high-technology equipment to track radio-collared animals.

Dr. Dennison's dental clinic enjoys a respectable level of income every year. Courtesy of increasing suburban sprawl in the Boston metropolitan region, Dr. Dennison sees more and more patients every year. In the past three years, he has grown his dental practice from about $1 million in gross revenues to just about $1.5 million this year.

Underwriting Analysis

Dr. Dennison welcomed an underwriting team to examine his office and operations, and to interview him and his staff regarding their business activities. The underwriters quickly focused their attention on the high number of part-time employees (eleven) and the lack of full-time employees aside from Dr. Dennison and his wife, Veronica. Carl explained that he cannot justify the high cost of employee benefits by elevating his employees to full-time status.

The underwriters anticipate that Dr. Dennison's practice may be subject to increased risk of liability in relation to his unique employment practices. All employers face the hazard of litigation from an aggrieved former employee, and defending against even one lawsuit can be tremendously expensive for a small medical practice. Moreover, a lawsuit by one employee may have the cascading effect of resulting in liability for multiple employees aggrieved by the same practice.

Another issue that came up during the inspection was that Dr. Dennison's office is located in a flood- and storm-prone area of Boston. One good Nor'easter (tropical storm/hurricane) could wield catastrophic damage to his building, which he owns, as well as his equipment and records. The time taken to rebuild the facility would also impose a substantial loss of income.

Flood insurance is difficult to purchase in many coastal areas and sometimes must be bought from the federal government. Wind and hail policies also provide critical protection against violent weather. A medical practice in Indianapolis or St. Louis may not have to take into account hurricane activity, but an allergy clinic in Boston should.

Dr. Dennison currently has flood insurance. Unfortunately, the premiums are very high, and they are only likely to climb with time. Therefore, the underwriters recommend a flood insurance deductible reimbursement policy. This enables Dr. Dennison to keep his current flood insurance while increasing the deductible amount and lowering the cost of flood insurance.

The medical practice can then seek a reimbursement from the captive for any deductible actually paid.

One area where the underwriters did not see the need for a change was with Dr. Dennison's malpractice liability insurance. The coverage appeared to be competent and reasonably priced. The deductible on his current policy was sufficiently low enough as to make a deductible-reimbursement policy unnecessary.

Here are the lines of coverage that the underwriters recommended for Dr. Dennison's practice. Consider how these lines of coverage differ from those recommended to Dr. Walker in the previous chapter:

Employment Practices Liability

Given the unique employment practices pursued by Nr. Dennison's firm, an employment practices liability policy seems like a smart decision. A comprehensive policy of this type reimburses the medical practice for legal expenses associated with defending against a lawsuit, as well as amounts paid in settlement to an aggrieved employee.

Administrative Actions

Dr. Dennison practices in a state in which patient complaints generally obligate the state's review board to investigate. Many dentists facing such an investigation have no choice but to spend significant sums engaging legal counsel to handle any inquiries.

As mentioned earlier, a policy covering regulatory risks protects the dental practice in three ways: First, the policy reimburses the practice for all costs associated with defending the practice against the regulatory action, extending to lost earnings as a result of personnel being occupied with attending to the regulatory action. Second, a policy protecting against administrative actions reimburses the medical practice for any fines or assessments. Third, a good policy in this area reimburses the dental practice for income lost as the result of a regulatory action that prevents the business from carrying on, such as if the state review board suspends Dr. Dennison's dentistry license.

Computer Data Restoration Expense

Dr. Dennison's dental practice is required by law to maintain patient records and archive them for several years. Several years ago, Carl invested in a state-of-the-art computerized patient record system that has expedited patient services and improved return visits, but which requires careful attention to ensure its continued performance. The loss of patient records would entail a loss of income, liability to patients for lost records, and the time and expense required to restore the data. The underwriters recommend a line of coverage to reimburse the dental practice for these types of expenses.

Work Stoppage (Business Interruption)

As previously mentioned, this type of policy protects the dental practice from the risk of events that do not damage the premises of the medical practice but which still end up interrupting the flow of business. Natural disasters might include windstorms, tornados, or floods. Given the location of the practice in a hurricane-prone area, coverage here would be extremely valuable. Other possible covered risks would include power outages or the unavailability of staff due to illness, such as a virus outbreak.

Legal Expenses

The objective with this particular line of coverage is to reimburse the dental practice for legal expenses that are not covered by other policies or which are limited by other policies. This type of policy may cover legal expenses incurred as both a defendant and as a plaintiff in certain instances.

Tax Audit Expenses

The underwriters suggest that Dr. Dennison acquire a line of coverage that reimburses his practice for the expenses incurred undergoing a tax audit. Most insurance policies do not cover the costs of a tax audit, making this type of policy very meaningful.

Wrongful Acts

In Chapter Four, we saw that a captive insurance company can provide cover for wrongful acts in a manner designed to fill the gaps in traditional insurance coverage. In Dr. Dennison's case, the underwriters recommended a comprehensive policy covering all forms of negligence, errors and omissions, and similar acts. In addition to addressing a gap in coverage, the underwriters suggested expanding the existing coverage to include lost income attributable to a wrongful act claim.

Loss of Income due to Reputational Damage

As discussed earlier in this book, all medical practitioners run the risk that a black mark on one's reputation may result in a serious loss of income. Reputational risk is one of the top tens areas of risk that business insurance is designed to address. Dr. Dennison's risk is no less important in this respect, particularly given that most of his patients hail from the Boston metropolitan area. If his dental clinic takes on a bad reputation, patients will flock to one of several competing dental clinics in the area.

Excess Accounts Receivable

The underwriters noted that Dr. Dennison's dental practice is particularly sensitive to the timing of collections on receivables for patient billings. In Massachusetts, this can be a thorny issue, with some insurers taking much longer than others to pay on patient claims. Many standard policies provide some form of coverage for excess accounts receivable, but the typical policy only covers record reconstruction.

Instead, the underwriters recommend that Dr. Dennison consider a policy that would reimburse the dental practice if uncollected receivables were to fall below a pre-determined amount. Over the past three years, the underwriters observe that Dr. Dennison has incurred a collections rate of at least 68%. Therefore, they recommend a policy that pays should collections fall below 65% in any given billing period.

Flood Insurance Deductible Reimbursement

The dental clinic is in a flood-prone hurricane zone near the coastline. Past storms of the Nor'easter variety resulted in significant flooding in the area. The dental practice currently carries flood insurance, but the coverage is extremely expensive and could stand to be mitigated by increasing the deductible.

Dr. Dennison can choose to increase the deductible on his flood insurance and reduce his premium costs by roughly one-third. He can then purchase a deductible reimbursement policy from his captive insurance company, ensuring that he remains covered but can now profit from favorable weather patterns. If the unfortunate Nor'easter makes its way into Boston, Dr. Dennison is comfortable in the knowledge that he retains comprehensive coverage with his existing insurer.

Wind/Hail Deductible Reimbursement

Similar to the flood insurance deductible reimbursement policy, a wind/hail deductible reimbursement policy permits the medical practice to continue with its existing wind/hail policy. However, to conserve on insurance costs and profit from favorable weather conditions, Dr. Dennison increases the deductible payable on his retail wind/hail policy and purchases deductible reimbursement coverage from his very own captive. This way, if an adverse weather event occurs, the dental practice can still look to deep-pocket coverage from a retail insurance company.

Earthquake Deductible Reimbursement

Coastal regions incur greater seismic activities than in the heartland of the United States. While earthquake insurance in Boston is not particularly expensive, it is not free either. The underwriters propose a high deductible on the existing earthquake insurance policy for the business, supplementing this with a deductible reimbursement policy issued by the captive.

Actuarial Analysis

Dr. Dennison reviewed the underwriting report and the lines of coverage that would be extending to protect his dental practice. The actuaries then stepped in to tell us what these various policies would cost if underwritten by the captive insurance company to be established by Dr. Dennison. As in other cases, the actuaries rated the proposed insurance program to illustrate the projected losses that might be incurred.

The underwriters proposed the following lines of coverage.

Please note that several of these lines were subject to aggregate limits or limits per event which are not detailed here:

	Limit
Employment Practices Liability	$250,000
Administrative Actions	$250,000
Computer Data Restoration	$100,000
Work Stoppage (Business Interruption)	$250,000
Legal Expenses	$250,000
Tax Audit Expenses	$100,000
Wrongful Acts	$250,000
Reputational Damage/Loss of Income	$250,000
Excess Accounts Receivable	$250,000
Deductible Reimbursement (Flood)	$100,000
Deductible Reimbursement (Wind/Hail)	$100,000
Deductible Reimbursement (Earthquake)	$100,000
Total (12 lines of coverage)	*$2,250,000*

The actuarial assumptions took into account whether Dr. Dennison's dental practice would continue to perform as projected, the fact that projections could only be made annually and would have to be adjusted with time, and the fact that loss rates and cost factors would be projected based on claim frequency and severity statistics. The actuaries also warned that actual losses would almost certainly deviate from expected losses.

As a result of their analysis, the actuaries priced the coverage out at $205,418 per year. Specifically, they calculated the aggregate premium amount by pricing each line of coverage as follows:

	Annual Premium
Employment Practices Liability	$23,260
Administrative Actions	$23,260
Computer Data Restoration	$16,001
Work Stoppage (Business Interruption)	$28,307
Legal Expenses	$15,070
Tax Audit Expenses	$4,912
Wrongful Acts	$19,206
Reputational Damage/Loss of Income	$5,255
Excess Accounts Receivable	$21,200
Deductible Reimbursement (Flood)	$10,724
Deductible Reimbursement (Wind/Hail)	$10,724
Deductible Reimbursement (Earthquake)	$5,640
Removal of Aggregate Deductible and Limit	$25,000
Total (12 lines of coverage)	$205,418

One thing to note here is that the underwriters designed Dr. Dennison's policy to include a waiver of the policy aggregate deductible and limit. This resulted in an additional $25,000 of premium cost for the insurance to be provided by the captive insurance company, but it would make Dr. Dennison's insurance expenses much simpler to understand and far more predictable in the event of a claim.

Captive Analysis

Dr. Dennison is particularly fee conscious, and so we set out to find a good value service provider for him. We ultimately settled on a North Carolina incorporated cell company (ICC) with a captive manager known for transparent service pricing. An ICC is a type of company that is similar to the Cayman Islands SPC: A host parent company, a North Carolina protected cell company (PCC), sponsors multiple ICCs, and each ICC serves a separate entity with its own distinct assets and liabilities. The advantage with an ICC over a "stand-alone" captive insurance company is that an ICC is far simpler to establish and maintain.

Boston Dental Insurance opened its doors with a Belize limited liability company ("LLC") as its shareholder. Much like a Belize asset protection trust, a Belize LLC enjoys extensive protection from unanticipated creditors. In particular, Belize LLC law provides that creditors cannot reach amounts contributed to the capital of a Belize LLC in exchange for a membership interest. Moreover, any creditor wishing to go after Carl's Belize LLC interest must first post a bond equal to one half the claim amount with a Belize bank. As you might expect, creditors do not bring litigation in Belize because of these rules. While the LLC is not as efficient for estate and gift tax planning purposes, the LLC is much simpler and cost effective to operate. Dr. Dennison's captive, Boston Dental Insurance, therefore offers two distinct layers of protection for Dr. Dennison's assets: First, premiums paid into the captive from Dr. Dennison's dental practice should be respected as arm's length insurance payments. Second, profits accumulating inside the captive accrue to the benefit of the Belize LLC, which is generally immune to the claims of Carl's creditors.

Tax and Financial Analysis

The dental clinic paid a premium of $205,418 to Boston Dental Insurance. Dr. Dennison figures that this deduction saved him roughly $100,000 in state and federal income taxes.

Prior to establishing his captive insurance company, Dr. Dennison consistently saved about $40,000 per year in retirement plan contributions. Carl figured that it would take him almost 15 years to save $500,000 with his traditional retirement plan.

By comparison, Dr. Dennison was able to accumulate just under $600,000 in savings inside his captive within three years. The captive paid out on two separate insurance claims filed by the dental practice over that three-year period. Fortunately, the claims were settled at modest values, but they did come at a cost to the captive.

Last year, after having operated his captive for over three years, Dr. Dennison took a dividend of $300,000 from the captive. The dividend was paid up into his Belize LLC, which Dr. Dennison manages. Carl promptly invested the $300,000 in a Swiss bank account titled in the LLC's name and managed by a registered investment advisor living in Carl's neighborhood. The captive still retains almost an equal amount.

By taking the dividend, Dr. Dennison took advantage of the 20% qualifying dividends tax rate. He incurred a federal income tax liability of $45,000 on the distribution, leaving $255,000 left over to manage in the Swiss bank account. One may argue over the timing of Dr. Dennison's distribution, but one cannot dispute that taking advantage of the qualifying dividends tax rate is a pretty smart move. Dr. Dennison's CPA determined that Carl would have had to earn twice as much money in his practice in order to have the money that he has in the LLC and the captive today.

CHAPTER 6.

CASE #3: THE MULTI-PHYSICIAN CLINIC

Client Background

Derrick Mickevicius and Michael Moore are two highly successful eye surgeons practicing in Henderson, Nevada. They first built their practice in Henderson before a number of well-known casinos expanded into the area, and the once-sleepy town of Henderson now resembles a seamless extension of its much larger neighbor, Las Vegas.

Patients of M&M VisionCare may visit one of seven different locations scattered through the Las Vegas metropolitan region, although all surgeries are conducted at the M&M Surgical Center in downtown Henderson. The professional staff consists of both ophthalmologists who perform routine eye exams as well as surgeons attending to corneal transplants, glaucoma, cataracts, and laser refractive surgery.

M&M VisionCare enjoys gross annual revenue of approximately $5 million, while the M&M Surgical Center generates slightly less than $3.5 million per year. M&M VisionCare has 32 staff distributed among its seven offices; 10 employees work for the surgical center.

Underwriting Analysis

Derrick and Michael were used to dealing with insurance underwriters visiting their building. It was no different when the insurance underwriters spent a few days on the ground inspecting the premises and interviewing staff to determine lines of insurance to be underwritten by a captive.

The underwriters honed in on several factors that they felt contributed to substantial risks in the medical practice, several of which were underinsured or uninsured altogether:

- M&M VisionCare has a significant number of employees and many locations.
- M&M Surgical Center engages in state-of-the-art surgical procedures with cutting edge equipment.

In consultation with the underwriters, we determined that a single captive insurance company could provide valuable insurance coverage to both businesses. The underwriters then set about recommending the individual lines of coverage for each business:

Employment Practices Liability

Employment liability insurance is one of the fastest-growing risk categories for insurance underwriting nationwide. M&M VisionCare has enjoyed tremendous growth in the Las Vegas metropolitan region and is poised for further expansion, meaning that more people are likely to be hired in the near future. Obtaining this type of coverage for both businesses (VisionCare and the surgery center) ensures that neither business is left unprotected.

Administrative Actions

Laser refractive surgery involves a slightly higher rate of complaints to the state medical board than many other outpatient surgical techniques. Although the surgery center has never incurred a complaint, the underwriters worry that it is merely a function of time before a patient lodges a formal complaint over the outcome of a laser refractive operation.

A policy covering regulatory risks protects the surgery center in three ways: First, the policy reimburses the practice for all costs associated with defending the practice against the regulatory action, extending to lost earnings as a result of personnel being occupied with attending to the regulatory action. Second, a policy protecting against administrative actions reimburses the medical practice for any fines or assessments. Third, a good policy in this area reimburses the medical practice for income lost as the result of a regulatory action that prevents the business from carrying on. For example, a suspended medical license warrants reimbursement from the captive with this type of coverage.

Computer Data Restoration Expense

The underwriters determined, after a thorough site inspection, that neither VisionCare nor the surgery center face significant exposure to a loss attributable to computer data restoration. Nevertheless, a catastrophic loss of patient records would entail a loss of income, liability to patients for lost records, and the time and expense required to restore the data. For this reason, the underwriters suggested that the captive could underwrite a small policy covering both of the businesses from any losses attributable to this particular risk.

Work Stoppage (Business Interruption)

Business interruption insurance guards against the risk of events that do not damage the premises of the medical practice but which still end up interrupting the flow of business. Natural disasters might include windstorms, tornados, or floods. Henderson experiences seasonal flooding and the periodic windstorm. This type of policy also protects against power outages or the unavailability of staff due to illness, such as a virus outbreak.

Legal Expenses

Both VisionCare and the surgery center incurred only modest legal expenses over the previous three years. The underwriters recommended coverage sufficient to reimburse both businesses for legal expenses that are not covered by other policies or which are limited by other policies. This type of policy may cover legal expenses incurred as both a defendant <u>and</u> as a plaintiff in certain instances.

Tax Audit Expenses

The underwriters proposed that both businesses acquire insurance that reimburses expenses incurred undergoing a tax audit. This type of coverage is normally not available with most conventional business insurance policies, making the captive an ideal candidate to underwrite this kind of risk.

Wrongful Acts

One benefit of captive insurance is that you can design a policy that provides broad coverage for wrongful acts, particular if the conventional business insurance policy available at the retail level does not provide any form of coverage for this category of risk. A comprehensive policy of this nature covers all forms of negligence, errors and omissions, and similar acts. The underwriters recommended that both businesses be insured for any lost income attributable to a wrongful act claim.

Loss of Income Due to Reputational Damage

This particular line of coverage is becoming increasingly valuable for doctors engaged in a multi-physician practice, where the damage from one doctor can ripple outward and affect all of his or her partners. The underwriters also found that the type of practice involved here – cutting edge surgical techniques for the eyes – and the large number of employees suggest substantial risk.

Contamination and Infection – Loss of Income and Cost of Cleanup

Clinics and surgical centers are particularly exposed to the risk of biohazardous or chemical contamination. Once a contaminating incident is identified and reported, a medical facility may be unusable until the contamination is cleaned up. Many times, remediation must be arranged under the close supervision of medical or environmental regulators.

The underwriters determined that M&M Surgical Center would be at risk of losing substantial revenue if their one and only surgical facility became unavailable due to biohazardous or chemical contamination. The surgeons and other medical staff would be unable to treat patients at any of the VisionCare centers, which are not equipped to handle proper surgical procedures. The surgeons informed the underwriters that such an event would require that they reschedule long-awaited procedures for many patients and refer still other patients to competing doctors and facilities. Thus, the surgical center would lose patients and their fees to their competitors.

Loss of Use of Surgical Center – Loss of Income and Extra Expense

M&M Surgical Center purchased property insurance through a large commercial carrier, and the property insurance covered loss of income due to business interruption and work stoppage. However, in examining the policies for both VisionCare and the surgery center, the underwriters determined that VisionCare had no similar business interruption insurance, even though VisionCare depends on the surgical center to handle VisionCare patient referrals. Accordingly, the underwriters suggested that VisionCare acquire a business interruption policy from the captive that covers the loss of VisionCare's patient access to the surgical center.

Inability to Practice – Loss of Revenue and Extra Expense

Both VisionCare and the surgical center would have continuing fixed overhead costs in the event that either doctor was absent from the practice for a sustained period of time, rendering that doctor unable to produce substantial revenue. Derrick and Michael acknowledged that it would take a considerable amount of time to locate a suitable replacement doctor so as to restore revenue. Complex business issues such as compensating the departing doctor and his family, and negotiating the buy-in of a new surgeon into the practice, would necessarily arise with a prolonged absence.

The underwriters encouraged Derrick and Michael to

consider acquiring a policy that pays out if either of them is unable to practice, whether for a temporary period of time or longer. Such a policy would not pay out if the absence were due to loss of life or a critical illness. Yet, events such as travel delay, jury service, and even imprisonment of either doctor would be covered, particularly if the absence were prolonged enough to jeopardize either doctor's medical license.

Actuarial Analysis

After confirming the underwriters' observations and conclusions, Derrick and Michael then consulted with a team of actuaries to help assess the cost of insurance to be issued by their captive insurance company. The actuaries made a point to rate the proposed insurance program to illustrate the projected losses that might be incurred. Certain of these lines were subject to aggregate limits or limits per event which are not detailed here:

	Limit
Employment Practices Liability	$750,000
Work Stoppage (Business Interruption)	$750,000
Administrative Actions	$500,000
Computer Data Restoration	$250,000
Legal Expenses	$750,000
Tax Audit Expenses	$500,000
Wrongful Acts	$750,000
Reputational Damage/Loss of Income	$750,000
Contamination and Infection	$750,000
Loss of Use of Surgical Center	$750,000
Inability to Practice	$750,000
Total (11 lines of coverage)	$7,000,000

The actuaries considered that the VisionCare business and surgical center would continue to perform as projected, the fact that projections could only be made annually and would have to be adjusted with time, and the fact that loss rates and cost factors would be projected based on claim frequency and severity statistics. The actuaries also warned that actual losses would almost certainly deviate from expected losses.

As a result of their analysis, the actuaries determined an aggregate annual premium of $205,418 per year for the two businesses. Specifically, they calculated the aggregate premium amount by pricing each line of coverage as follows. For simplicity, I have not included the separate calculations for each business entity (VisionCare and the surgical center):

	Annual Premium
Employment Practices Liability	$39,489
Work Stoppage (Business Interruption)	$95,224
Administrative Actions	$24,169
Computer Data Restoration	$58,111
Legal Expenses	$38,216
Tax Audit Expenses	$17,960
Wrongful Acts	$38,216
Reputational Damage/Loss of Income	$36,817
Contamination and Infection	$73,111
Loss of Use of Surgical Center	$73,111
Inability to Practice	$92,972
Total (11 lines of coverage)	*$602,396*

The underwriters recommended, and subsequently designed the insurance coverage to include, a waiver of the policy aggregate deductible and limit. The actuaries factored this in at an additional $25,000 of aggregate premium cost from the captive insurance company.

Captive Analysis

Derrick and Michael became co-owners of a Nevis captive insurance company (SAC) licensed to write insurance: M&M Insurance Ltd. Unlike the Cayman Islands SPC or the North

Carolina ICC discussed in previous chapters, Derrick's and Michael's Nevis captive is a stand-alone insurance company: They formed it, they own it, and they direct its activities. Nevis requires that their captive be managed by a licensed insurance manager in that jurisdiction, which is fine for them because they could use the assistance of an expert manager.

M&M Insurance Ltd. underwrites insurance lines of coverage for both M&M VisionCare and M&M Surgical Center. While a captive insurance company cannot offer insurance to the general public, it can offer insurance to multiple businesses that are all owned by the same group of affiliated shareholders. This helps to economize by enabling Derrick and Michael to form just one captive insurance company to insure all their related businesses.

Both surgeons agreed that they did not want their captive insurance company to fall victim to unanticipated creditors. In particular, Michael underwent a difficult divorce a few years ago, losing a substantial sum to alimony and legal fees. He is keen to marry again one day and does not want to experience the same financial loss twice.

I suggested that both surgeons consider a Nevis asset protection trust to own the captive insurance company. Each surgeon has his own personal trust which holds a variety of investment assets and a fifty percent interest in M&M Insurance Ltd. Under the laws of Nevis, creditors cannot reach the assets of a Nevis asset protection trust. This leaves Derrick and Michael free to focus with their trustees on the prudent management of their investments as well as their captive insurance company.

Derrick and Michael have achieved two distinct layers of asset protection: First, premiums paid by VisionCare and the surgical center flow into the captive as arm's length insurance payments. This means that excess cash is not sitting inside either business where it might be exposed to the creditors of the business. Second, profits accumulating inside the captive accrue to the benefit of each surgeon's Nevis asset protection trust. Creditors cannot reach assets of a Nevis asset protection trust, leaving those funds to provide for the surgeons and their families.

Tax and Financial Analysis

VisionCare and the surgical center paid, in the aggregate, $602,396 to M&M Insurance. The surgeons' accountants have calculated approximately $250,000 in federal income tax savings attributable to the deduction (Nevada does not have a state income tax).

Two years ago, the captive reimbursed VisionCare on a substantial employment liability claim. A staff member who was passed up for a promotion filed an age discrimination complaint against the company. Shortly after the original complaint was lodged, the plaintiff's attorney signed up three other employees to join in on the lawsuit. Rather than face ongoing legal defense fees and the prospect of a hostile civil jury, VisionCare's lawyers negotiated a settlement that resulted in a claim for reimbursement at the policy's limit: $750,000.

When the captive made the $750,000 reimbursement, the captive was able to make a claim on its reinsurance for $375,000. Thus, the captive itself paid $375,000 out on its claim, and another $375,000 was born by the reinsurance pool (and spread proportionately among all the other insurance company pool participants). Thus, an added value of the captive was the ability to mitigate the impact of any one large claim by sharing the cost of that claim with the reinsurance pool. Fortunately, given the large number of participants in the reinsurance pool, the relative cost to each of the pool participants was nominal in relation to the value of the claim itself.

Derrick and Michael are thrilled with their captive insurance arrangement. They regard the employment liability coverage as a critical benefit for their practice. Had they purchased retail commercial coverage, Michael figures that the combined businesses would have spent close to $60,000 per year, or $120,000 by the second year when they incurred the employment liability claim. Also, they would have incurred the cost of a $25,000 deductible on the retail policy, meaning that their total cost would have been $145,000 with retail insurance versus $375,000 with their own captive. Notwithstanding this, Derrick and Michael calculate that they are still both ahead with captive insurance, as they still managed to save close to $900,000 in underwriting profits inside the captive in its first two years.

A large Nevada-based bank manages the investment portfolio for M&M Insurance. With time, Derrick and Michael expect that they will be able to bring on additional surgeons and open a second surgery center in Reno within the next few years. Any insurance savings captured inside M&M Insurance would be instrumental in helping the surgeons finance their business expansion.

CHAPTER 7.

CASE #4: THE PHYSICIAN-OWNED HOSPITAL

Client Background

The Irvine Burn Center is a medical practice in based in Irvine, California, and is owned by four principal doctors, Mario Cusabo, Walter Brams, Joseph McIntosh, and Sam Orista. The medical practice was established to serve as a dedicated resource for people seeking the most advanced methods of post-burn cosmetic reconstructive surgery utilizing the body's own tissue. The Irvine Burn Center employs approximately 40 doctors, nurses, and support staff.

Doctors Sam Orista and Walter Brams specialize exclusively in state-of-the-art surgery techniques that allow for post-burn facial reconstruction without the sacrifice of important functional muscles. They are international leaders in the treatment of lost and damaged skin following severe burns, pioneering groundbreaking procedures in reconstructive surgical techniques.

The Irvine Burn Center was founded in 1979 and is the only practice in North America that performs all available types of post-burn facial reconstructive surgery. In 1988, the founding partners of the Irvine Burn Center created the Newport Institute, the first and only hospital in the world dedicated to cosmetic reconstructive surgery for burn patients. The 120,000 square foot facility, located adjacent to the world-renowned

Irvine Burn Center, houses over 150 employees who provide total, state-of-the-art care from initial consultation through recovery. Cutting edge technology provides patients undergoing facial reconstructive surgery the latest in pre-surgical imaging, microsurgical monitoring, and pain management. A full service inpatient pharmacy, along with radiology and anesthesiology departments, provides comprehensive inpatient care.

The Irvine Burn Center and the hospital enjoy an international reputation with patients travelling from all over the world to obtain state-of-the-art patient care in Irvine, California. Dr. Cusabo, the visionary behind the hospital, believes in the clinical advantages of a highly specialized facility. He points out that other regional hospitals cannot cope with the volume of procedures performed by the Irvine Burn Center's practitioners.

The Newport Institute is a fully licensed hospital and registered for Medicare, although it does not actually serve any Medicare patients. Because its patients travel long distances to receive treatment at the Newport Institute, the hospital does not have an emergency room.

The procedures performed by the Irvine Burn Center are so unique that it is not a member of any insurer network. All procedures performed by the medical practitioners at the hospital are consisted "out of network" for insurance reimbursement purposes. This means that all insured cases require the insurance company's pre-approval, and almost every patient's billing goes through an appeals procedure with the insurance carrier. Standardized insurance billing codes do not accommodate the complicated, advanced procedures performed at the Newport Institute.

Over the past two years, the Newport Institute has enjoyed revenues averaging $35 million. The Irvine Burn Center averages $22 million in revenue per year, although its revenue declined in the past year, most likely as a result of a slowdown in the U.S. economy. The physicians anticipate that the revenues of the Irvine Burn Center will pick back up with any improvement in the economy.

Underwriting Analysis

The Irvine Burn Center and the Newport Institute have extensive insurance needs and work with a number of leading commercial carriers. In fact, the hospital has an employee dedicated just to negotiating and maintaining the hospital's insurance policies.

We asked a team of underwriters to work with the hospital's dedicated insurance manager to examine the scope of existing insurance coverage and identify the key areas of risk, regardless of whether insurance existed to cover the risk. The underwriters quickly identified a number of key risks that would be pertinent to their analysis:

- Both the burn center and the hopsital have employ a significant number of staff members.

- The Irvine Burn Center and the Newport Institute are located in an earthquake-prone region of the United States.

- The City of Irvine has also experienced rapid development over the past twenty years, resulting in increased urbanization. Whereas crime was not an issue in Irvine when the Newport Institute opened its doors, crime is now a regular facet of working in downtown Irvine.

The underwriters then set about outlining their insurance recommendations for the burn clinic and separately for the hospital.

Risks of the Irvine Burn Center

Administrative Actions

A policy covering regulatory risks protects the Irvine Burn Center in three ways:

1. The policy reimburses the practice for all costs associated with defending the practice against the regulatory action. This extends to lost earnings as a result of personnel having to sacrifice revenue hours in order to attend to a defense against the regulatory action.
2. A policy protecting against administrative actions reimburses the burn center for any fines or assessments.
3. A competent policy on administrative actions reimburses the burn center for income lost as the result of a regulatory action that prevents the business from carrying on. For example, a suspended medical license warrants reimbursement from the insurance carrier with this type of coverage.

Loss of Key Employee

Drs. Cusabo, Brams, McIntosh, and Orista are essential to the revenue of the Irvine Burn Center and cannot easily be replaced, if at all, due to their unique experience, proprietary techniques, and reputation in the field earned over decades of practice. The policy would cover any fortuity other than death that prevents them from temporarily or permanently working for the burn center. A voluntary absence is excluded under this type of coverage. The Irvine Burn Center would be reimbursed up to $150,000 per month per doctor for a loss in this category.

Contamination and Infection – Loss of Income and Cost of Clean Up

As discussed in the previous chapter, clinics and outpatient surgical centers run the risk of biohazardous or chemical contamination to their facilities. Once a contaminating incident is identified and reported, use of the facility typically has to be suspended until the contamination is cleaned up. Usually, medical or environmental regulators closely supervise the cleanup and must sign off before the facility may be put back to use.

One mitigating factor in this risk category is that the Irvine Burn Center conducts procedures at both its own facility and at the adjacent hospital. The underwriters calculated that the doctors would be able to transport their outpatient procedures to the hospital if the burn center were rendered unusable for any period of time, albeit the increased use of the hospital's facilities would hinder the hospital's ability to maintain its own volume of procedures.

Work Stoppage (Business Interruption)

As discussed in several of the preceding chapters, business interruption insurance guards against the risk of events that do not damage the premises of the operating business but which nevertheless interrupt the flow of business. Natural disasters might include earthquakes, windstorms, tornados, and floods.

The City of Irvine is in an earthquake "hot zone." Almost every day, the city experiences tremors that are practically imperceptible. Coverage in this area would help protect the Irvine Burn Center should a significant seismic event prevent the burn center from operating for a sustained period of time. This type of coverage also protects a business from losses incurred due to a significant power outage or the unavailability of staff due to a public health emergency, such as a virus outbreak.

Legal Expenses

The Irvine Burn Center routinely experiences litigation, particularly as it is located in California, which enjoys a reputation as a plaintiff-friendly jurisdiction. While the burn center maintains comprehensive coverage, that coverage comes at a significant cost due to the burn center's history of litigation, and the underwriters identified numerous gaps in coverage.

The underwriters recommended that insurance coverage be sufficient to reimburse the burn center for its out-of-pocket expenses that are not covered by other policies or which are limited by other policies. The underwriters also suggested that the insurance coverage extend to legal expenses incurred by the burn center as a plaintiff.

Tax Audit Expenses

The underwriters proposed that the Irvine Burn Center acquire insurance that reimburses its expenses incurred undergoing a tax audit. This type of coverage is normally not available with most conventional business insurance policies, leaving a gap in coverage that can be filled in with a customized policy issued by a captive insurance carrier.

Loss of Income Due to Reputational Damage

Reputational damage is a serious risk for any medical practice. The underwriters consider this risk to be enhanced in practices that specialize in the treatment of conditions that are life-threatening. Life-threatening conditions carry with them a significant emotional impact for the patients.

Highly emotional patients are considered more likely to complain publicly. The reputation of the Irvine Burn Center and its doctors is carefully nurtured. A begrudged patient governed by the high emotions of a life-threating condition could easily harm that reputation.

Computer Data Restoration

The Irvine Burn Center keeps patient records pursuant to a number of legal requirements. Those records are archived both on-site and in a backup facility located elsewhere in the State of California.

The computer systems at the Irvine Burn Center are customized to the unique style of practice and medical procedures performed by its physicians. Certain aspects of the systems integrate very tightly with the Newport Institute's records and retrieval systems so that same-patient data may pass between the two organizations.

The underwriters interviewed the technology staff as well as the outside contractor that designed the underlying software used by the burn center. They mutually determined that damage to the systems and loss of patient records would yield substantial financial harm for the business. This risk is mitigated by the fact that the burn center regularly follows an off-site backup plan. However, the outside contractor pointed out to the underwriters that a loss of system functionality in the burn center would have an adverse impact on the Newport Institute's computer systems, and vice versa, due to the unique manner in which their two distinct systems depend on each other to exchange patient data.

Even with the extensive backup regimen that is religiously followed by the technology staff at the burn center, the software programmers are convinced that a significant interruption in the burn center's computer systems would require significant labor to resurrect, and access to patient data would be limited or nonexistent for a material period of time. Accordingly, the underwriters proposed that the Irvine Burn Center purchase insurance coverage to reimburse the medical practice for these types of expenses, as well as for liability to patients for the temporary or permanent loss of records.

Risks of the Newport Institute

Administrative Actions

As with the Irvine Burn Center, the underwriters advised that the Newport Institute procure insurance to protect it from administrative (regulatory) actions. Coverage in this risk category would protect the hospital in three ways:

1. The policy protects the hospital from any costs incurred while defending the hospital from a regulatory action. The protection would include lost earnings as a result of hospital staff having to spend time fighting a regulatory action rather than helping to generate revenue for the hospital.
2. A policy protecting against administrative actions reimburses the hospital for any fines or assessments.
3. The hospital may be reimbursed for income lost as the result of a regulatory action that prevents the hospital from conducting its business.

Loss of Key Employee

Drs. Cusabo, Brams, McIntosh, and Orista are each essential to the revenue of the Newport Institute. The loss of any of these four physicians would put the hospital in a bind, requiring an international recruitment effort to find a suitable replacement. Even then, a replacement physician may not be available.

This form of "key man" coverage would protect the hospital from any fortuity (other than the death of the physician) preventing the physician from working, whether temporarily or permanently. The voluntary absence of a doctor would be excluded from coverage. The hospital would be reimbursed up to $150,000 per month on account of any losses arising from the doctor's absence.

Contamination and Infection – Loss of Income and Cost of Clean Up

Hospital premises are particularly exposed to the risk of contamination or infection, which renders them unusable until cleaned up. Because hospitals are made subject to a uniquely comprehensive set of environmental regulations, hospital operations may be suspended while a contamination or infection is mitigated. Regulators may be on hand to supervise the cleanup or disinfection.

The underwriters determined that the hospital would incur significant losses from an incident of contamination or infection. They therefore recommended insurance that would help protect the hospital from the cost of mitigation. Also, a comprehensive insurance policy in this risk category would reimburse the hospital for lost income arising from the incident.

Work Stoppage (Business Interruption)

This type of coverage protects the Newport Institute from the risk that external forces such as a natural disaster may not damage the hospital facility itself, but which nevertheless prevent the hospital from conducting business. Many years ago, an earthquake in the Los Angeles metropolitan area damaged the Santa Monica Freeway, forcing business commuters to seek alternate routes to work or refrain from commuting altogether.

At least some people had an alternate route to pursue. By contrast, the City of Irvine, further south in Orange County, resides in a geographic pinch point in which earthquake damage to the nearby freeway system, or a wildfire in the surrounding hills, may choke off traffic from outside areas.

Business interruption insurance protects the hospital from more than just natural disasters. Hospitals need to be concerned about a flu epidemic or other public health crises affecting the availability of staff and patients. Power outages, while infrequent, may prove catastrophic for a hospital. Procurement of this type of insurance assures the hospital management that business at the hospital may continue unabated, and that insurance coverage will step in to protect the hospital from any material interruption.

Patient Evacuation

Hospitals need to prepare for disasters and the distinct possibility that patients may need to be evacuated to other hospital facilities in neighboring communities. A particular concern in this regard for the Newport Institute is that a majority of its patients hail from beyond Southern California, and many patients travel from far overseas just to obtain treatment at the Newport Institute. Adding to the complexity is that some burn patients require specialized accommodations before they can be moved from one hospital to another. If a nearby hospital does not have the requisite facilities for a severe burn patient, the patient may need to be airlifted (or flown by specially-equipped private aircraft) to a remote location. Competent insurance coverage reimburses the hospital for the cost of transporting patients to area facilities and housing them in alternate locations.

Legal Expenses

California-based hospitals such as the Newport Institute are frequent targets of litigation. In addition to experienced in-house legal counsel, the Newport Institute relies on an area law firm to help manage its ongoing litigation. Insurance to protect the hospital from legal expenses is expensive to procure in Southern California.

The underwriters proposed that the hospital purchase insurance coverage that would indemnify the hospital for its out-of-pocket expenses incurred in prosecuting claims and defending itself from lawsuits. They recommended that the insurance coverage be carefully designed to help plug the gaps in the hospital's existing web of commercial insurance coverage.

Tax Audit Expenses

As with the burn center, the underwriters determined that the Newport Institute should purchase coverage for expenses incurred undergoing a tax audit. This type of coverage is normally not available with most conventional business insurance policies, leaving a gap in coverage that can be filled in with a customized policy issued by a captive insurance carrier.

Loss of Income Due to Reputational Damage

This is a serious risk for any hospital, but particular a hospital that enjoys a unique international reputation and draws patients from the world over. The underwriters recommended insurance coverage for this particular type of loss, but only extending to loss of income in respect of damage to the Newport Institute's reputation (to the exclusion of reputational damage to an attending physician or the burn center). The underwriters also suggested that insurance coverage be drawn up to cover reputational damage arising from a connection between the Newport Institute and the Irvine Burn Center, but that the policy limit for this type of risk be lower than the policy limit for coverage on the reputational risk confronting the Newport Institute in isolation.

Excess Charge Adjustment

All hospital billings are subject to adjustments from patients' health insurers. From time to time, a health insurer may change its reimbursement practices, including the amount of reimbursement for a given procedure as well as the manner in which a procedure is considered for insurance. These changes may be instigated by similar changes in the way Medicare reimburses service providers.

Changes in reimbursement levels and procedures by health insurers are par for the course in the hospital business. The underwriters suggested that the hospital protect itself from changes that exceed a defined level, at which point the changes would yield a serious impact on the hospital's earning or "net patient revenues." Insurance coverage would step in to reimburse the hospital to the extent that those changes exceed the threshold level, subject to an overall policy limit.

Actuarial Analysis – Irvine Burn Center

Following the recommendations of the underwriters, the insurance and legal staff from the burn center met with a team of actuaries to assess the cost of insurance proposed to be underwritten through a captive insurance company. The actuaries prepared their rating of the proposed insurance program with a view to projecting losses that might be incurred. Certain of these lines were subject to aggregate limits or limits per event which are not detailed here.

	Limit
Administrative Actions	$1,000,000
Loss of Key Employee	$1,000,000
Contamination and Infection	$1,000,000
Work Stoppage (Business Interruption)	$1,000,000
Legal Expenses	$1,000,000
Tax Audit Expenses	$500,000
Reputational Damage/Loss of Income	$1,000,000
Computer Data Restoration	$1,000,000
Total (8 lines of coverage)	*$7,500,000*

The actuaries factored into their projections the assumptions that the business would continue to perform as projected, the fact that projections could only be made annually and would have to be adjusted with time, and the fact that loss rates and cost factors would be projected based on claim frequency and severity statistics. The actuaries also warned that actual losses would almost certainly deviate from expected losses.

As a result of their analysis, the actuaries determined an aggregate annual premium of $922,277 per year for the burn center. Specifically, they calculated the aggregate premium amount by pricing each line of coverage as follows:

	Annual Premium
Administrative Actions	$140,041
Loss of Key Employee	$41,910
Contamination and Infection	$160,758
Work Stoppage (Business Interruption)	$225,256
Legal Expenses	$23,556
Tax Audit Expenses	$38,414
Reputational Damage/Loss of Income	$127,149
Computer Data Restoration	$165,193
Total (8 lines of coverage)	$822,277

The underwriters recommended, and subsequently designed the insurance coverage to include, a waiver of the policy aggregate deductible and limit. The actuaries factored this in at no additional premium cost from the captive insurance company.

Actuarial Analysis – Newport Institute

The hospital's insurance manager and in-house legal counsel, along with additional hospital staff, reviewed the recommendations of the underwriters to confirm the proposed lines of coverage. They then consulted with the actuaries to assess the cost of insurance proposed to be underwritten through a captive insurance company. The actuaries prepared their rating of the proposed insurance program with a view to projecting losses that might be incurred. Certain of these lines were subject to aggregate limits or limits per event which are not detailed here.

	Limit
Administrative Actions	$1,500,000
Loss of Key Employee	$1,500,000
Contamination and Infection	$2,000,000
Work Stoppage (Business Interruption)	$2,000,000
Legal Expenses	$1,000,000
Tax Audit Expenses	$500,000
Reputational Damage/Loss of Income	$1,000,000
Excess Charge Adjustment	$1,500,000
Patient Evacuation	$500,000
Total (8 lines of coverage)	$11,500,000

The actuaries assumed that the hospital's business and financial performance would continue as projected, the fact that projections could only be made annually and would have to be adjusted with time, and the fact that loss rates and cost factors would be projected based on claim frequency and severity statistics. The actuaries also warned that actual losses would almost certainly deviate from expected losses.

As a result of their analysis, the actuaries determined an aggregate annual premium of $1,844,058 per year for the hospital. Specifically, they calculated the aggregate premium amount by pricing each line of coverage as follows:

	Annual Premium
Administrative Actions	$298,986
Loss of Key Employee	$47,662
Contamination and Infection	$341,563
Work Stoppage (Business Interruption)	$307,140
Legal Expenses	$58,792
Tax Audit Expenses	$41,670
Reputational Damage/Loss of Income	$232,408
Excess Charge Adjustment	$255,656
Patient Evacuation	$60,181
Total (8 lines of coverage)	*$1,644,058*

The underwriters recommended, and subsequently designed the insurance coverage to include, a waiver of the policy aggregate deductible and limit. The actuaries factored this in at no additional premium cost from the captive insurance company.

Captive Analysis

Each of the four principal doctors desired to own a captive insurance company that would serve as a means of accumulating underwriting profits for the benefit of themselves and their family members. Accordingly, four separate captive insurance companies were established, each of which participated in some of the coverages for both the burn center and the hospital.

The doctors settled on Tennessee, and its "series" limited liability company (LLC) law, as the basis for the formation of their captive insurance companies. A series LLC is similar to a segregated portfolio company, segregated account company, or similar cell company found in other insurance jurisdictions: Each LLC series constitutes a distinct entity with its own assets and liabilities, separate and apart from the host LLC and any sister series. In this particular case, a licensed captive manager supervised by the Tennessee Department of Insurance manages the host LLC. Establishing a new series for each new captive insurance company is a relatively straightforward matter of filing a written declaration for the series, notifying the insurance commissioner of the series formation, and obtaining the insurance license for the new series.

One concern that was at the forefront of all our discussions was the fact that each of the four physicians faces substantial personal liability arising from the business. Not only are they doctors, but they are also treating burn patients, which is an emotionally-charged field of practice.

I cautioned the physicians that a domestic LLC, including a Tennessee series LLC, offers absolutely no protection from outside creditors. Many purveyors of domestic asset protection trusts and LLCs claim that, by forming a trust in Alaska or Nevada, or an LLC in a state like Delaware, somehow your assets are miraculously protected from the claims of creditors. Nothing could be further from the truth.

It is important for you to understand why it is that I think domestic asset protection does not work. You need to be careful before following the advice of anyone who tells you that your assets are safe inside an Alaska, Delaware, or Nevada trust, or a Delaware or Wyoming LLC. I refer to these types of structure as "domestic asset protection structures."

The United States Constitution contains a provision known as the "Full Faith and Credit" clause[13]. This clause provides, very simply, that a judgment rendered in one state is entitled to full faith and credit (i.e., enforceability) in any other state in the U.S. If a creditor in California sues you in that state and obtains a judgment against you, that creditor can enforce that judgment in any other state.

Advocates of domestic asset protection structures argue that your creditor would still need to sue the trust or LLC in order to reach your assets held in that entity. From experience, I can assure you that the only barrier preventing a creditor from suing your domestic asset protection structure is the mere cost of filing a piece of paper with the court that names your domestic asset protection structure as an additional defendant in the lawsuit. In most states, the cost of adding an additional named defendant is less than $100. Do you really believe that a creditor will spend thousands of dollars suing you but somehow will not spend another $100 to add your domestic asset protection structure to the lawsuit?

I believe that domestic asset protection structures only work in two circumstances. First, there is a sophisticated planning technique called the "SWIFT Trust" under which you establish a hybrid Swiss-Wyoming trust. The details are far beyond the scope of this book. In fact, I have a separate book outlining this technique with precision for those who are interested. Second, domestic asset protection structures *may* work for people who actually reside in a state that offers domestic asset protection laws, but only if the creditor is also a sole resident of that state. For example, if you live in Nevada and your creditor is a Nevada-based company, odds are that Nevada's asset protection trust law might shield your trust assets from that particular creditor. Unfortunately, Nevada law will not protect your trust assets from creditors of any other state. The reason for this is that a creditor in another state will sue you in federal court and seek to apply the laws of a state (such as California) that does not recognize domestic asset protection structures.

Advocates of domestic asset protection structures raise all forms of ultra-legalistic arguments for why a judge in California or Connecticut would be required to abide by the asset protection laws of Alaska or Nevada. I simply cannot buy into that nonsense. More importantly, I would not want my client to be the guinea pig who loses his life's savings to something that, to date, has not been thoroughly tested in the courts. The Alaska asset protection trust has already been found not to work in bankruptcy.[14] Therefore, a domestic asset protection structure established in any other state, including Delaware, Nevada, or Wyoming, just as likely leaves your assets exposed to creditors.

I agreed in consultation with the four principal doctors of the Irvine Burn Center and the Newport Institute that a foreign asset protection structure would be superior to a domestic asset protection structure. At the same time, we could not change the fact that each of their four captive insurance companies were established as Tennessee LLC series.

The strategy we settled on was to form a separate Belize limited liability company for each captive insurance company. Belize is the first country in the world to offer an asset protection LLC law wherein capital contributions by members to an LLC cannot be challenged as fraudulent transfers. Belize also limits creditors to a charging order as the exclusive remedy for any claim against a member of a Belize LLC.

It is worth pointing out that, under Belize law, a creditor must post a bond with the court equal to <u>one half</u> of the value of the claim. For example, if a creditor is suing you for $1 million, the creditor must post a cash bond with the court of $500,000 before the claim will be entertained by the court. Even then, Belize law does not honor foreign judgments against a Belize LLC. Instead, the creditor must bring an original claim in the Belize courts, and only after posting the aforementioned bond.

Dr. McIntosh's captive, Newport Insurance, owns a Belize LLC, aptly named Newport (Belize), LLC. Dr. McIntosh has filed what is called a "disregarded entity" election with the IRS whereby the Belize LLC is treated as a disregarded entity for U.S. Federal income tax purposes. All of the income and assets of the Belize LLC are reported on the tax return for Newport Insurance. At the same time, the Belize LLC holds all of the captive's investment assets. Because Belize protects capital contributions, no creditor may reach the assets of the Belize LLC under any circumstance.

Each of Dr. McIntosh's partners established a similar foreign asset protection trust structure. While the captive insurance company for each partner remains a domestic entity (a Tennessee series LLC), each doctor is comforted in the knowledge that the core assets of his captive are safely tucked away in a Belize LLC that is shielded from creditors.

Tax and Financial Analysis

The Irvine Burn Center paid premiums in the first year of slightly more than $800,000 to a group of four separate captive insurance companies, each owned by one of the four principal physicians. Given that each of the four physicians is subject to California state income tax, the combined Federal and state taxes that would otherwise apply to $800,000 of income would be approximately $400,000.

Separately, the Newport Institute paid aggregate premiums of roughly $1.6 million to the same four captives. Again, had premiums not been paid and the doctors instead withdrew the $1.6 million as excess profits from the business, the doctors would have incurred combined Federal and California income tax liabilities of about $800,000. They also would have left themselves and their two businesses, the burn center and the hospital, seriously exposed to substantial risks.

Given the size and scope of the activities of the captive insurance companies in this case, claims are routine. A wildfire west of Irvine a few years ago threatened the ability of many staff members living on the coast from reaching the work facilities, and a handful of staff members had to evacuate their houses. Still, the burn center and the hospital have been diligent in mitigating their losses, and the four captives have collectively accumulated over $10 million in slightly over four years.

Shortly before the expiration of the 15% capital gains tax rate, each of the four physicians received a handsome dividend from his respective captive. Not only were they able to benefit from the lowest possible tax rate on dividends from their captives, but the dividend helped each captive to ensure that its earnings would not accumulate to such a large level as to invoke the application of the accumulated earnings tax.

Even though the 15% long-term capital gains tax rate is now history, the rate is now 20%, which is still better than 39.6% on ordinary income. Please note that a captive insurance company cannot be intentionally used to exploit the tax rate "arbitrage" between the 20% capital gains tax rate and the 39.6% ordinary income tax rate. However, when established for the right reasons and properly maintained, a captive insurance company can pay out dividends that are taxed at half the rate of ordinary income.

13 U.S. Const. art. IV, § 1.
14 See Battley v. Mortensen, No. A09-90036-DMD (Adv. D.Alaska, May 26, 2011).

CHAPTER 8.

CONCLUSION

Over the past fifty years, captive insurance has become an established area of insurance planning for American businesses. Virtually all of the Fortune 500 companies utilizes a captive insurance plan, and increasing numbers of privately-held and family-run companies are taking advantage of the important financial savings that can be achieved with captive insurance. The widespread adoption of captive insurance planning has only accelerated with the IRS's acquiescence to the validity of captive insurance as an important planning tool for businesses.

I wrote this book specifically for physicians and hospital owners who may be considering captive insurance for a medical business. However, captives also exist for a variety of other businesses, whether or not medically related. Moreover, within the medical profession, captive insurance has been successfully utilized to protect surgical centers, laser centers, and a wide variety of other medical practices.

The forms of insurance coverage described in the foregoing chapters are representative only. There are a wide variety of risks that can be successfully mitigated with a captive insurance company. Many of these risks will vary from industry to industry. For example, an auto parts factory cannot possibly use "patient evacuation" insurance, just as a doctor's office has no need for insurance protecting against supply chain disruptions.

To best understand the types of risks that can be insured in your business, I recommend that you speak with someone experienced in the field of captive insurance.

Given the limited scope of this book, I have not devoted many pages to describing the mechanics and procedures behind the successful operation and maintenance of a captive insurance company. An entire book could be written on that subject alone, and it would likely be more technical a discussion than you would care to read. However, as with any business, there is a lot that goes into operating and maintaining a captive, and an entire industry of service professionals exists to aid in this effort. Underwriters evaluate the business and recommend the lines of coverage to be insured through the captive. Actuaries calculate the premiums to be paid and the potential risks faced by the captive. Insurance administrators and legal staff design the insurance policies in close consultation with the underwriters and the insured business' representatives. Accountants maintain books for the captive insurance company and work with auditors to provide recurring audits of the captive's financial status. Insurance adjusters evaluate claims and process payments from the captive to the insured business. Reinsurance specialists work with the captive's managers to ensure that the captive has the financial resources to pay claims on the policies issued by the captive, and that any reinsurance maintained by the captive is financial- and tax-compliant. Still more accountants work on the tax filings for the captive, and still other staff focus on maintaining the bank and investment accounts owned by the captive. Just as well, there are investment managers selected by the client to manage the captive's portfolio of investment assets.

Notwithstanding the tremendous savings that can be achieved on insurance costs with a captive, there are people out there who cut corners and market captives for less honorable purposes. A profitable captive insurance plan may yield some tax savings. However, those tax savings cannot serve as a primary motive for the captive insurance plan. More importantly, if you engage in a captive insurance plan for tax reasons alone, you are likely to be disappointed. Red flags to consider when evaluating a captive insurance plan or a service provider include the following:

- Marketing that seems entirely focused on tax savings, with no discussion of the way in which insurance costs can be mitigated as a profit-making business of a captive.

- Recommended lines of insurance coverage that have little or no applicability to the business, or which are in amounts that are far in excess of the reasonable needs of the business.

- Promoters who offer "boilerplate" forms in which the client decides on the lines of coverage and the amount of insurance to be purchased in the business, with no credible underwriting assessment of the reasonable insurance needs of the business or any actuarial analysis of the practical costs of insurance.

- Advisors suggesting the use of cash value life insurance with a captive insurance company. I do not endorse such ideas and would caution anyone considering a captive insurance company to not incorporate life insurance into the plan. Keep your personal life insurance planning separate from your business insurance planning.

- Insurance managers who are unable to document the manner in which a captive insurance company satisfies the risk distribution requirements of U.S. income tax law. A credible service provider should be able to provide a thorough actuarial analysis that, ideally, can serve as the foundation for obtaining a private letter ruling from the IRS.

Most importantly, if you have any questions or are interested in a further evaluation of captive insurance for your business, I invite you to contact me. We work with lawyers and their clients in establishing, licensing, and administering captive insurance companies on a daily basis. I would be pleased to walk you through the process in greater detail and help you evaluate the viability of a captive insurance plan specific to your needs.

KEY CASES AND RULINGS ON CAPTIVE INSURANCE

Throughout this book, I have referenced a number of key cases and rulings concerning captive insurance taxation. This appendix contains these key authorities (reformatted for this book) along with notations concerning their importance. These authorities may be summarized as follows:

1. <u>Helvering</u> v. <u>Le Gierse</u>, 312 U.S. 531 (1941): In this case, the U.S. Supreme Court introduces us to the concepts of "risk shifting" and "risk distribution" as required elements of "insurance" for tax purposes.
2. <u>Humana Inc. v. Commissioner</u>, 881 F.2d 247 (6th Cir. 1989): The Sixth Circuit Court of Appeals, ruling against the IRS, finds that a captive insurance company achieves sufficient risk distribution by insuring risks of subsidiaries underneath a common corporate parent.
3. <u>Harper Group v. Commissioner</u>, 979 F.2d 1341 (9th Cir. 1992): Sufficient risk distribution exists even if the captive only insures between 29% and 33% unrelated party risks.
4. <u>Sears, Roebuck and Co. v. Commissioner</u>, 972 F.2d 858 (7th Cir. 1992): Writing for the Seventh Circuit, Judge Easterbrook concludes that (i) a captive insurance subsidiary may achieve risk distribution by insuring risks of its parent in conjunction with unrelated party risks, and (ii) insurance against mortgage loan defaults is "insurance."
5. <u>United Parcel Service v. Commissioner</u>, 254 F.3d 1014 (11th

Cir. 2001): The Eleventh Circuit, reversing the Tax Court, sustains an arrangement whereby UPS's captive reinsures almost all the risks associated with customer shipping insurance through an unrelated "fronting" carrier.

6. Rent-A-Center v. Commissioner, 142 T.C. No. 1 (2014): Consistent with Sears, Roebuck (above), the Tax Court sustained a captive that insured only the activities of its parent holding company and its affiliates. "Risk distribution" was measured by the number of individual risks insured by the captive, rather than the number of legal entities (as in Humana (above)) within the corporate family procuring insurance from the captive.

7. Securitas Holdings, Inc. v. Commissioner, T.C. Memo. 2014-225 (2014): The Tax Court sustained a captive insurance arrangement almost identical to Rent-A-Center, concluding that "risk distribution" was adequately measured based on the number of insured risks, rather than on the number of participating legal entities within the same corporate ownership group.

8. R.V.I. Guaranty Co., Ltd. v. Commissioner, 145 T.C. No. 9 (2015): In concluding that insuring against the decline in the residual value of leased automobiles is "insurance," the Tax Court rejects the IRS theory that "investment risk" is different from "insurance risk."

9. Revenue Ruling 77-316: In this old IRS ruling, the Service indicates that it will disallow deductions of insurance premiums paid to captive insurance company under "economic family" doctrine. Fortunately for taxpayers and unfortunately for the IRS, no court has ever accepted the Service's argument on this point.

10. Revenue Ruling 2001-31: This is the seminal ruling in which the IRS announces that it will no longer disallow deductions of insurance premiums paid to a captive insurance company under the "economic family" doctrine.

11. Revenue Ruling 2002-89: This ruling contains a set of

examples indicating that, for sufficient risk distribution to exist, the captive insurance company must not insure more than 50% unrelated party risks. The ruling also alludes to reinsurance pooling as a means of satisfying the risk distribution requirement.

12. Revenue Ruling 2002-90: Conceding the taxpayer's position in Humana, the IRS rules that sufficient risk distribution exists where all the insured parties are related through a common parent holding company.

13. Revenue Ruling 2002-91: The IRS approves a hypothetical group or association captive arrangement in which (i) no member owns more than 15% of the captive and (ii) no member holds more than 15% of the vote on any corporate governance issues.

14. Revenue Ruling 2005-40: The IRS outlines four hypothetical situations concerning captive insurance and then offers its opinion on the tax consequences. The ruling emphasizes the number of tax-recognized legal entities participating in the risk pool as critical to risk distribution, going so far as to indicate that one structure involving LLCs disregarded for tax purposes would not be acceptable, whereas the same structure with LLCs taxed as corporation would be fine. Ultimately, this position was rejected by the Tax Court in Rent-A-Center, above, and Securitas, above, which emphasize that risk distribution may be achieved based on the number of insured risks, regardless of the number of legal entities insured.

15. Revenue Ruling 2008-8: The IRS explains that "cell" captive insurance companies will be evaluated individually on a cell-by-cell basis.

16. Revenue Ruling 2009-26: In stark contrast to Revenue Ruling 2005-40, where the IRS engaged in the artificial practice of counting entity-insureds to determine whether risk distribution was adequate, in this ruling the IRS looks

through a reinsurance agreement to find sufficient risk distribution.

17. <u>Revenue Ruling 2014-15</u>: Consistent with the position taking in <u>Revenue Ruling 2009-26</u>, the IRS determines adequate risk distribution exists in a captive insurance arrangement. While there is only one insured, a voluntary employee benefits association (VEBA), the IRS looks through the VEBA to finds multiple underlying risks.

18. <u>Proposed Treasury Regulations § 301.7701-1(a)(5)</u>: In 2010, the Treasury Department issued proposed regulations that would govern the tax treatment of "cell" captive insurance companies consistent with the approach outlined in <u>Revenue Ruling 2008-8</u>, above.

19. <u>Private Letter Ruling 200402001</u>: Following the issuance of <u>Revenue Procedure 2002-75</u>, which invited taxpayers to apply to the IRS for rulings concerning their captive insurance arrangements, this was one of the first private letter rulings actually issued.

20. <u>Private Letter Ruling 200907006</u>: The IRS approves an arrangement in which the captive cedes all of its insured risk to a reinsurance pool, and the captive then assumes a quota share of the risk in the overall pool.

21. <u>Private Letter Rulings 200950016</u>: In two substantially identical private letter rulings (the companion ruling is <u>Private Letter Ruling 200950017</u>), the IRS affirms quota share reinsurance arrangements as "insurance." Use of a fronting carrier was not regarded as affecting the underlying merits of the reinsurance arrangements.

22. <u>Private Letter Ruling 201030014</u>: The IRS confirms that a reinsurance pool offers genuine risk distribution where no one insured's risk exceeds 15% of the overall risks of the pool.

23. <u>Private Letter Ruling 201126036</u>: The IRS finds inadequate risk distribution where related party risk constitutes 69.4% of the overall risk pool. The IRS distinguishes <u>Harper Group</u>

by emphasizing that the 69-71% of related party risk in Harper Group was attributable to legally distinct business entities within the same corporate family.

24. Private Letter Rulings 201219009: In the first of three similar rulings, the IRS concludes that risk distribution may be achieved through participation in a quota share reinsurance agreement with a reinsurance pool.

25. Private Letter Ruling 201350008: This was one of a series of private letter rulings issued in 2013 in which the IRS staked out its argument that "investment risks" are distinguishable from "insurance risks" and cannot be the proper subject of captive insurance. This position was overruled by the Tax Court in R.V.I. Guaranty, above.

HELVERING V. LEGIERSE

Helvering v. LeGierse, 312 U.S. 531 (1941)
CERTIORARI TO THE CIRCUIT COURT OF APPEALS
FOR THE SECOND CIRCUIT

Syllabus

- Within the meaning of § 302(g) of the Revenue Act of 1926, as amended, amounts "receivable as insurance" are amounts receivable as the result of transactions which involved, at the time of their execution, an actual insurance risk.

- Risk shifting and risk distribution are essentials of a contract of life insurance.

- A contract in the standard form of a life insurance policy, containing the usual provisions, including those for assignment or surrender, was issued to a woman of eighty years of age, without physical examination, for a single premium less than the face of the policy, together with an annuity policy for another premium calling for annual payments to her until her death. Although both policies were, on the face, separate contracts, neither referring to the other, and each was treated as independent in the matters of application, computation of premium, report and book entry of premium payment, maintenance of reserve, etc., they were issued at the same time, and the making of the annuity contract was a condition to the issuance of the life policy, and the combined effect was such that, in case of premature death, the gain to the insurance company under one would neutralize its loss under the other.

Held:

- That the contracts must be considered together.

- They created no insurance risk. Any risk that the prepayment would earn less than the amount paid by the insurance company as an annuity was an investment risk, not an insurance risk.

- The amount payable to the beneficiary named in the life policy, upon the death of the "insured," was not in the scope of § 302(g), supra, but was properly taxed in the decedent's estate under § 302(c) as a transfer to take effect in possession or enjoyment at or after death.

110 F.2d 734 reversed.

Certiorari, 311 U.S. 625, to review the affirmance of a decision of the Board of Tax Appeals, 39 B.T.A. 1134, reversing a deficiency assessment of estate tax.

MR. JUSTICE MURPHY delivered the opinion of the Court.

Less than a month before her death in 1936, decedent, at the age of 80, executed two contracts with the Connecticut General Life Insurance Co. One was an annuity contract in standard form entitling decedent to annual payments of $589.80 as long as she lived. The consideration stated for this contract was $4,179. The other contract was called a "Single Premium Life Policy-Non Participating" and provided for a payment of $25,000 to decedent's daughter, respondent Le Gierse at decedent's death. The premium specified was $22,946. Decedent paid the total consideration, $27,125 at the time the contracts were executed. She was not required to pass a physical examination or to answer the questions a woman applicant normally must answer.

The "insurance" policy would not have been issued without the annuity contract, but, in all formal respects, the two were treated as distinct transactions. Neither contract referred to the other. Independent applications were filed for each. Neither premium was computed with reference to the other. Premium payments were reported separately and entered in different accounts on the company's books. Separate reserves were maintained for insurance and annuities. Each contract was in standard form. The "insurance" policy contained the usual provisions for surrender, assignment, optional modes of settlement, etc.

Upon decedent's death, the face value of the "insurance" contract became payable to respondent Le Gierse, the beneficiary. Thereafter, a federal estate tax return was filed which excluded from decedent's gross estate the proceeds of the "insurance" policy. The Commissioner notified respondents Bankers Trust Co. and Le Gierse, as executors of decedent's estate, that he proposed to include the proceeds of this policy in the gross estate, and to assess a deficiency. Suit in the Board of Tax Appeals followed, and the Commissioner's action was reversed. 39 B.T.A. 1134. The Circuit Court of Appeals affirmed. 110 F.2d 734. We brought the case here because of conflict with *Commissioner v. Keller's Estate*, 113 F.2d 833, and *Helvering v. Tyler*, 111 F.2d 422. 311 U.S. 625.

The ultimate question is whether the "insurance" proceeds may be included in decedent's gross estate.

Section 302 of the Revenue Act of 1926, 44 Stat. 9, 70, as amended, 47 Stat. 169, 279, 48 Stat. 680, 752, provides:

> The value of the gross estate of the decedent shall be determined by including the value at the timeof his death of all property, real or personal, tangible or intangible * * *.
>
> (g) To the extent of the amount receivable by the executor as insurance under policies taken out by the decedent upon his own life, and to the extent of the excess over $40,000 of the amount

receivable by all other beneficiaries as insurance under policies taken out by the decedent upon his own life.

Thus, the basic question is whether the amounts received here are amounts "receivable as insurance" within the meaning of § 302(g).

Conventional aids to construction are of little assistance here. Section 302(g) first appeared in identical language in the Revenue Act of 1918 as § 402(f). 40 Stat. 1057, 1098. It has never been changed. [Footnote 1] None of the acts has ever defined "insurance." Treasury Regulations, interpreting the original provision, stated simply:

"The term 'insurance' refers to life insurance of every description, including death benefits paid by fraternal beneficial societies, operating under the lodge system."

Treasury Regulations No. 37, 1921 edition, p. 23. This statement has never been amplified. [Footnote 2] The committee report accompanying the Revenue Act of 1918 merely noted that the provision taxing insurance receivable by the executor clarified existing law, and that the provision taxing insurance in excess of $40,000 receivable by specific beneficiaries was inserted to prevent tax evasion. House Report No. 767, 65th Cong., 2d Sess., p. 22. [Footnote 3] Subsequent committee reports do not mention § 302(g). Transcripts of committee hearings in 1918 and since are equally uninformative. [Footnote 4]

Necessarily, then, the language and the apparent purpose of § 302(g) are virtually the only bases for determining what Congress intended to bring within the scope of the phrase "receivable as insurance." In fact, in using the term "insurance," Congress has identified the characteristic that determines what transactions are entitled to the partial exemption of § 302(g).

We think the fair import of subsection (g) is that the amounts must be received as the result of a transaction which involved an actual "insurance risk" at the time the transaction was executed. Historically and commonly, insurance involves risk shifting and risk distributing. That life insurance is desirable from an economic and social standpoint as a device to shift and distribute risk of loss from premature death is unquestionable. That these elements of risk shifting and risk distributing are essential to a life insurance contract is agreed by courts and commentators. *See, for example, Ritter v. Mutual Life Ins. Co.,* 169 U. S. 139; *In re Walsh,* 19 F.Supp. 567; *Guaranty Trust Co. v. Commissioner,* 16 B.T.A. 314; *Ackerman v. Commissioner,* 15 B.T.A. 635; Couch, Cyclopedia of Insurance, Vol. I, § 61; Vance, Insurance, §§ 1-3; Cooley, Briefs on Insurance, 2d edition, Vol. I, p. 114; Huebner, Life Insurance, Ch. 1. Accordingly, it is logical to assume that, when Congress used the words "receivable as insurance" in § 302(g), it contemplated amounts received pursuant to a transaction possessing these features. *Commissioner v. Keller, supra; Helvering v. Tyler, supra; Old Colony Trust Co. v. Commissioner,* 102 F.2d 380; *Ackerman v. Commissioner, supra.*

Analysis of the apparent purpose of the partial exemption granted in § 302(g) strengthens the assumption that Congress used the word "insurance" in its commonly accepted sense. Implicit in this provision is acknowledgement of the fact that, usually, insurance payable to specific beneficiaries is designed to shift to a group of individuals the risk of premature death of the one upon whom the beneficiaries are dependent for support. Indeed, the pith of the exemption is particular protection of contracts and their proceeds intended to guard against just such a risk. *See Commissioner v. Keller, supra; United States Trust Co. v. Sears,* 29 F.Supp. 643; Hughes, Federal Death Tax, p. 91; Comment, 38 Mich.L.Rev. 526, 528; *compare Chase National Bank v. United States,* 28 F.Supp. 947; *In re Walsh, supra; Moskowitz v. Davis,* 68 F.2d 818. Hence, the next question is whether the transaction in suit in fact involved an "insurance risk" as outlined above.

We cannot find such an insurance risk in the contracts between decedent and the insurance company.

The two contracts must be considered together. To say they are distinct transactions is to ignore actuality, for it is conceded on all sides, and was found as a fact by the Board of Tax Appeals, that the "insurance" policy would not have been issued without the annuity contract. Failure, even studious failure, in one contract to refer to the other cannot be controlling. Moreover, authority for such consideration is not wanting, however unrealistic the distinction between form and substance may be. *Commissioner v. Keller, supra; Helvering v. Tyler, supra. See* Williston, Contracts, Vol. III, § 628; Paul, Studies in Federal Taxation, 2d series, p. 218; *compare Pearson v. McGraw*, 308 U. S. 313. [Footnote 5]

Considered together, the contracts wholly fail to spell out any element of insurance risk. It is true that the "insurance" contract looks like an insurance policy, contains all the usual provisions of one, and could have been assigned or surrendered without the annuity. Certainly the mere presence of the customary provisions does not create risk, and the fact that the policy could have been assigned is immaterial, since, no matter who held the policy and the annuity, the two contracts, relating to the life of the one to whom they were originally issued, still counteracted each other. It may well be true that, if enough people of decedent's age wanted such a policy, it would be issued without the annuity, or that, if the instant policy had been surrendered, a risk would have arisen. In either event, the essential relation between the two parties would be different from what it is here. The fact remains that annuity and insurance are opposites; in this combination, the one neutralizes the risk customarily inherent in the other. From the company's viewpoint, insurance looks to longevity, annuity to transiency. *See Commissioner v. Keller, supra; Helvering v. Tyler, supra; Old Colony Trust Co. v. Commissioner, supra; Carroll v. Equitable Life Assur. Soc.*, 9 F.Supp. 223; Note, 49

Yale L.J. 946; Cohen, Annuities and Transfer Taxes, 7 Kan.B.A.J. 139.

Here, the total consideration was prepaid, and exceeded the face value of the "insurance" policy. The excess financed loading and other incidental charges. Any risk that the prepayment would earn less than the amount paid to respondent as an annuity was an investment risk similar to the risk assumed by a bank; it was not an insurance risk as explained above. It follows that the sums payable to a specific beneficiary here are not within the scope of § 302(g). The only remaining question is whether they are taxable.

We hold that they are taxable under § 302(c) of the Revenue Act of 1926, as amended, as a transfer to take effect in possession or enjoyment at or after death. *See Helvering v. Tyler, supra; Old Colony Trust Co. v. Commissioner, supra; Kernochan v. United States,* 29 F.Supp. 860; *Guaranty Trust Co. v. Commissioner, supra; compare Gaither v. Miles,* 268 F. 692; Comment, 38 Mich.L.Rev. 526; Comment, 32 Ill.L.Rev. 223.

The judgment of the Circuit Court of Appeals is
Reversed.

THE CHIEF JUSTICE and MR. JUSTICE ROBERTS think the judgment should be affirmed for the reasons stated in the opinion of the Circuit Court of Appeals.

[Footnote 1]
Act of 1921; 42 Stat. 227, 279, § 402(f); Act of 1924; 43 Stat. 253, 305, § 302(g); Act of 1926; 44 Stat. 9, 71, § 302(g); Code of 1939; 53 Stat. 1, 122.

[Footnote 2]
Regulations No. 63, p. 26; Regulations No. 68, p. 31; Regulations No. 70, 1926 edition, p. 30; Regulations No. 70, 1929 edition, p. 33; Regulations No. 80, p. 62.

[Footnote 3]

"... [Insurance payable to specific
beneficiaries does] not fall within
the existing provisions defining

gross estate. It has been brought to the attention of the committee that wealthy persons have and now anticipate resorting to this method of defeating the estate tax. Agents of insurance companies have openly urged persons of wealth to take out additional insurance payable to specific beneficiaries for the reason that such insurance would not be included in the gross estate. A liberal exemption of $40,000 has been included, and it seems not unreasonable to require the inclusion of amounts in excess of this sum."

Id., p. 22. The same comment appears in Senate Report No. 617, 65th Cong., 3d Sess., p. 42.

[Footnote 4]

The curious consistency and inadequacy of section 302(g) have not escaped notice. *See* Paul, Life Insurance and The Federal Estate Tax, 52 Har.L.Rev. 1037; Paul, Studies in Federal Taxation, 3d Series, p. 351; *United States Trust Co. v. Sears,* 29 F.Supp. 643, 650.

[Footnote 5]

Legg v. St. John, 296 U. S. 489, is not to the contrary. There, nothing indicated that the one contract would not have been issued without the other; there was no necessary connection between the two.

HUMANA, INC. V. COMMISSIONER

Humana, Inc. v. Commissioner, 881 F.2D 247 (6th Cir. 1989)
ON APPEAL FROM THE UNITED STATES TAX COURT
Before: Martin and Milburn, Circuit Judges; and Hackett, *
District Judge.

BOYCE F. MARTIN, JR., CIRCUIT JUDGE. Humana Inc. and its wholly owned subsidiaries with which it files a consolidated federal income tax return appeal the decision of the United States Tax Court determining deficiencies against them with respect to their 1976-1979 fiscal years on the basis that: 1) sums paid by Humana Inc. to its captive insurance subsidiary, Health Care Indemnity, on its own behalf and on behalf of other wholly owned subsidiaries did not constitute deductible insurance premiums under the Internal Revenue Code section 162(a) (1954), and 2) such payments are not deductible under the Internal Revenue Code section 162 (1954) as ordinary and necessary business expenses as payments to a captive insurance company are equivalent to additions to a reserve for losses.

Humana Inc. and its subsidiaries operate hospitals whose insurance coverage was cancelled. Humana Inc. incorporated Health Care Indemnity, Inc., as a Colorado captive insurance company. In order to facilitate the incorporation of Health Care Indemnity, Humana Inc. also incorporated Humana Holdings, N.V., as a wholly owned subsidiary in the Netherland Antilles. The only business purpose of Humana Holdings was to assist in the capitalization of Health Care Indemnity. /1/ At the time of the initial capitalization, Health Care Indemnity issued 150,000 shares of preferred stock and 250,000 shares of common stock. Of these, Humana Holdings, the wholly owned Netherland subsidiary, purchased the preferred stock for $250,000.00 in cash (its entire capitalization) and Humana Inc. purchased 150,000 shares of Health Care Indemnity's common stock for $750,000.00 in the form of irrevocable letters of credit (as provided by Colorado statute).

Health Care Indemnity, the captive insurance subsidiary of Humana Inc., provided insurance coverage for Humana Inc. and its other subsidiaries. Humana Inc. paid to Health Care Indemnity amounts which it treated as insurance premiums. Humana Inc. allocated and charged to the subsidiaries portions of the amounts paid representing the share each bore for the hospitals each operated. The remainder represented Humana Inc.'s share for the hospitals which it operated. The total sums, $21,055,575.00, were deducted on a consolidated income tax return as insurance premiums.

The Commissioner, in accordance with the position outlined in Rev. Rul. 77-316, 1977-2 C.B. 52, disallowed the deductions and asserted deficiencies against Humana Inc. and the subsidiaries. Humana Inc. and its subsidiaries filed petitions in the tax court for redeterminations of the deficiencies assessed against them. On August 14, 1985, the tax court issued a memorandum opinion upholding the Commissioner's determination. Following a petition for reconsideration, the tax court withdrew that opinion. Humana Inc. requested full court review. On January 26, 1987, the tax court, after review by the entire nineteen member court, upheld the Commissioner. Humana Inc. and Subsidiaries v. Commissioner, 88 T.C. 197 (1987).

The opinion of the tax court contains a twelve member majority written by Judge Goffe, an eight member concurrence written by Judge Whitaker and joined by seven members of the majority, a two member concurring opinion written by Judge

Hamblen and joined by Judge Whitaker, and a seven member dissent written by Judge Korner. The twelve member majority relied on its prior decisions in Carnation Company v. Commissioner, 71 T.C. 400 (1978), affd. 640 F.2d 1010 (9th Cir. 1981), cert. denied, 454 U.S. 965 (1981) and Clougherty Packing Company v. Commissioner, 84 T.C. 948 (1985), affd. 811 F.2d 1297 (9th Cir. 1987), and held 1) that sums paid by Humana Inc. to Health Care Indemnity on its own behalf (described as the "parent- subsidiary" issue) were not deductible as ordinary and necessary business expenses for insurance premiums, and 2) the sums charged by Humana Inc. to the operating subsidiaries (described as the "brother- sister" issue) were also not deductible on the consolidated income tax returns as ordinary and necessary business expenses for insurance premiums. The majority reasoned that there was no insurance because the risks of loss were not shifted from Humana Inc. and its subsidiaries to Health Care Indemnity. In so holding, the majority specifically rejected adoption of the economic family concept argued by the Commissioner.

The tax court noted that the second issue, the brother-sister issue — whether the sums charged by Humana Inc. to its operating subsidiaries were deductible on the consolidated income tax returns as ordinary and necessary business expenses as insurance premiums — was an issue of first impression before the court. The court claimed that the issue had been decided in favor of denying the premiums as deductible in two other cases, Stearns-Roger Corp. v. United States, 774 F.2d 414 (10th Cir. 1985) and Mobil Corp. v. United States, 8 Cl. Ct. 555 (1985). The majority stated that Stearns-Roger and Mobil extended the rationale of Carnation and Clougherty to the "brother- sister" factual pattern. In holding that Humana Inc. did not shift the risk from the subsidiaries to Health Care Indemnity by charging its subsidiaries portions of the amounts paid representing the share each bore for the hospitals each operated, the tax court accepted the joint opinion of two experts, Dr. Plotkin and Mr. Stewart. Dr. Plotkin and Mr. Stewart stated:

> Commercial insurance is a mechanism for transferring the financial uncertainty arising from pure risks faced by one firm to another in exchange for an insurance premium.... The essential element of an insurance transaction from the standpoint of the insured (e.g. Humana and its hospital network), is that no matter what perils occur, the financial consequences are known in advance. . . . A firm placing its risk in a captive insurance company in which it holds a sole . . . ownership position, is not relieving itself of financial uncertainty. . . . True insurance relieves the firm's balance sheet of any potential impact of the financial consequences of the insured peril. . . . [However] as long as the firm deals with its captive, its balance sheet cannot be protected from the financial vicissitudes of the insured peril.

Humana, 88 T.C. at 219-25 (1987).

The majority also declared that payments to a captive insurance company are equivalent to additions to a reserve for losses and, therefore, not deductible under the Internal Revenue Code section 162 (1954) as ordinary and necessary business expenses paid or incurred during the taxable years in issue. Stearns-Roger Corp. v. United States, 774 F.2d 414 (10th Cir. 1985); Mobil Oil Corp. v. United States, 8 Cl. Ct. 555 (1985).

The eight member concurrence agreed with the majority's conclusion on both issues but felt uncomfortable with the majority's reliance on the expert witnesses, Dr. Plotkin and Mr. Stewart, whose theories rested heavily upon the economic family concept of captive insurance companies. They wrote to affirm that they were holding against Humana solely on the basis that the contracts between Humana Inc. and Health Care Indemnity and the contracts between Humana Inc.'s subsidiaries and Health Care Indemnity were not insurance contracts because of the lack of risk shifting. Humana, 88 T.C. at 231 (1987) (Whitaker, J., concurring).

A two member concurrence wrote to express concern about the "economic family" concept. They noted that the Commissioner's discussions of the economic family concept did not square with Moline Properties v. Commissioner, 319 U.S. 436 (1943). The Supreme Court in Moline Properties held that each corporate taxpayer was a separate entity for tax purposes. The two person concurrence felt that the Moline Properties issue was injected unnecessarily by way of the economic family concept analogy. The two member concurrence noted that the majority cites proponents of the economic family concept and felt that this was neither appropriate nor necessary. The two member concurrence stated that they "strongly believe that we should decide the issue solely on a lack of risk shifting and risk distribution basis." Humana, 88 T.C. at 237 (1987) (Hamblen, J., concurring).

The seven member dissent concurred in part with the majority that the premiums paid to Health Care Indemnity by Humana Inc. for insurance on itself may not be deducted as insurance premiums. They dissented with respect to the majority's holding that the same result applies to premiums paid by Humana Inc.'s subsidiaries to Health Care Indemnity for comparable insurance on THEM and THEIR EMPLOYEES. The dissent stated that neither Carnation nor Clougherty decided the issue of deductability of insurance premiums where the insurance contract was between corporations related as brother and sister. The dissent stated that the record in this case showed that 1) the wholly owned subsidiaries of Humana Inc. were insured under the subject policies, 2) the subsidiaries were related to Health Care Indemnity as brother-sister, not as parent-subsidiaries, 3) the amounts due under the subject policies as premiums were billed by Health Care Indemnity to Humana on a monthly basis,

4) Humana paid the total amount billed by Health Care Indemnity on a monthly basis, 5) later, the foregoing amounts were allocated and charged back by Humana, Inc. to its appropriate subsidiaries.

The dissent further noted that the majority rested heavily upon the joint opinion of the experts Plotkin and Stewart. However, these opinions gave no support to the position of the majority on the brother-sister question. The thrust of the Plotkin, Stewart testimony was aimed at the parent-subsidiary question, the reasoning being that the subsidiary's stock was shown as an asset on the parent's balance sheet. If the parent suffered an insured loss which a subsidiary had to pay, the assets of the subsidiary insurer would be depleted by the amount of the payment. This, in turn, reduced the value of the subsidiary shares as an asset of the parent. In effect, the assets of the insured parent were bearing the loss as far as the true economic impact was concerned. The dissent claimed that the reasoning presented by the experts provided no support for the majority's position in the brother-sister context. Humana, 88 T.C. at 243-44 (1987) (Korner J., dissenting). Humana Inc.'s insured subsidiaries owned no stock in Health Care Indemnity, nor vice versa. The subsidiarys' balance sheets and net worth were in no way affected by the payment of an insured claim by Health Care Indemnity. When the subsidiaries paid their own premiums for their own insurance, they shifted their risks to Health Care Indemnity. The dissent argued that the rationale of Carnation and Clougherty thus did not apply. Id. at 247.

The dissent further noted that the cases cited by the tax court, Stearns-Roger, Mobil Oil, and Beech Aircraft v. United States, 797 F.2d 920 (10th Cir. 1986), each explicitly or implicitly adopted the economic family concept. However, Health Care Indemnity and the hospital subsidiaries were valid separate business entities conducting active legitimate businesses devoid of sham. No facts stated the contrary. The dissent argued that to hold the insurance contracts between them invalid because they are one "economic family" and what happens to one happens to all of them ignored the separate entities of Humana Inc., its hospital subsidiaries, and Health Care Indemnity. Such a holding violated the time honored rule under Moline Properties that each taxpayer is a separate entity for tax purposes.

I.

We review de novo the legal standard applied by the tax court in determining whether Humana Inc.'s payments to its captive insurance company, Health Care Indemnity, for itself and on behalf of its subsidiaries constitute ordinary and necessary business expenses for insurance. Rose v. Commissioner, 868 F.2d 851 (6th Cir. 1989). The tax court's findings of fact shall not be overturned unless clearly erroneous. Id. at 853.

The Internal Revenue Code section 162(a) (1954) allows a deduction for all ordinary and necessary business expenses paid or incurred during the taxable year in carrying on a trade or business. Insurance premiums in the case of a business are generally deductible business expenses. Treas. Reg. section 1.1621(a) (1954). Although the term "insurance" is not self-defined by the Internal Revenue Code, the Supreme Court in Helvering v. Le Gierse, 312 U.S. 531 (1943), provided the test for defining "insurance" for federal tax purposes.

An insurance contract involves (1) risk shifting and (2) risk distribution. Helvering v. Le Gierse, 312 U.S. 539 (1943) (where an annuity contract completely neutralized the risk inherent in a life insurance contract when both contracts were considered together as one transaction). Risk shifting involves the shifting of an identifiable risk of the insured to the insurer. The focus is on the individual contract between the insured and the insurer. Risk distribution involves shifting to a group of individuals the identified risk of the insured. The focus is broader and looks more to the insurer as to whether the risk insured against can be distributed over a larger group rather than the relationship between the insurer and any single insured. Commissioner of

Internal Revenue v. Treganowan, 183 F.2d 288, 291 (2nd Cir.), cert. denied, 340 U.S. 853 (1950).

We believe that the tax court correctly held on the first issue, the parent-subsidiary issue, that under the principles of Clougherty and Carnation the premiums paid by Humana Inc., the parent to Health Care Indemnity, its wholly owned subsidiary, did not constitute insurance premiums and, therefore, were not deductible. Humana Inc. did not shift the risk to Health Care Indemnity. As the Tenth Circuit stated in Stearns-Roger:

The comparison of the arrangement here made to self-insurance cannot be ignored. The parent provided the necessary funds to the subsidiary by way of what it called "premiums" to meet the casualty losses of the parent. The subsidiary retained these funds until paid back to the parent on losses. . . . In the case before us we must again consider economic reality. The sums were with the subsidiary for future use and would be included in the Stearns-Roger balance sheet. Again the risk of loss did not leave the parent corporation.

Stearns-Roger, 744 F.2d at 416-1 7. We believe the tax court also correctly held that IF the subject payments made by the wholly owned subsidiaries were not deductible as insurance premiums, they likewise should be considered additions to a reserve for losses and not deductible under the Internal Revenue Code section 162 (1954) as ordinary and necessary business expenses. Stearns-Roger, 774 F.2d at 415; Mobil Oil, 8 Cl. Ct. at 567; Steere Tank Lines, Inc. v. United States, 577 F.2d 279, 280 (5th Cir. 1978), cert. denied 440 U.S. 946 (1979); Spring Canyon Coal v. Commissioner, 43 F.2d 78 (10th Cir. 1930), cert. denied 284 U.S. 654 (1931). We find no error in fact or law with regard to this first issue.

With regard to the second issue, the brother-sister issue, we believe that the tax court incorrectly extended the rationale of Carnation and Clougherty in holding that the premiums paid by the subsidiaries of Humana Inc. to Health Care Indemnity,

parent and stated that the "risk of loss remains with the parent," and thus there was no insurance. Mobil Oil 8 Cl. Ct. at 570.

The Tenth Circuit in Stearns-Roger v. United States, 774 F.2d 414 (1985), rested its holding impliedly if not expressly on the economic family theory. On appeal pursuant to certification under section 1292(b), the Tenth Circuit affirmed the district court's holding, 577 F.Supp. 833, 838 (1984), in which the district court concluded:

Its [Glendale Insurance Company] only business is to insure its parent corporation which wholly owns it and ultimately bears any losses or enjoys any profits it produces. Both profits and losses stay within the Stearns-Roger "economic family." I conclude that since the agreement between Stearns-Roger and Glendale did not shift the risk of losses, it was not an insurance contract for federal tax purposes. /2/

The tax court cannot avoid direct confrontation with the separate corporate existence doctrine of Moline Properties by claiming that its decision does not rest on "economic family" principles because it is merely RECLASSIFYING or RECHARACTERIZING the transaction as nondeductible additions to a reserve for losses. The tax court argues in its opinion that such "recharacterization" does not disregard the separate corporate status of the entities involved, but merely disregards the particular transactions between the entities in order to take into account SUBSTANCE over form and the economic reality" of the transaction that no risk has shifted.

The tax court misapplies this substance over form argument. The substance over form or economic reality argument is not a broad legal doctrine designed to distinguish between legitimate and illegitimate transactions and employed at the discretion of the tax court whenever it feels that a taxpayer is taking advantage of the tax laws to produce a favorable result for the taxpayer. Higgins v. Smith, 308 U.S. 473, 476 (1940) (where the Court stated, "The Government urges that the principle underlying Gregory v. Helvering finds expression in the rule calling for a realistic approach to tax situations. As so broad and unchallenged a principle furnishes only a general direction, it is of little value in the solution of tax problems."). The substance over form analysis, rather, is a distinct and limited exception to the general rule under Moline Properties that separate entities must be respected as such for tax purposes. The substance over form doctrine applies to disregard the separate corporate entity where "Congress has evinced an intent to the contrary. . . ." Clougherty, 811 F.2d at 1302. As the Court stated in Le Gierse, 319 U.S. at 439, "A particular legislative purpose, such as the development of the merchant marine, . . . may call for the disregarding of the separate entity, Munson S.S. Line v. Commissioner, 77 F.2d 849, as may the necessity of striking down frauds on the tax statute, Continental Oil v. Jones, 113 F.2d 557." However, as the Ninth Circuit pointed out in Clougherty, "Congress . . . has remained silent with respect to the taxation of captive insurers. . . ." 811 F.2d at 1302. In general, absent specific congressional intent to the contrary, as is the situation in this case, a court cannot disregard a transaction in the name of economic reality and substance over form absent a finding of sham or lack of business purpose under the relevant tax statute. Clougherty, 811 F.2d at 1302; Gregory v. Helvering, 239 U.S. 465, 469 (1935); Higgins v. Smith, 308 U.S. 473, 477 (1940).

In the instant case, the tax court found that Humana had a valid business purpose for incorporating Health Care Indemnity. Congress has manifested no intent to disregard the separate corporate entity in the context of captive insurers. In short, the substance over form or economic reality argument under current legal application does not provide any justification for the tax court to reclassify the insurance premiums paid by the subsidiaries of Humana Inc. as nondeductible additions to a reserve for losses. The test to determine whether a transaction under the Internal Revenue Code section 162(a) (1954) is legitimate or illegitimate is not a vague and broad "economic reality" test. The test is whether there is risk shifting and risk distribution. Only if a transaction fails to meet the above two-pronged test can the court justifiably RECLASSIFY the transaction as something other than insurance.

We have both risk shifting and risk distribution involved in the transactions between the Humana subsidiaries and Health Care Indemnity. The transactions between Health Care Indemnity and the separate affiliates of Humana, therefore, are properly within the statutory language of the Internal Revenue Code section 162(a) (1954) as interpreted in Le Gierse. As long as the transactions meet the purposes of the tax statute, Higgins, 308 U.S. at 477, the substance of the transactions are valid and legitimate regardless of its form and regardless of the tax motivation on the part of the taxpayers involved, Gregory, 293 U.S. at 469.

We, therefore, find no credence in the distinction between disregarding the particular transactions between the Humana affiliates and Health Care Indemnity and disregarding the separate entities. Absent a fact pattern of sham or lack of business purpose, a court should accept transactions between related though separate corporations as proper and not disregard them because of the relationship between the parties. As the Second Circuit stated in Kraft Foods Company v. Commissioner, 232 F.2d 118, 123-24 (2nd Cir. 1956):

[I]t is one thing to say that transactions between affiliates should be carefully scrutinized and sham transactions disregarded, and quite a different thing to say that a genuine transaction affecting legal relations should be disregarded for tax purposes merely because it is a transaction between affiliated corporations. We think that to strike down a genuine transaction because of a parent's subsidiary relation would violate the scheme of the statute and depart from the rules of law heretofore governing intercompany transactions.

Id. 123-24.

Finally, the tax court argues that if it did not deny the deductions in the brother-sister context, Humana Inc. could avoid the tax court's holding on issue one, the parent-captive issue, that insurance premiums paid by the parent to a captive insurance company are not deductible and accomplish the same purpose through its subsidiaries. Such an argument provides no LEGAL justification for denying the deduction in the brother-sister context. The legal test is whether there has been risk distribution and risk shifting, not whether Humana Inc. is a common parent or whether its affiliates are in a brother-sister relationship to Health Care Indemnity. We do not focus on the relationship of the parties per se or the particular structure of the corporation involved. We look to the assets of the insured. Clougherty, 811 F.2d at 1305. If Humana changes its corporate structure and that change involves risk shifting and risk distribution, and that change is for a legitimate business purpose and is not a sham to avoid the payment of taxes, then it is irrelevant whether the changed corporate structure has the side effect of also permitting Humana Inc.'s affiliates to take advantage of the Internal Revenue Code section 162(a) (1954) and deduct payments to a captive insurance company under the control of the Humana parent as insurance premiums.

The Commissioner argues for us to adopt its economic family approach because this approach recognizes the economic reality of the transaction between Humana affiliates and the captive insurance company, Health Care Indemnity. We do not, however, as the government argues, look to Humana Inc., the parent, to determine whether premiums paid by the affiliates to Health Care Indemnity are deductible. To do so would be to treat Humana Inc., its affiliates and Health Care Indemnity as one "economic unit" and ignore the reality of their separate corporate existence for tax purposes in violation of Moline Properties. Even the tax court explictly rejected the Commissioner's economic family argument. Humana, 88 T.C. at 230. /3/

The Commissioner has also argued that even if we do not adopt the economic family argument, we should look through the form of the transaction between the Humana affiliates and

Health Care Indemnity to the substance of the transaction and hold that in substance there was no risk shifting. It would appear that this is just another way of stating that transactions between affiliates for tax purposes shall be disregarded if devoid of business purposes or a sham. We have already discussed in detail this exception to Moline Properties, supra. However, if the Commissioner's form over substance or "economic reality" argument is an attempt to broaden the "sham" exception or fashion a new exception, we reject the argument.

B. RISK DISTRIBUTION

Treating the Humana affiliates and Health Care Indemnity as separate entities and rejecting the economic family argument leads to the conclusion that the first prong of the Le Gierse test for determining "insurance" has been met — there is risk shifting between the Humana affiliates and Health Care Indemnity. However, we must also satisfy the second prong of Le Gierse and find risk distribution. As stated, supra, risk distribution involves shifting to a group of individuals the identified risk of the insured. The focus is broader and looks more to the insurer as to whether the risk insured against can be distributed over a larger group rather than the relationship between the insurer and any single insured. Commissioner of Internal Revenue v. Treganowan, 183 F.2d 288, 291 (2nd Cir.), cert. denied, 340 U.S. 853 (1950). There is little authority adequately discussing what constitutes risk distribution if there is risk shifting. Just recently, the tax court in Gulf Oil v. Commissioner, 89 T.C. 1010, 1035 (1987), noted that insurance must consist of both risk shifting and risk distribution and that the definition of an insurance contract depended on meeting both of the prongs. /4/ With this we firmly agree. Risk transfer and risk distribution are two separate and distinct prongs of the test and both must be met to create an insurance contract. An arrangement between a parent corporation and a captive insurance company in which the captive insures only the risks of the parent might not result in risk distribution. Any loss by the parent is not subject to the premiums of any other entity. However, we see no reason why there would not be risk distribution in the instant case where the captive insures several separate corporations within an affiliated group and losses can be spread among the several distinct corporate entities.

III.

In conclusion, we affirm the tax court on issue one, the parent-subsidiary issue. The contracts between Humana, Inc., the parent, and Health Care Indemnity, the wholly owned captive insurance company, are not insurance contracts and the premiums are not deductible under the Internal Revenue Code section 162(a) (1954). We reverse the tax court on issue two, the brother-sister issue. The contracts between the affiliates of Humana Inc. and Health Care Indemnity are in substance insurance contracts and the premiums are deductible. Under Moline Properties, we must recognize the affiliates as separate and distinct corporations from Humana Inc., the parent company, and, as such, they shifted their risk to Health Care Indemnity. Furthermore, we find there was risk distribution on the part of Health Care Indemnity given the number of separate though related corporations insured by Health Care Indemnity. Under no circumstances do we adopt the economic family argument advanced by the government.

Thus the Tax Court is affirmed on Issue One, Reversed on Issue Two and the case remanded for recomputation of the tax due.

FOOTNOTES

* The Honorable Barbara K. Hackett, United States District Judge for the Eastern District of Michigan, sitting by designation.

/1/ Humana Incorporated owns 75% of Health Care Indemnity and Human's Netherland affiliate owns 25%. Technically, therefore, Humana is not a 100% owner of Health Care Indemnity. However, the tax court stated, and both parties agreed, that the only business purpose of the offshore affiliate was to provide capital for Health Care Indemnity. Therefore, the court and both parties agreed to treat Health Care Indemnity as a wholly-owned subsidiary of Humana.

/2/ The Carnation case involved an undercapitalized foreign captive, with a capitalization agreement running to the captive from the parent. Stearns-Roger, although involving an adequately capitalized domestic captive, involved an indemnification agreement running from the parent to the captive. A third case, Beech Aircraft 797 F.2d 920 (10th Cir. 1986), mentioned as support for the majority position, also involved an undercapitalized captive. These weaknesses alone provided a sufficient basis from which to find no risk shifting and to decide the cases in favor of the Commissioner. The Humana case contained no such indemnification agreement and Health Care Indemnity was adequately capitalized.

/3/ Although the tax court in the present case disclaims reliance on the economic family theory, its holding appears ultimately premised on the same type of analysis. In effect the tax court holds that one corporate entity cannot shift risk of loss in an insurance transaction to another corporate entity if they are in the same affiliated group. This approach conflicts with the Moline Properties rule of separate corporate entities. As the eight member concurrence written by Judge Whitaker pointed out:

> However, the majority refers repeatedly with apparent approval to decisions of other courts, including the opinion of the Court of Appeals of the Ninth Circuit affirming our opinion in Carnation, all of which follow Carnation and adopt the economic family concept. The majority also quotes extensively with approval from the testimony of respondent's experts, Dr. Plotkin and Mr. Stewart, who have fully swallowed respondent's economic family concept. . . . For these reasons, I strongly believe that we should

decide the issue solely on a lack of risk shifting
and risk distribution basis.

Humana, 88 T.C. 197, 231 (1987) (Whitaker, J., concurring).

It is this argument that we consider more logically sound than the majority. We disagree, however, in the application of the argument and find the existence of risk shifting and risk distribution.

/4/ The tax court noted in Gulf Oil, decided shortly after this Humana case, that if a captive insurance company insured unrelated interests outside the affiliated group of the captive insurance company, then there might be adequate risk transfer created by insuring the risks of independent third parties. The majority held that the addition of 2% of unrelated premiums is de minimis and would not satisfy the majority that the risk was transferred. However, if the premium income from unrelated parties was at least 50%, the majority stated that there would be sufficient risk transfer so that the arrangement would constitute insurance and premiums paid by the parent and affiliates to the captive insurance company would be deductible under the Internal Revenue Code section 162(a) (1954). It is unclear in the language employed by the tax court majority in Gulf Oil whether the appearance of unrelated third-party premiums constitutes risk shifting or risk distribution. The tax court majority refers to the appearance of unrelated third-parties as sufficient to constitute "risk transfer." If the appearance of unrelated third-parties creates "risk transfer" and by this the tax court means both risk shifting and risk distribution, the tax court majority ignores the fact that risk shifting and risk distribution are two separate and distinct prongs. The tax court majority cannot collapse the two prong test into one and claim that the appearance of unrelated third- parties creates enough risk transfer. Such is not the law. If the presence of unrelated third-parties goes to the question of risk distribution, then the tax court majority should never have reached that issue as its prior opinions, especially its opinion in Humana, stated that there can be no risk shifting as between a captive insurance company and a parent and its affiliated corporations where both are owned by a common parent, as was the situation in Gulf Oil. Thus the tax court has created its own conflict between its holding in Humana and its holding in Gulf.

HARPER GROUP V. COMMISSIONER

Harper Group v. Commissioner, 979 F.2d 1341 (9th Cir. 1992)
APPEAL FROM A DECISION OF THE UNITED STATES
TAX COURT
Before: POOLE, FERNANDEZ, and T.G. NELSON, Circuit
Judges.
FERNANDEZ, Circuit Judge:

1

The Harper Group (Harper) and certain of its domestic
subsidiaries purchased insurance policies from Rampart
Insurance Co., Ltd. (Rampart) and deducted the premiums for
income tax purposes. Rampart is a wholly owned subsidiary of
two of Harper's subsidiaries. The Commissioner of Internal
Revenue (Commissioner) determined that because of the
relationship among the parties the transactions did not
constitute insurance. A notice of deficiency was issued by the
Commissioner, and Harper and its subsidiaries petitioned the
Tax Court for a redetermination. The Tax Court found that the
transactions were insurance./1/ It, therefore, held against the
Commissioner who now appeals. We affirm.

2

In AMERCO, Inc. v. Commissioner, 979 F.2d 162 (9th
Cir.1992) we decided that it is possible to have a true insurance
transaction between a corporation and its wholly owned
insurance company if that captive does substantial unrelated
insurance business. Likewise other members of the corporate

group can have true insurance transactions with the captive. The result is that insurance premiums paid by the parent or the other members of the group are deductible by them. The only relevant way in which this case differs from AMERCO is that here the unrelated business of the captive was from 29 percent to 33 percent of its total business, rather than the 52 percent to 74 percent found in AMERCO.

3

Prior cases which have found true insurance have also included higher percentages of unrelated business than those found here. See Sears Roebuck & Co. v. Commissioner, 972 F.2d 858, 860 (7th Cir.1992) (99.75 percent from others); Ocean Drilling & Exploration Co. v. United States, 24 Cl.Ct. 714, 730 (1991) (44 percent to 66 percent from others).

4

Cases which have found no true insurance have found much lower percentages of unrelated business. See, e.g., Beech Aircraft Corp. v. United States, 797 F.2d 920, 921-22 (10th Cir.1986) (.5 percent from others); Gulf Oil Corp. v. Commissioner, 89 T.C. 1010, 1028 (1987) (2 percent from others), rev'd in part on other grounds, 914 F.2d 396 (3d Cir.1990); Clougherty Packing Co. v. Commissioner, 811 F.2d 1297, 1299 (9th Cir.1987) (none from others).

5

Thus, it is undoubtedly true that the existence of insurance is obvious in some cases. Moreover, there is a point at which the amount of outside business is insubstantial, so true insurance does not exist.

6

The Tax Court found that the point of insubstantiality had not been reached in this case. We cannot say that it committed clear error in so deciding.

7

AFFIRMED.

/1/

Harper Group and Includible Subsidiaries v. Commissioner, 96 T.C. 45 (1991).

SEARS, ROEBUCK AND CO. V. COMMISSIONER OF INTERNAL REVENUE SERVICE

Sears, Roebuck and Co. v. Commissioner, 972 F.2d 858 (7th Cir. 1992)
APPEAL FROM A DECISION OF THE UNITED STATES TAX COURT
EASTERBROOK, Circuit Judge.

Several subsidiaries of Sears, Roebuck & Co. sell insurance. One, Allstate Insurance Co., underwrote some of the risks of the parent corporation. Two others wrote mortgage insurance, promising to pay lenders if borrowers defaulted. Because Sears and all other members of the corporate group file a consolidated tax return, disputes about the tax consequences of these transactions affect the taxes of the entire group. The Commissioner of Internal Revenue assessed the group with deficiencies exceeding $2.5 million for the tax years 1980-82. Whether the group owes this money depends on the proper characterization of the two kinds of transaction.

An insurer may deduct from its gross income an amount established as a reserve for losses. 26 U.S.C. § 832. Until 1986 it could deduct the entire reserve; today it must discount this reserve in recognition of the fact that a dollar payable tomorrow is worth less than a dollar today. Tax Reform Act of 1986 § 1023, 100 Stat. 2085, 2399 (1986). These transactions occurred before 1986, and in any event we deal with the existence rather than the size of the deduction. Allstate created and deducted reserves to cover casualties on policies it issued to Sears. The Commissioner disallowed these deductions (and made some related adjustments), reasoning that the shuffling of money from one corporate pocket to another cannot be "insurance." The Tax Court disagreed. It distinguished captive subsidiaries (which write policies for the parent corporation but few or no others) from bona fide insurance companies that deal with their corporate parents or siblings at market terms. 96 T.C. 61 (1991).

The two subsidiaries underwriting mortgage insurance estimated losses as of the time the underlying loans went into default. The Commissioner contended that these insurers could not establish deductible loss reserves until the lenders obtained good title to the mortgaged property, because the insurance policies made a tender of title a condition precedent to the insurers' obligation to pay. The Tax Court agreed with this conclusion, rejecting the insurers' argument that the Internal Revenue Code permits them to deduct loss reserves required by state law, as these reserves were.

The judges of the Tax Court split four ways. Judges Körner, Shields, Hamblen, Swift, Gerber, Wright, Parr, Colvin, and Halpern joined Judge Cohen's opinion for the majority. Judges Chabot and Parker would have ruled for the Commissioner on both issues; Chief Judge Nims and Judge Jacobs would have ruled for Sears on both issues. Judge Whalen concluded that the majority had things backward: that Sears should have prevailed on the mortgage insurance issue but lost on the subsidiary issue. We join Chief Judge Nims and Judge Jacobs.

I

Allstate is a substantial underwriter, collecting more than $5 billion in premiums annually and possessing more than $2 billion in capital surplus. During the years at issue, Allstate charged Sears approximately $14 million per year for several kinds of insurance. Some 99.75% of Allstate's premiums came from customers other than Sears, which places 10% to 15% of its insurance with Allstate. The Commissioner's brief concedes that "[p]olicies issued to Sears by Allstate were comparable to policies issued to unrelated insureds. With respect to the execution, modification, performance and renewal of all of the policies in issue, Allstate and Sears observed formalities similar to those followed with respect to the insurance policies issued by Allstate to unrelated insureds. In addition, the premium rates charged by Allstate to Sears were determined by means of the same underwriting principles and procedures that were used in determining the premium rates charged to unrelated insureds, and were the equivalent of arm's-length rates." The Tax Court made similar findings, although not nearly so concisely.

Allstate, founded in 1931, has been selling insurance to Sears since 1945. Everyone, including the Commissioner, has taken Allstate as the prototypical non-captive insurance subsidiary. Until 1977 the Internal Revenue Service respected transactions between non-captive insurers and their parents. In that year the Commissioner decided that a wholly owned subsidiary cannot "insure" its parent's operations, even if the subsidiary's policies are identical in terms and price to those available from third parties. Rev.Rul. 77-316, 1977-2 C.B. 53. Examples given in this revenue ruling all dealt with captives that had no customers *861 outside the corporate family. After issuing the ruling the Service continued to believe that subsidiaries engaged in "solicitation and acceptance of substantial outside risks" could provide insurance to their parents. G.C.M. 38136 (Oct. 12, 1979). But in 1984 the General Counsel reversed course, G.C.M. 39247 (June 27, 1984), and the Commissioner later announced that all wholly owned insurance subsidiaries should be treated alike. Rev.Rul. 88-72, 1988-2 C.B. 31, clarified, Rev.Rul. 89-61, 1989-1 C.B. 75. Our task is to decide whether this is correct. We therefore disregard details, which may be found in the Tax Court's opinion. Like the Commissioner, we deem immaterial the nature of the risks Allstate accepted, the terms the parties negotiated, and the precise deductions taken.

If Sears did no more than set up a reserve for losses, it could not deduct this reserve from income. United States v. General Dynamics Corp., 481 U.S. 239, 107 S.Ct. 1732, 95 L.Ed.2d 226 (1987). Firms other than insurance companies may deduct business expenses only when paid or accrued; a reserve is deductible under § 832 only if the taxpayer issued "insurance." "Self-insurance" is just a name for the lack of insurance-for bearing risks oneself. According to the Commissioner, "insurance" from a subsidiary is self-insurance by another name. Moving funds from one pocket to another does nothing, even if the pocket is separately incorporated. If Subsidiary pays out a dollar, Parent loses the same dollar. Nothing depends on whether Subsidiary has other customers; there is still a one-to-one correspondence between its payments and Parent's wealth. So although Allstate may engage in the pooling of risks, and thus write insurance, Sears did not purchase the shifting of risks, and thus did not buy insurance. Unless the transaction is insurance from both sides-unless it "involves risk-shifting [from the client's perspective] and risk-distributing [from the underwriter's]", Helvering v. Le Gierse, 312 U.S. 531, 539, 61 S.Ct. 646, 649, 85 L.Ed. 996 (1941)-it is not insurance for purposes of the Internal Revenue Code. The Commissioner asks us to pool the corporate family's assets to decide whether risk has been shifted. This is the "economic family" approach of Rev.Rul. 77-316, which the Service sometimes supplements with a "balance sheet" inquiry under which a transaction is not insurance if it shows up on both sides of a corporation's balance sheet.

No judge of the Tax Court has ever embraced the IRS's "economic family" approach, which is hard to reconcile with the doctrine that tax law respects corporate forms. Molien Properties, Inc. v. CIR, 319 U.S. 436, 63 S.Ct. 1132, 87 L.Ed. 1499 (1943). Although the Commissioner may recharacterize intra-corporate transactions that lack substance independent of their tax effects, cf. Gregory v. Helvering, 293 U.S. 465, 55 S.Ct. 266, 79 L.Ed. 596 (1935); Yosha v. CIR, 861 F.2d 494 (7th Cir.1988)-which supports disregarding captive insurance subsidiaries-the "economic family" approach asserts that all transactions among members of a corporate group must be disregarded. Even the ninth circuit, which in citing Rev.Rul. 77-316 favorably has come the closest to the Commissioner's position, has drawn back by implying that subsidiaries doing substantial outside business cannot be lumped with true captives into a single pot. Carnation Co. v. CIR, 640 F.2d 1010 (9th Cir.1981); Clougherty Packing Co. v. CIR, 811 F.2d 1297, 1298 n. 1 (9th Cir.1987).

What is "insurance" for tax purposes? The Code lacks a definition. Le Gierse mentions the combination of risk shifting and risk distribution, but it is a blunder to treat a phrase in an opinion as if it were statutory language. Zenith Radio Corp. v. United States, 437 U.S. 443, 460-62, 98 S.Ct. 2441, 2450-51, 57 L.Ed.2d 337 (1978). Cf. United States v. Consumer Life Insurance Co., 430 U.S. 725, 740-41, 97 S.Ct. 1440, 1448-49, 52 L.Ed.2d 4 (1977). The Court was not writing a definition for all seasons and had no reason to, as the holding of Le Gierse is only that paying the "underwriter" more than it promises to return in the event of a casualty is not insurance by any standard. Life insurance passes outside a decedent's estate, making it advantageous to turn (taxable) assets of *862 the estate into insurance proceeds. Less than a month before her death, an elderly woman bought a policy denominated life insurance. The policy named a death benefit of $25,000 and carried a premium of $23,000. As part of the package, the "insurer" required the beneficiary to buy an annuity contract for $4,000. If the beneficiary died immediately, the insurer was $2,000 to the good; if she lived, the premiums were more than enough to fund the promised annuity payment and death benefit. So no risks were being spread, transferred, pooled, whatever.

As the Court observed, there was no insurance risk; the buyer of the policy expected to die soon, and the issuer expected to turn the proceeds over to the heirs, keeping an administrative fee for the service of removing the assets from the estate. Le Gierse, like Gregory and Yosha, shows that substance prevails over empty forms. Sears, by contrast, had insurable risks. The Commissioner does not deny that if Sears had purchased from Hartford or Aetna the same policies it purchased from Allstate, these would have been genuine "insurance." Forms there were, but not empty ones-and taxes usually depend on form, as the Commissioner trumpets whenever this enlarges the revenue. E.g., Howell v. United States, 775 F.2d 887 (7th Cir.1985). Distinctions with little meaning to the populace-for example, income at 11:59 p.m. on December 31 versus income at 12:01 a.m. on January 1, or wages plus the promise of a pension versus higher wages used to purchase an annuity-produce large differences in tax.

Doubtless a casualty that leads Allstate to reimburse Sears does not bring cash into the corporate treasury the same way a payment from Hartford would. A favorable loss experience for Sears cuts Allstate's costs, and thus augments the group's aggregate wealth, by more than the same reduction in losses would produce if Hartford issued the policy. Yet the Commissioner does not push this as far as he could. Corporate liability is limited by corporate assets. Corporations accordingly do not insure to protect their wealth and future income, as natural persons do, or to provide income replacement or a substitute for bequests to their heirs (which is why natural persons buy life insurance). Investors can "insure" against large risks in one line of business more cheaply than do corporations, without the moral hazard and adverse selection and loading costs: they diversify their portfolios of stock. Instead corporations insure to spread the costs of casualties over time. Bad experience concentrated in a single year, which might cause bankruptcy (and its associated transactions costs), can be paid for over several years. See generally David Mayers & Clifford W. Smith, Jr., On the Corporate Demand for Insurance, 55 J. Bus. 281 (1982). Much insurance sold to corporations is experience-rated. An insurer sets a price based on that firm's recent and predicted losses, plus a loading and administrative charge. Sometimes the policy is retrospectively rated, meaning that the final price is set after the casualties have occurred. Retrospective policies have minimum and maximum premiums, so the buyer does not bear all of the risk, but the upper and lower bounds are set so that almost all of the time the insured firm pays the full costs of the losses it generates. Both experience rating and retrospective rating attempt to charge the firm the full cost of its own risks over the long run, a run as short as one year with retrospective rating. The client buys some time-shifting (very little in the case of retrospective rating) and a good deal of administration. Insurers are experts at evaluating losses, settling with (or litigating against) injured persons, and so on. A corporation thus buys loss-evaluation and loss-administration services, at which insurers have a comparative advantage, more than it buys loss distribution. If retrospectively rated policies, called "insurance" by both issuers and regulators, are insurance for tax purposes-and the Commissioner's lawyer conceded for purposes of this case that they are-then it is impossible to see how risk shifting can be a sine qua non of "insurance."

The Commissioner insists that "shifting risk to third-party insureds" is an essential ingredient of insurance, but what does this mean? Take term life insurance. One *863 thousand persons at age 30 pay $450 each for a one-year policy with a death benefit of $200,000. In a normal year two of these persons will die, so the insurer expects to receive $450,000 and disburse $400,000. Of course more may die in a given year than the actuarial tables predict. But as the size of the pool increases the law of large numbers takes over, and the ratio of actual to expected loss converges on one. The absolute size of the expected variance increases, but the ratio decreases.

Risk-averse buyers of insurance shuck risk. Risk-neutral insurers match risks. No third party gets extra risk. Each person's chance of dying is unaffected; the financial consequences of death are shared. Joseph E. Stiglitz, professor of economics at Stanford, one of the leading students of risk and insurance, and an expert witness for Sears, put things nicely in saying that insurance does not shift risk so much as the pooling transforms and diminishes risk. See Richard A. Posner, Economic Analysis of Law 103 (4th ed. 1992). Insurance companies, with diversified investors and oodles of potential claims, are effectively risk-neutral. So everyone gains. The insureds willingly pay the loading charge to reduce their financial variance. The investors in the underwriters make a profit.

Convergence through pooling is an important aspect of insurance. Allstate puts Sears's risks in a larger pool, performing one of the standard insurance functions in a way that a captive insurer does not. More: Allstate furnishes Sears with the same hedging and administration services it furnishes to all other customers. It establishes reserves, pays state taxes, participates in state risk-sharing pools (for insolvent insurers), and so on, just as it would if Sears were an unrelated company. States recognize the transaction as "real" insurance for purposes of mandatory-insurance laws (several of the policies were purchased to comply with such laws for Sears's auto fleet, and for workers' compensation in Texas). From Allstate's perspective this is real insurance in every way. It must maintain the reserves required by state law (not to mention prudent management). Sears cannot withdraw these reserves on whim, and events that affect their size for good or ill therefore do not translate directly to Sears's balance sheet. It therefore does not surprise us that the Tax Court, while accepting the Commissioner's view that true captives do not write insurance, believes that insurance affiliates with substantial business from outside the group are genuine insurers. E.g., Gulf Oil Corp. v. CIR, 89 T.C. 1010, 1025-27 (1987) (dictum), aff'd in relevant part, 914 F.2d 396 (3d Cir.1990); AMERCO v. CIR, 96 T.C. 18 (1991) (52% to 74% writing for unrelated parties); Harper Group v. CIR, 96 T.C. 45 (1991) (30% writing for unrelated parties). So, too, courts of appeals have allowed the Commissioner to recharacterize "captive" cases as self-insurance without extending this principle to firms with substantial outside business. Beech Aircraft Corp. v. United States, 797 F.2d 920 (10th Cir.1986); Stearns-Roger Corp. v. United States, 774 F.2d 414 (10th Cir.1985). One court has held that fraternal corporations may write genuine "insurance" for each other, although they do no business outside the corporate group. Humana Inc. v. CIR, 881 F.2d 247 (6th Cir.1989).

Power to recharacterize transactions that lack economic substance is no warrant to disregard both form and substance in the bulk of cases. The Tax Court has given up the effort to find a formula, instead listing criteria such as insurance risk, risk shifting, risk distribution, and presence of forms commonly accepted as insurance in the trade. 96 T.C. at 99-101 (this case); Harper, 96 T.C. at 57-58 (opinion by Judge Jacobs describing this as a "facts and circumstances" test); AMERCO, 96 T.C. at 38 (opinion by Judge Körner rejecting any unified "test" and remarking that the considerations "are not independent or exclusive. Instead, we read them as informing each other and, to the extent not fully consistent, confining each other's potential excesses.").

No set of criteria is a "test." Lists without metes, bounds, weights, or means of resolving conflicts do not identify necessary or sufficient conditions; they never prescribe concrete results. Perhaps a list is all we can expect when the statute is silent and both sides of a dispute have solid points. For the Commissioner is right to say that Sears does not buy insurance in the same sense as a natural person buys auto insurance, and that it transfers less risk when buying a policy from Allstate than when buying the same policy from Nationwide. Sears is right to say that Allstate sells Sears a product that passes for insurance in the industry, identical to what Allstate sells to its other clients and having economic consequences differing from a self-insurance reserve. Perhaps disputes of this kind do little more than illustrate the conundrums inherent in an effort to collect a tax from corporations, as opposed to a tax measured by the changes in wealth of corporate investors (or measured by their withdrawals for consumption, so as to encourage investment). The experts who labored during this trial to define "insurance" all would have agreed that this dispute is an artifact of the corporate income tax, which by divorcing taxation from real persons' wealth, income, or consumption is bound to combine tricky definitional problems with odd incentives.

Suppose we ask not "What is insurance?" but "Is there adequate reason to recharacterize this transaction?", given the norm that tax law respects both the form of the transaction and the form of the corporate structure. It follows from putting the matter this way that the decision of the Tax Court must be affirmed. For whether a transaction possesses substance independent of tax consequences is an issue of fact-something the Commissioner harps on when she prevails in the Tax Court. E.g., Yosha, 861 F.2d at 499 (citing cases). The transaction between Sears and Allstate has some substance independent of tax effects. It increases the size of Allstate's pool and so reduces the ratio between expected and actual losses; it puts Allstate's reserves at risk; it assigns claims administration to persons with a comparative advantage at that task. These effects are no less real than those of loans and interest payments within corporate groups-which the Commissioner usually respects even though they are occasionally recharacterized as contributions to capital. E.g., National Farmers Union Service Corp. v. United States, 400 F.2d 483 (10th Cir.1968); Crosby Valve & Gage Co. v. CIR, 380 F.2d 146 (1st Cir.1967). Hartford is a subsidiary of ITT, as Allstate is of Sears. Suppose Sears were to buy from Hartford the same policies it obtained from Allstate, and Allstate were to serve ITT's needs. Then even the Commissioner would concede that both ITT and Sears had "insurance," yet nothing of substance would differ-not given the Commissioner's concession that Allstate wrote policies with standard commercial terms at competitive premiums. A trier of fact may, and did, conclude that Allstate furnished Sears with insurance.

II

PMI Mortgage Insurance Company, another part of the Sears group, writes mortgage insurance. PMI Mortgage Insurance and its own subsidiary, PMI Insurance Company (collectively PMI), insure lenders against the risk that borrowers will not pay. The Tax Court's opinion marshals the facts, 96 T.C. at 73-85, which are unnecessary to recount at length. Two dominate: (1) The insured risk is a borrower's default in payment. (2) Mortgage insurers insist that the lender try to collect from borrowers or realize on the collateral; until the lender has foreclosed on or otherwise obtained title to the property securing the loan (which also fixes the amount of the loss), the insurer does not pay. The last statement is a simplification. Sometimes PMI compromises with the lender in advance of foreclosure, but the policy does not require PMI to pay until the lender has good title.

Lenders must tell PMI about defaults and the steps they have taken to collect. PMI establishes reserves for losses when one of the following occurs: (a) the property has been conveyed to the lender but not sold to a third party; (b) the property is in the process of foreclosure; or (c) the loan has been in default for four months or *865 more. PMI also estimates the number of loans for which one of these three things has occurred but not been reported. Such reserves for incurred but not reported (IBNR) casualties are staples of the insurance business, and the Commissioner does not contest the establishment of IBNR reserves, provided that an identical reported event would support a loss reserve deductible under § 832.

Obviously not all of these events will lead to obligations on the insurance. Borrowers may catch up on overdue payments and retire their loans. Property sold at foreclosure may generate proceeds adequate to cover the outstanding balance of the loan. Insurers, including PMI, therefore discount their reserves to reflect their experience (and the industry's). PMI discounted too heavily, as things turned out. For 1982 PMI established year-end reserves of $35.9 million. The amounts disbursed in later years on account of these defaulted loans came to $51.5 million.

So its reserve was too small. But the Commissioner believes that PMI's reserves were too big for tax purposes. She limited the loss reserve deduction to $19.5 million for 1982, making comparable cuts for other years, and the Tax Court sustained her decisions. The court held that an "insurer cannot incur a loss until the insured has suffered the defined economic loss, to wit, after the lender takes title to the mortgaged property and submits a claim for loss." 96 T.C. at 114. By this time, of course, there is no need for a "reserve"; payment is a current obligation. The court's approach does not affect the taxes of insurers in a steady state but substantially increases the taxes of those with growing businesses (or growing losses) by postponing the time when the losses may be deducted.

Sears contests this decision on two grounds: first, that § 832 does not limit loss deductions to casualties that have reached the point of being payable; second, that the Tax Court erred in deciding when an insurer's obligation attaches. Judge Whalen (joined in this respect by Chief Judge Nims and Judge Jacobs) agreed with the former argument, concluding that the majority's holding "is a radical departure from the annual statement method of accounting, which section 832 and its predecessors have required property and casualty insurance companies to use in reporting underwriting and investment income for Federal income tax purposes since 1921." 96 T.C. at 114-15.

The "annual statement method of accounting" to which Judge Whalen referred is prescribed by the National Association of Insurance Commissioners, a body comprising state insurance regulators that has filed a brief as amicus curiae in support of Sears. The NAIC's annual statement requires property and casualty insurers to take certain things into income and prescribes reserves. A mortgage insurer must include in its reserves the three categories of losses that PMI used, plus reserves for IBNR losses. The Commissioner concedes that PMI complied with the NAIC's requirements. Federal agencies such as the Federal Housing Administration engaged in guaranteeing loans account for loss reserves exactly as PMI did. The insurance regulators believe that PMI erred, if at all, in understating its loss reserves. No surprise here. State regulators strive to assess and preserve the solvency of insurers. Accurate estimates of losses are essential to the former task, and high estimates contribute to the latter by requiring insurers to obtain additional capital or curtail the writing of new policies. Regulators therefore favor generous estimates of losses, while the federal tax collector prefers low estimates. The majority of the Tax Court stressed this when concluding that PMI could not follow the NAIC's method: "The objectives of State regulation ... are not identical to the objectives of Federal income taxation. State insurance regulators are concerned with the solvency of the insurer.... In contrast, Federal tax statutes are concerned with the determination of taxable income on an annual basis." 96 T.C. at 110.

Generalities about what "[f]ederal tax statutes are concerned with" do not control concrete cases. Section 832 is no ordinary rule. It expressly links federal taxes to the NAIC's annual statement:

> (a) In the case of [a property or casualty] insurance company ... the term "taxable income" means the gross income as defined in subsection (b)(1) less the deductions allowed by subsection (c).
>
> (b)(1) The term "gross income" means the sum of-
>
> . . . . .
>
> (A) the combined gross amount earned during the taxable year, from investment income and from underwriting income as provided in this subsection, computed on the basis of the underwriting and investment exhibit of the annual statement approved by the National Association of Insurance Commissioners....
>
> . . . . .
>
> (b)(3) The term "underwriting income" means

the premiums earned on insurance contracts during the taxable year less losses incurred and expenses incurred.

. . . . .

(b)(5)(A) The term "losses incurred" means losses incurred during the taxable year on insurance contracts computed as follows:

(i) To losses paid during the taxable year, deduct salvage and reinsurance recovered during the taxable year.

(ii) To the result so obtained, add all unpaid losses ... outstanding at the end of the taxable year and deduct all unpaid losses ... outstanding at the end of the preceding taxable year.

This quotation includes changes made in 1988, but these do not affect the current dispute. Section 832(b)(1)(A) requires an insurer to use "the underwriting and investment exhibit of the annual statement approved by the National Association of Insurance Commissioners" to determine its "gross income." Contrary to usual notions of "gross income," this concept in § 832 does not denote all inflows of revenue. Instead it refers to "premiums earned" (a premium is not "earned" until the period for which it purchases coverage occurs) less "losses incurred." For purposes of § 832, then, "gross income" is a version of net earned income. Both the "premiums earned" and "losses incurred" go into determining "gross income"-which is to be "computed on the basis of the underwriting and investment exhibit of the annual statement approved by the National Association of Insurance Commissioners". State insurance commissioners' preferences about reserves thus are not some intrusion on federal tax policy; using their annual statement is federal tax law. See Brown v. Helvering, 291 U.S. 193, 201, 54 S.Ct. 356, 360, 78 L.Ed. 725 (1934): "[T]he deductions allowed for additions to the reserves of insurance companies are technical in character and are specifically provided for in the Revenue Acts. These technical reserves are required to be made by the insurance laws of the several States."

True enough, the definition of loss reserves in § 832(b)(5) does not refer to the annual statement. Yet subsection (b)(5) losses are a component of subsection (b)(1) income, which is to be computed according to the NAIC's statement. It is scarcely possible to use the statement when determining one but not the other. Although it is not impossible-almost nothing is impossible in tax law-divorcing (b)(5) losses from the annual statement computations would make no sense in terms of the structure of the statute or its genesis. Subsection (b)(5) prescribes a method of toting up losses derived almost verbatim from the annual statement used in 1921, when Congress enacted the provision.

If annual statements were to depart from an effort to approximate actual "losses" then subsections (b)(1) and (b)(5) might come into conflict. This occurred when states required insurers to mark up their loss reserves by a percentage. The Commissioner objected to the deduction of these marked up losses, issuing regulations in 1943 and 1944 requiring insurers to use experience, and not formulas prescribed by state rules, as the basis of loss reserves. Modified versions of these regulations are still in force but no longer present the insurers with conflicting state and federal demands. In 1950 the NAIC came 'round *867 to the Commissioner's point of view, changing its annual statement so that both federal and state governments require insurers to reserve "only actual unpaid losses ... stated in amounts which, based upon the facts in each case and the company's experience with similar cases, represent a fair and reasonable estimate of the amount the company will be required to pay." Treas.Reg. 1.832-4(b). Charles W. Tye, The Convention Form and Insurance Company Tax Problems, 6 Tax L.Rev. 245 (1951), narrates the history of this dispute and the details of its resolution. PMI used actual cases to generate its loss reserves, and in the event underestimated losses; it complied with both the NAIC's requirements and the Treasury's regulations. Having followed the NAIC's annual statement approach, PMI is entitled to deduct the loss reserves so computed.

For what it is worth, we believe that PMI would be entitled to prevail under the regulation independent of the requirements of the NAIC's annual statement. The regulation says "actual unpaid losses" but omits any requirement that these losses be quantified and immediately payable. Once an obligation is quantified, an accrual-basis taxpayer may deduct it. Yet § 832 and the regulation suppose that insurers may deduct losses denied to any old accrual-basis taxpayer, a supposition the Supreme Court confirmed in General Dynamics when holding that an employer paying for its employees' medical care without an insurer's intermediation could not deduct IBNR expenses (in this context, the cost of medical services already rendered to employees but for which the employer did not have bills in hand).

Consider some standard issues in establishing reserves. A policy of auto insurance requires the issuer to pay if its insured is at fault in a collision. An accident occurs during December. May the insurer add to its reserves? The liability is not fixed, for the insurer is not legally obliged to pay until a court determines that its policy-holder was at fault (or the underwriter so concedes), and even then the firm may not be called on to pay if the loss turns out to be less than the deductible or the victim collects from his own carrier, which decides not to pursue the other driver's carrier. It may take years before the amount of the loss is quantified and the negligent driver is identified. Yet reserves established for such a case meet the regulatory definition of actual, case-based losses, and it would be insane of an insurer not to establish reserves for such casualties. Or consider health insurance. An insured has a heart attack on December 31. Medical care will be required over the next months (or years), and the insurance policy conditions the obligation to pay on receipt of a physician's bill at rates usual and customary in the vicinity (with a provision for arbitration if the fee seems high or the medical services unnecessary). Once again it may be some time before services have been rendered and billed at rates agreeable to the carrier. Does it follow that the insurer must wait till it receives the bill before establishing a reserve? At oral argument counsel for the Commissioner answered "yes," but the Commissioner cannot mean it, for this answer collapses all distinction between "reserves" and bills payable by return mail. Cf. Harco Holdings, Inc. v. United States, 969 F.2d 440, 442 (7th Cir.1992).

Just so with the Tax Court's conclusion about mortgage insurance. It has confused quantification of the loss, which does not occur until the lender tenders title, with the occurrence of the covered loss. Perhaps it seems artificial to speak of a borrower's failure to make a few payments as a "loss." The borrower may catch up, or the sale of the property may reimburse the lender. Default is not an immediate casualty in the sense that a collision between two automobiles crushes the cars (and people) on the spot, and it does not portend outlays with the high probability that a myocardial infarction does. Yet the acid test is whether the default leaves the insurer responsible for payment. Let us suppose that PMI issues a policy for 1982 only, and the borrower omits the last four payments of the year. The lender neglects to renew the policy (or purchase a substitute) for 1983. Eventually the lender forecloses and sends PMI a bill. Must PMI pay? The answer is yes; the default is the event triggering coverage under the policy. (Neither the Commissioner nor the Tax Court disagrees with PMI's representations about its obligations under the policy.) Thus to state its statutory "gross income" for 1982 accurately, PMI must take into income the premiums earned during 1982 and exclude a reserve for losses attributable to those premiums, including the bills that will straggle in during future years on account of defaults that began in 1982. The Tax Court's observation that federal law calls for "determination of taxable income on an annual basis", 96 T.C. at 110, turns out to support PMI, once we see that default is the event triggering coverage under the policy and leaving the insurer on the hook, waiting to see how things turn out, even if it never receives another penny in premiums.

Corporate taxation teems with artificial and formal distinctions, and the taxation of insurers has more than its share of them. Whether § 832 is attributable to some finely honed sense of the economics of the insurance business or to political pressure is not for us to say. Provisions of the Internal Revenue Code do not conflict with "tax policy," as the Commissioner seems to believe. They are tax policy and are to be enforced. Usually this enlarges the revenue. E.g., Holywell Corp. v. Smith, 503 U.S. 47, 112 S.Ct. 1021, 117 L.Ed.2d 196 (1992); INDOPCO v. CIR, 503 U.S. 79, 112 S.Ct. 1039, 117 L.Ed.2d 226 (1992). An Internal Revenue Service eager to dish out the medicine of literalism must be prepared to swallow it. Sears is entitled to prevail on both branches of this case. The judgment of the Tax Court is affirmed with respect to the Allstate dispute and reversed with respect to the PMI dispute. The case is remanded for the redetermination of the deficiency in accord with this opinion. The Tax Court is free to consider the Commissioner's argument, which it did not need to reach before, that PMI's returns for 1980 and 1981 did not use a proper case-based method of approximating its loss reserves.

NOLAND, Senior District Judge, concurring in part and dissenting in part.

While I join the majority's opinion on the insurance premiums issue, finding the same to be well-reasoned, I must respectfully dissent on the mortgage guarantee insurance issue for the reason stated in Tax Court Judge Mary Ann Cohen's fifty-three (53) page majority opinion (approximately twelve (12) pages of which were dedicated to this issue). As Judge Cohen states in her opinion:

> In common understanding, an insurance contract is an agreement to protect the insured (or a third-party beneficiary) against a direct or indirect economic loss arising from a defined contingency." Allied Fidelity Corp. v.

Commissioner, 66 T.C. 1068, 1074 (1976), affd. 572 F.2d 1190 (7th Cir.1978). The defined contingency in this case was the insured's loss on the mortgage loan. It follows that the insurer cannot incur a loss until the insured has suffered the defined economic loss, to wit, after the lender takes title to the mortgaged property and submits a claim for loss.

Sears, Roebuck & Co. v. Commissioner, 96 U.S.T.C. 61, 113-114 (T.C.1991). Judge Cohen's analysis regarding the timing of the insurer's loss, i.e., the taxable event, is compelling.

*1 Judge Cohen authored the majority opinion. Two (2) of the judges on the Tax Court, Judges Wells and Ruwe, did not participate in the consideration of the Court's opinion. Judge Whalen authored a dissenting opinion signaling his disagreement with the majority on both issues. Chief Judge Nims, joined by Judge Jacobs, concurred with respect to the insurance premiums issue and dissented with respect to the mortgage guarantee insurance issue. Judge Chabot, joined by Judge Parker, concurred with respect to the mortgage insurance issue and dissented with respect to the insurance premiums issue. Thus, only three (3) members of the Tax Court dissented with respect to the mortgage guarantee insurance issue.

UNITED PARCEL SERVICE V. COMMISSIONER OF INTERNAL REVENUE SERVICE

United Parcel Service v. Commissioner, 254 F.3d 1014 (11th Cir. 2001)
APPEAL FROM A DECISION OF THE UNITED STATES TAX COURT

Cox, Circuit Judge.

As amended July 2, 1001

The tax court held United Parcel Service of America, Inc. and (UPS) liable for additional taxes and penalties for the tax year 1984. UPS appeals, and we reverse and remand.

I. Background

UPS, whose main business is shipping packages, had a practice in the early 1980s of reimbursing customers for lost or damaged parcels up to $100 in declared value.

Above that level, UPS would assume liability up to the parcel's declared value if the customer paid 25 per additional $100 in declared value, the "excess-value charge." If a parcel were lost or damaged, UPS would process and pay the resulting claim. UPS turned a large profit on excess-value charges because it never came close to paying as much in claims as it collected in charges, in part because of efforts it made to safeguard and track excess-value shipments. This profit was taxed; UPS declared its revenue from excess-value charges as income on its 1983 return, and it deducted as expenses the claims paid on damaged or lost excess-value parcels.

UPS's insurance broker suggested that UPS could avoid paying taxes on the lucrative excess-value business if it restructured the program as insurance provided by an overseas affiliate. UPS implemented this plan in 1983 by first forming and capitalizing a Bermuda subsidiary, Overseas Partners, Ltd. (OPL), almost all of whose shares were distributed as a taxable dividend to UPS shareholders (most of whom were employees; UPS stock was not publicly traded). UPS then purchased an insurance policy, for the benefit of UPS customers, from National Union Fire Insurance Company. By this policy, National Union assumed the risk of damage to or loss of excess-value shipments. The premiums for the policy were the excess-value charges that UPS collected. UPS, not National Union, was responsible for administering claims brought under the policy. National Union in turn entered a reinsurance treaty with OPL. Under the treaty, OPL assumed risk commensurate with National Union's, in exchange for premiums that equal the excess-value payments National Union got from UPS, less commissions, fees, and excise taxes.

Under this plan, UPS thus continued to collect 25per $100 of excess value from its customers, process and pay claims, and take special measures to safeguard valuable packages. But UPS now remitted monthly the excess-value payments, less claims paid, to National Union as premiums on the policy. National Union then collected its commission, excise taxes, and fees from the charges before sending the rest on to OPL as payments under the reinsurance contract. UPS reported neither revenue from excess-value charges nor claim expenses on its 1984 return, although it did deduct the fees and commissions that National Union charged.

The IRS determined a deficiency in the amount of the excess-value charges collected in 1984, concluding that the excess-value payment remitted ultimately to OPL had to be treated as gross income to UPS. UPS petitioned for a redetermination. Following a hearing, the tax court agreed with the IRS.

It is not perfectly clear on what judicial doctrine the holding rests. The court started its analysis by expounding on the assignment-of-income doctrine, a source rule that ensures that income is attributed to the person who earned it regardless of efforts to deflect it elsewhere. See United States v. Basye, 410 U.S. 441, 450, 93 S.Ct. 1080, 1086, 35 L.Ed.2d 412 (1973).

The court did not, however, discuss at all the touchstone of an ineffective assignment of income, which would be UPS's control over the excess-value charges once UPS had turned them over as premiums to National Union. See Comm'r v. Sunnen, 333 U.S. 591, 604, 68 S.Ct. 715, 722, 92 L.Ed. 898 (1948). The court's analysis proceeded rather under the substantive-sham or economic-substance doctrines, the assignment-of-income doctrine's kissing cousins. See United States v. Krall, 835 F.2d 711, 714 (8th Cir.1987) (treating the assignment-of-income doctrine as a sub-theory of the sham-transaction doctrine). The conclusion was that UPS's redesign of its excess-value business warranted no respect. Three core reasons support this result, according to the court: the plan had no defensible business purpose, as the business realities were identical before and after; the premiums paid for the National Union policy were well above industry norms; and contemporary memoranda and documents show that UPS's sole motivation was tax avoidance. The revenue from the excess-value program was thus properly deemed to be income to UPS rather than to OPL or National Union. The court also imposed penalties.

UPS now appeals, attacking the tax court's economic-substance analysis and its imposition of penalties. The refrain of UPS's lead argument is that the excess value plan had economic substance, and thus was not a sham, because it comprised genuine exchanges of reciprocal obligations among real, independent entities. The IRS answers with a before-and-after analysis, pointing out that whatever the reality and enforceability of the contracts that composed the excess-value plan, UPS's post-plan practice equated to its pre-plan, in that it collected excess-value charges, administered claims, and generated substantial profits. The issue presented to this court, therefore, is whether the excess-value plan had the kind of economic substance that removes it from "sham-hood," even if the business continued as it had before. The question of the effect of a transaction on tax liability, to the extent it does not concern the accuracy of the tax court's fact-finding, is subject to de novo review. Kirchman v. Comm'r, 862 F.2d 1486, 1490 (11th Cir.1989); see Karr v. Comm'r, 924 F.2d 1018, 1023 (11th Cir.1991). We agree with UPS that this was not a sham transaction, and we therefore do not reach UPS's challenges to the tax penalties.

II. Discussion

I.R.C. §§ 11, 61, and 63 together provide the Code's foundation by identifying income as the basis of taxation. Even apart from the narrower assignment-of-income doctrine-which we do not address here-these sections come with the gloss, analogous to that on other Code sections, that economic substance determines what is income to a taxpayer and what is not.

See Caruth Corp. v. United States, 865 F.2d 644, 650 (5th Cir.1989) (addressing, but rejecting on the case's facts, the argument that the donation of an income source to charity was a sham, and that the income should be reattributed to the donor); United States v. Buttorff, 761 F.2d 1056, 1061 (5th Cir.1985) (conveying income to a trust controlled by the income's earner has no tax consequence because the assignment is insubstantial); Zmuda v. Comm'r, 731 F.2d 1417, 1421 (9th Cir.1984) (similar). This economic-substance doctrine, also called the sham-transaction doctrine, provides that a transaction ceases to merit tax respect when it has no "economic effects other than the creation of tax benefits." Kirchman, 862 F.2d at 1492. *fn3 Even if the transaction has economic effects, it must be disregarded if it has no business purpose and its motive is tax avoidance. See Karr, 924 F.2d at 1023 (noting that subjective intent is not irrelevant, despite Kirchman's statement of the doctrine); Neely v. United States, 775 F.2d 1092, 1094 (9th Cir.1985); see also Frank Lyon Co. v. United States, 435 U.S. 561, 583-84, 98 S.Ct.

1291, 1303, 55 L.Ed.2d 550 (1978) (one reason requiring treatment of transaction as genuine was that it was "compelled or encouraged by business or regulatory realities"); Gregory v. Helvering, 293 U.S. 465, 469, 55 S.Ct. 266, 267, 79 L.Ed. 596 (1935) (reorganization disregarded in part because it had "no business or corporate purpose").

The kind of "economic effects" required to entitle a transaction to respect in taxation include the creation of genuine obligations enforceable by an unrelated party. See Frank Lyon Co., 435 U.S. at 582-83, 98 S.Ct. at 1303 (refusing to deem a sale-leaseback a sham in part because the lessor had accepted a real, enforceable debt to an unrelated bank as part of the deal). The restructuring of UPS's excess-value business generated just such obligations. There was a real insurance policy between UPS and National Union that gave National Union the right to receive the excess-value charges that UPS collected. And even if the odds of losing money on the policy were slim, National Union had assumed liability for the losses of UPS's excess-value shippers, again a genuine obligation. A history of not losing money on a policy is no guarantee of such a future. Insurance companies indeed do not make a habit of issuing policies whose premiums do not exceed the claims anticipated, but that fact does not imply that insurance companies do not bear risk. Nor did the reinsurance treaty with OPL, while certainly reducing the odds of loss, completely foreclose the risk of loss because reinsurance treaties, like all agreements, are susceptible to default.

The tax court dismissed these obligations because National Union, given the reinsurance treaty, was no more than a "front" in what was a transfer of revenue from UPS to OPL. As we have said, that conclusion ignores the real risk that National Union assumed. But even if we overlook the reality of the risk and treat National Union as a conduit for transmission of the excess-value payments from UPS to OPL, there remains the fact that OPL is an independently taxable entity that is not under UPS's control. UPS really did lose the stream of income it had earlier reaped from excess-value charges. UPS genuinely could not apply that money to any use other than paying a premium to National Union; the money could not be used for other purposes, such as capital improvement, salaries, dividends, or investment. These circumstances distinguish UPS's case from the paradigmatic sham transfers of income, in which the taxpayer retains the benefits of the income it has ostensibly forgone. See, e.g., Zmuda v. Comm'r, 731 F.2d at 1417 (income "laundered" through a series of trusts into notes that were delivered to the taxpayer as "gifts"). Here that benefit ended up with OPL. There were, therefore, real economic effects from this transaction on all of its parties.

The conclusion that UPS's excess-value plan had real economic effects means, under this circuit's rule in Kirchman, that it is not per se a sham. But it could still be one if tax avoidance displaced any business purpose. The tax court saw no business purpose here because the excess-value business continued to operate after its reconfiguration much as before. This lack of change in how the business operated at the retail level, according to the court, betrayed the restructuring as pointless.

It may be true that there was little change over time in how the excess-value program appeared to customers. But the tax court's narrow notion of "business purpose"-which is admittedly implied by the phrase's plain language-stretches the economic-substance doctrine farther than it has been stretched. A "business purpose" does not mean a reason for a transaction that is free of tax considerations. Rather, a transaction has a "business purpose," when we are talking about a going concern like UPS, as long as it figures in a bona fide, profit-seeking business. See ACM P'ship v. Comm'r, 157 F.3d 231, 251 (3d Cir.1998). This concept of "business purpose" is a necessary corollary to the venerable axiom that tax-planning is permissible. See Gregory v. Helvering, 293 U.S. 465, 469, 55 S.Ct. 266, 267, 79 L.Ed. 596 (1935) ("The legal right of a taxpayer to decrease the amount of what otherwise would be his taxes, or altogether avoid them, by means which the law permits, cannot be doubted."). The Code treats lots of categories of economically similar behavior differently. For instance, two ways to infuse capital into a corporation, borrowing and sale of equity, have different tax consequences; interest is usually deductible and distributions to equity holders are not. There may be no tax-independent reason for a taxpayer to choose between these different ways of financing the business, but it does not mean that the taxpayer lacks a "business purpose." To conclude otherwise would prohibit tax-planning.

The case law, too, bears out this broader notion of "business purpose." Many of the cases where no business purpose appears are about individual income tax returns, when the individual meant to evade taxes on income probably destined for personal consumption; obviously, it is difficult in such a case to articulate any business purpose to the transaction. See, e.g., Gregory, 293 U.S. at 469, 55 S.Ct. at 267 (purported corporate reorganization was disguised dividend distribution to shareholder); Knetsch v. United States, 364 U.S. 361, 362-65, 81 S.Ct. 132, 133-35, 5 L.Ed.2d 128 (1960) (faux personal loans intended to generate interest deductions); Neely v. United States, 775 F.2d 1092, 1094 (9th Cir.1985) (one of many cases in which the taxpayers formed a trust, controlled by them, and diverted personal earnings to it). Other no-business-purpose cases concern tax-shelter transactions or investments by a business or investor that would not have occurred, in any form, but for tax-avoidance reasons. See, e.g., ACM P'ship, 157 F.3d at 233-43 (sophisticated investment partnership formed and manipulated solely to generate a capital loss to shelter some of Colgate-Palmolive's capital gains); Kirchman, 862 F.2d at 1488-89 (option straddles entered to produce deductions with little risk of real loss); Karr, 924 F.2d at 1021 (façade of energy enterprise developed solely to produce deductible losses for investors); Rice's Toyota World, Inc. v. Comm'r,, 752 F.2d 89, 91 (4th Cir.1985) (sale-leaseback of a computer by a car dealership, solely to generate depreciation deductions). By contrast, the few cases that accept a transaction as genuine involve a bona fide business that-perhaps even by design-generates tax benefits. See, e.g., Frank Lyon, 435 U.S. at 582-84, 98 S.Ct. at 1302-04 (sale-leaseback was part of genuine financing transaction, heavily influenced by banking regulation, to permit debtor bank to outdo its competitor in impressive office space); Jacobson v. Comm'r, 915 F.2d 832, 837-39 (2d Cir.1990) (one of many cases finding that a bona fide profit motive provided a business purpose for a losing investment because the investment was not an obvious loser ex ante).

The transaction under challenge here simply altered the form of an existing, bona fide business, and this case therefore falls in with those that find an adequate business purpose to neutralize any tax-avoidance motive. True, UPS's restructuring was more sophisticated and complex than the usual tax-influenced form-of-business election or a choice of debt over equity financing. But its sophistication does not change the fact that there was a real business that served the genuine need for customers to enjoy loss coverage and for UPS to lower its liability exposure.

We therefore conclude that UPS's restructuring of its excess-value business had both real economic effects and a business purpose, and it therefore under our precedent had sufficient economic substance to merit respect in taxation. It follows that the tax court improperly imposed penalties and enhanced interest on UPS for engaging in a sham transaction. The tax court did not, however, reach the IRS's alternative arguments in support of its determination of deficiency, the reallocation provisions of I.R.C. §§ 482 and 845(a). The holding here does not dispose of those arguments, and we therefore must remand for the tax court to address them in the first instance.

III. Conclusion

For the foregoing reasons, we reverse the judgment against UPS and remand the action to the tax court for it to address in the first instance the IRS's contentions under §§ 482 and 845(a).

REVERSED AND REMANDED.

Opinion Footnotes

*fn1 Honorable Kenneth L. Ryskamp, U.S. District Judge for the Southern District of Florida, sitting by designation.

*fn2 These facts synopsize the high points of the tax court's long opinion, which is published at 78 T.C.M. (CCH) 262, 1999 WL 592696.

*fn3 Kirchman, which is binding in this circuit, differs in this respect from the oft-used statement of the doctrine derived from Rice's Toyota World, Inc. v. Comm'r, 752 F.2d 89, 91-92 (4th Cir.1985). Rice's Toyota World, unlike Kirchman, requires a tax-avoidance purpose as well as a lack of substance; Kirchman explicitly refuses to examine subjective intent if the transaction lacks economic effects.

RENT-A-CENTER, INC. V. COMMISSIONER

Rent-A-Center, Inc. v. Commissioner, 142 T.C. No. 1 (2014)

FOLEY, Judge: Respondent determined deficiencies of $14,931,159, $13,409,628, $7,461,039, $5,095,222, and $2,828,861 relating, respectively, to Rent-A-Center, Inc. (RAC), and its subsidiaries' 2003,/1/ 2004, 2005, 2006, and 2007 (years in issue) consolidated Federal income tax returns. The issue for decision is whether payments to Legacy Insurance Co., Ltd. (Legacy), were deductible, pursuant to section 162,/2/ as insurance expenses.

FINDINGS OF FACT

RAC, a publicly traded Delaware corporation, is the parent of a group of approximately 15 affiliated subsidiaries (collectively, petitioner). During the years in issue, petitioner was the largest domestic rent-to-own company. Through stores owned and operated by RAC's subsidiaries, petitioner rented, sold, and delivered home electronics, furniture, and appliances. The stores were in all 50 States, the District of Columbia, Puerto Rico, and Canada. From 1993 through 2002, petitioner's company-owned stores increased from 27 to 2,623. During the years in issue, RAC's subsidiaries owned between 2,623 and 3,081 stores; had between 14,300 and 19,740 employees; and operated between 7,143 and 8,027 insured vehicles.

I. Petitioner's Insurance Program

In 2001, American Insurance Group (AIG), in response to a

claim against RAC's directors and officers (D&O), withdrew a previous offer to renew RAC's D&O insurance policy. To address this problem, RAC engaged Aon Risk Consultants, Inc. (Aon), which convinced AIG to renew the policy. Impressed with Aon's insurance expertise and concerned about its growing insurance costs, petitioner engaged Aon to analyze risk management practices and to broker workers' compensation, automobile, and general liability insurance. With Aon's assistance, petitioner developed a risk management department and improved its loss prevention program.

Prior to August 2002, Travelers Insurance Co. (Travelers) provided petitioner's workers' compensation, automobile, and general liability coverage through bundled policies. Pursuant to a bundled policy, an insurer provides coverage and controls the claims administration process (i.e., investigating, evaluating, and paying claims). Travelers paid claims as they arose and withdrew amounts from petitioner's bank account to reimburse itself for any claims less than or equal to petitioner's deductible (i.e., a portion of an insured claim for which the insured is responsible). Pursuant to a predetermined formula, each store was allocated, and was responsible for paying, a portion of Travelers' premium costs.

In 2001, after receiving a $3 million invoice from Travelers for "claim handling fees", petitioner became dissatisfied with the cost and inefficiency associated with its bundled policies. On August 5, 2002, petitioner, with the assistance of Aon, obtained unbundled workers' compensation, automobile, and general liability policies from Discover Re. Pursuant to an unbundled policy, an insurer provides coverage and a third-party administrator manages the claims administration process. Discover Re underwrote the policies; multiple insurers provided coverage;/3/ and Specialty Risk Services, Inc. (SRS),/4/ a third-party administrator, evaluated and paid claims. Petitioner and its staff of licensed adjusters had access to SRS' claims management system and monitored SRS to ensure the proper handling of claims. This arrangement gave petitioner greater control over the claims administration process.

Petitioner, pursuant to the Discover Re policies' deductibles, was liable for a specific amount of each claim against its workers' compensation, automobile, and general liability policies (e.g., pursuant to its 2002 workers' compensation policy, petitioner was liable for the first $350,000 of each claim). Petitioner's retention of a portion of the risk resulted in lower premiums.

II. Legacy's Inception

Between 1993 and 2002, petitioner rapidly expanded and became increasingly concerned about its growing risk management costs. In 2002, after analyzing petitioner's insurance program, Aon suggested that petitioner form a wholly owned insurance company (i.e., a captive). Aon representatives informed David Glasgow, petitioner's director of risk management, about the financial and nonfinancial benefits of forming a captive. Aon convincingly explained that a captive could help petitioner reduce its costs, improve efficiency, obtain otherwise unavailable coverage, and provide accountability and transparency. Mr. Glasgow presented the proposal to petitioner's senior management, who concurred with Mr. Glasgow's recommendation to further explore the formation of a captive. Petitioner's senior management directed Aon to conduct a feasibility study (i.e., relying on petitioner's workers' compensation, automobile, and general liability loss data) and to prepare loss forecasts and actuarial studies. Petitioner engaged KPMG to analyze the feasibility study, review tax considerations, and prepare financial projections.

Aon, in the feasibility study, recommended that the captive be capitalized with no less than $8.8 million. Before deciding where to incorporate the captive, RAC analyzed projected financial data and reviewed multiple locations. On December 11, 2002, RAC incorporated, and capitalized with $9.9 million,/5/ Legacy, a wholly owned Bermudian subsidiary./6/ Legacy opened an account with Bank of N.T. Butterfield and Son, Ltd., and, on

December 20, 2002, filed a class 1 insurance company registration application with the Bermuda Monetary Authority (BMA), which regulated Bermuda's financial services sector. A class 1 insurer may insure only the risk of its shareholders and affiliates; must be capitalized with at least $120,000; and must meet a minimum solvency margin calculated by reference to the insurer's net premiums, general business assets,/7/ and general business liabilities. See Insurance Act, 1978, secs. 4B, 6, Appleby (2008) (Berm.); Insurance Returns and Solvency Regulations, 1980, Appleby, Reg. 10(1), Schedule I, Figure B (Berm.). During the years in issue, the BMA had the authority to modify prescribed requirements through both prospective and retroactive directives for special allowances. See Insurance Act, 1978, sec. 56.

Legacy planned to insure petitioner's liabilities for the period beginning in 2002 and ending December 31, 2003 (proposed period). Aon informed petitioner that coverage provided by unrelated insurers would be more costly than Aon's estimate of Legacy's premiums and that some insurers would not be willing to offer coverage. In response to a quote request, Discover Re stated that it was not in the market to provide the coverage Legacy contemplated. Discover Re estimated, however, that its premium (i.e., if it were to write one relating to the proposed period) would be approximately $3 million more than Legacy's.

III. Petitioner's Policies

During the years in issue, petitioner obtained unbundled workers' compensation, automobile, and general liability policies from Discover Re. Pursuant to these policies, Discover Re provided petitioner with coverage above a predetermined threshold relating to each line of coverage. In addition, Legacy wrote policies that covered petitioner's workers' compensation, automobile, and general liability claims below the Discover Re threshold. Petitioner, depending on the amount of a covered loss, could seek payment from Legacy, Discover Re, or both companies.

The annual premium Legacy charged petitioner was actuarially determined using Aon loss forecasts and was allocated to each RAC subsidiary that owned covered stores. RAC was a listed policyholder pursuant to the Legacy policies. No premium was attributable to RAC, however, because it did not own stores, have employees, or operate vehicles. RAC paid the premiums relating to each policy,/8/ estimated petitioner's total insurance costs (i.e., Legacy policies, Discover Re policies, third-party administrator fees, overhead, etc.), and established a monthly rate relating to each store's portion of these costs. The monthly rate was based on three factors: each store's payroll, each store's number of vehicles, and the total number of stores. At the end of each year, RAC adjusted the allocations to ensure that its subsidiaries recognized their actual insurance costs. SRS administered all claims relating to petitioner's workers' compensation, automobile, and general liability coverage. During the years in issue, the terms of Legacy's coverage varied, Legacy progressively covered greater amounts of petitioner's risk, and Legacy did not receive premiums from any unrelated entity. From December 31, 2002, through December 30, 2007, Legacy earned net underwriting income of $28,761,402. See infra p. 16.

A. Legacy's Deferred Tax Assets

Pursuant to the Legacy policies, coverage began on December 31 of each year. Because petitioner was a calendar year accrual method taxpayer, these policies created temporary timing differences between income recognized for tax purposes and income recognized for financial accounting (book) purposes./9/ For example, on December 31, 2002, when Legacy's second policy became effective, Legacy recognized, for tax purposes, the full amount of the premium (i.e., $42,800,300) relating to the taxable year ending December 31, 2002. See sec. 832(b)(4). For book purposes, however, Legacy in 2002 recognized only 1/365 of the premium (i.e., $117,261), and the remaining $42,683,039 constituted a reserve. This timing difference created a deferred tax asset (DTA) because in 2002 Legacy "prepaid" its tax liability relating to income it recognized, for book purposes, in 2003. Each day Legacy recognized a portion of its premium income (i.e., $117,261) for book purposes and reduced its reserve by the same amount. On December 30, 2003, the reserve was fully depleted. Upon the issuance of a new policy on December 31, 2003, a new DTA was created because Legacy recognized, for tax purposes, in 2003 the full amount of the premium; a corresponding tax liability was incurred; the premium reserve increased; and most of the premium income attributable to the 2003 policy was recognizable, for book purposes, in 2004.

1. Bermuda's Minimum Solvency Margin Requirement

Pursuant to the Bermuda Insurance Act, an insurance company must maintain a minimum solvency margin. See Insurance Act, 1978, sec. 6. More specifically, a class 1 insurer's general business assets must exceed its general business liabilities by the greatest of: $120,000; 10% of the insurer's loss and loss expense provisions plus other insurance reserves; or 20% of the first $6 million of net premiums plus 10% of the net premiums which exceed $6 million. See Insurance Returns and Solvency Regulations, 1980, Appleby, Reg. 10(1), Schedule I, Figure B. DTAs generally may be treated as general business assets only with the BMA's permission.

2. Legacy Receives Permission To Treat DTAs as General Business Assets Through 2003

In the minimum solvency margin calculation set forth in its insurance company registration application, Legacy treated DTAs as general business assets. On March 11, 2003, Legacy petitioned the BMA for the requisite permission to do so. The following letter from RAC accompanied the request:

We write to confirm to you that Rent-A-Center, Inc., * * * will guarantee the payment to Legacy Insurance Company, Ltd. (the "Company"), * * * of all amounts reflected on the projected balance sheets of the Company previously delivered to you as deferred tax assets arising from timing differences in the amounts of taxes payable for tax and financial accounting purposes. This guaranty of payment will take effect in the event of any change in tax laws that would require recognition of an impairment of the deferred tax asset, and will be effective to the extent of the amount of the impairment.

On March 13, 2003, the BMA granted Legacy permission to treat DTAs as general business assets on its statutory balance sheet through December 31, 2003./10/ The BMA also informed Legacy that from December 31, 2002, through March 13, 2003, it "wrote insurance business without being in receipt of its Certificate of Registration and was therefore in violation of the [Bermuda Insurance] Act as it engaged in insurance business without a license." Despite this violation, the BMA registered Legacy as a class 1 insurer effective December 20, 2002 (i.e., the date Legacy filed its insurance registration request and before it issued policies relating to the years in issue).

3. The Parental Guaranty: Facilitating the Treatment of DTAs as General Business Assets Through 2006

In response to the recurring DTA issue, Legacy requested that RAC guarantee DTAs relating to subsequent years. On September 17, 2003, RAC's board of directors authorized the execution of a guaranty of "the obligations of Legacy to comply with the laws of Bermuda." On the same day, RAC's chairman and chief executive officer executed a parental guaranty and sent it to Legacy's board of directors. The parental guaranty provided:

The undersigned, Rent-A-Center, Inc. a Delaware corporation ("Rent-A-Center") is sole owner of 100% of the issued and outstanding shares in your share capital and as such DOES HEREBY GUARANTEE financial support for you, Legacy Insurance Co., Ltd., * * * and for your business, as more particularly set out below, which is to say:

Under the [Bermuda] Insurance Act * * * and related Regulations (the "Act"), Legacy Insurance Co., Ltd., must maintain certain solvency and liquidity margins and, in order to ensure continued compliance with the Act, it is necessary to support Legacy Insurance Co., Ltd. with a guarantee of its liabilities under the Act (the "Liabilities") not to exceed Twenty-Five Million US dollars (US $25,000,000).

Accordingly, Rent-A-Center DOES HEREBY GUARANTEE to you the payment in full of the Liabilities of Legacy Insurance Co., Ltd. and further to indemnify and hold harmless Legacy Insurance Co., Ltd. from the Liabilities up to the maximum dollar amount [$25,000,000] indicated in the foregoing paragraph.

Seeking regulatory approval to treat DTAs as general business assets in subsequent years, Legacy, on October 30, 2003, petitioned the BMA and attached the parental guaranty.

On November 12, 2003, the BMA issued a directive which "approved the Parental Guarantee from Rent-A-Center, Inc. dated 17 th September, 2003 up to an aggregate amount of $25,000,000 for utilization as part of * * * [Legacy]'s capitalization". This approval was granted for the years ending December 31, 2003, 2004, 2005, and 2006. Legacy used the parental guaranty only to meet the minimum solvency margin (i.e., to treat DTAs as general business assets)./11/ On December 30, 2006, RAC unilaterally canceled the parental guaranty because Legacy met the minimum solvency margin without it.

B. Legacy's Ownership of RAC Treasury Shares

Legacy purchased RAC treasury shares during 2004, 2005, and 2006. The BMA approved the purchases and allowed Legacy to treat the shares as general business assets for purposes of calculating its liquidity ratio (i.e., its ratio of general business assets to liabilities). Pursuant to Bermuda solvency regulations, an insurer fails to meet the liquidity ratio if the value of its general business assets is less than 75% of its liabilities. See Insurance Returns and Solvency Regulations, 1980, Appleby, Reg. 11(2). During the years in issue, Legacy met its liquidity ratio and did not resell the shares.

C. Legacy's Financial Reports

For each policy period, Legacy's auditor, Arthur Morris & Co. (Arthur Morris), prepared, and provided to RAC and the BMA, reports and financial statements. In these reports and statements, Arthur Morris calculated Legacy's DTAs,/12/ minimum solvency margin,/13/ premium-to-surplus ratio,/14/ and net underwriting income./15/ During each of the years in issue, Legacy's total statutory capital and surplus equaled or exceeded the BMA minimum solvency margin. In calculating total statutory capital and surplus, Arthur Morris took into account the following four components: contributed surplus, statutory surplus, capital stock, and other fixed capital (i.e., assets deemed to be general business assets). During 2003, 2004, and 2005, Legacy included portions of the parental guaranty as general business assets. During the years in issue, the amounts of Legacy's DTAs exceeded the portions of Legacy's parental guaranty treated as general business assets. See infra p. 16. Arthur Morris calculated Legacy's statutory surplus by adding statutory surplus at the beginning of the year and income for the year, subtracting dividends paid and payable, and making other adjustments relating to changes in assets.

The following table summarizes key details relating to Legacy's policies:

Policy Period	Premium	DTAs	Parental Guaranty Asset	Total Statutory Capital & Surplus	Minimum Solvency Margin	Premium-to-Surplus Ratio
2003	$42,800,300	$5,840,613	$4,805,764	$5,898,192	$5,898,192	8.983:1
2004	50,639,000	6,275,326	4,243,823	7,036,573	7,036,572	7.695:1
2005	54,148,912	7,659,009	3,987,916	8,379,436	8,379,435	6.369:1
2006	53,365,926	8,742,425	-0-	10,014,206	9,284,601	6.326:1
2007	63,345,022	9,689,714	-0-	12,428,663	10,888,698	5.221:1
2008	64,884,392	9,607,661	-0-	23,712,022	11,278,359	2.538:1

IV. Procedural History

Respondent sent petitioner, on January 7, 2008, a notice of deficiency relating to 2003; on December 22, 2009, a notice of deficiency relating to 2004 and 2005; and on August 5, 2010, a notice of deficiency relating to 2006 and 2007 (collectively, notices). In these notices, respondent determined that petitioner's payments to Legacy were not deductible pursuant to section 162. On April 6, 2009, March 22, 2010, and September 29, 2010, respectively, petitioner, whose principal place of business was Plano, Texas, timely filed petitions with the Court seeking redeterminations of the deficiencies set forth in the notices. After concessions, the remaining issue for decision is whether payments to Legacy were deductible.

OPINION

In determining whether payments to Legacy were deductible, our initial inquiry is whether Legacy was a bona fide insurance company. See Harper Grp. v. Commissioner, [Dec. 47,131] 96 T.C. 45, 59 (1991), aff'd, 979 F.2d 1341 (9th Cir. 1992); AMERCO v. Commissioner, [Dec. 47,130] 96 T.C. 18, 40-41 (1991), aff'd,

979 F.2d 162 (9th Cir. 1992). We respect the separate taxable treatment of a captive unless there is a finding of sham or lack of business purpose. See Moline Props., Inc. v. Commissioner, [43-1 ustc ¶9464] 319 U.S. 436, 439 (1943); Harper Grp. v. Commissioner, 96 T.C. at 57-59. Respondent contends that Legacy was a sham entity created primarily to generate Federal income tax savings.

I. Legacy Was Not a Sham

A. Legacy Was Created for Significant and Legitimate Nontax Reasons

After successfully resolving petitioner's D&O insurance problem, Aon evaluated petitioner's risk management department. Petitioner, with Aon's assistance, improved risk management practices, switched from bundled to unbundled policies, and hired SRS as a third-party administrator. Aon proposed that petitioner form a captive, and petitioner determined that a captive would allow it to reduce its insurance costs, obtain otherwise unavailable insurance coverage, formalize and more efficiently manage its insurance program, and provide accountability and transparency relating to insurance costs. Petitioner engaged KPMG to prepare financial projections and evaluate tax considerations referenced in the feasibility study. Federal income tax consequences were considered, but the formation of Legacy was not a tax-driven transaction. See Moline Props., Inc. v. Commissioner, 319 U.S. at 439; Britt v. United States, [70-1 ustc ¶9400] 431 F.2d 227, 235-236 (5th Cir. 1970); Bass v. Commissioner, [Dec. 29,055] 50 T.C. 595, 600 (1968). To the contrary, in forming Legacy, petitioner made a business decision premised on a myriad of significant and legitimate nontax considerations. See Jones v. Commissioner, [Dec. 33,434] 64 T.C. 1066, 1076 (1975) ("A corporation is not a 'sham' if it was organized for legitimate business purposes or if it engages in a substantial business activity."); Bass v. Commissioner, 50 T.C. at 600.

B. There Was No Impermissible Circular Flow of Funds

Respondent further contends that Legacy was "not an independent fund, but an accounting device". In support of this contention, respondent cites a purported "circular flow of funds" through Legacy, RAC, and RAC's subsidiaries. Respondent's expert, however, readily acknowledged that he found no evidence of a circular flow of funds, nor have we. Legacy, with the approval of the BMA, purchased RAC treasury shares but did not resell them. Furthermore, petitioner established that there was nothing unusual about the manner in which premiums and claims were paid. Finally, respondent contends that the netting of premiums owed to Legacy during 2003 is evidence that Legacy was a sham. We disagree. This netting was simply a bookkeeping measure performed as an administrative convenience.

C. The Premium-to-Surplus Ratios Do Not Indicate That Legacy Was a Sham

Respondent emphasizes that, during the years in issue, Legacy's premium-to-surplus ratios were above the ratios of U.S. property and casualty insurance companies and Bermuda class 4 insurers/16/ (collectively, commercial insurance companies). On cross-examination, however, respondent's expert admitted that his analysis of commercial insurance companies contained erroneous numbers. Furthermore, he failed to properly explain the profitability data he cited and did not include relevant data relating to Legacy. Moreover, his comparison, of Legacy's premium-to-surplus ratios with the ratios of commercial insurance companies, was not instructive. Commercial insurance companies have lower premium-to-surplus ratios because they face competition and, as a result, typically price their premiums to have significant underwriting losses. They compensate for underwriting losses by retaining sufficient assets (i.e., more assets per dollar of premium resulting in lower premium-to-surplus ratios) to earn ample amounts of investment income. Captives in Bermuda, however, have fewer assets per dollar of premium (i.e., higher premium-to-surplus ratios) but generate significant underwriting profits because their premiums reflect the full dollar value, rather than the present value, of expected losses. Simply put, the premium-to-surplus ratios do not indicate that Legacy was a sham.

D. Legacy Was a Bona Fide Insurance Company

Petitioner presented convincing, and essentially uncontradicted, evidence that Legacy was a bona fide insurance company. As respondent concedes, petitioner faced actual and insurable risk. Comparable coverage with other insurance companies would have been more expensive, and some insurance companies (e.g., Discover Re) would not underwrite the coverage provided by Legacy. In addition, RAC established Legacy for legitimate business reasons, including: increasing the accountability and transparency of its insurance operations, accessing new insurance markets, and reducing risk management costs. Furthermore, Legacy entered into bona fide arm's-length contracts with petitioner; charged actuarially determined premiums; was subject to the BMA's regulatory control; met Bermuda's minimum statutory requirements; paid claims from its separately maintained account; and, as respondent's expert readily admitted, was adequately capitalized. See Humana Inc. & Subs. v. Commissioner, [89-2 ustc ¶9453] 881 F.2d 247, 253 (6th Cir. 1989), aff'g in part, rev'g in part and remanding [Dec. 43,666] 88 T.C. 197, 206 (1987); Harper Grp. v. Commissioner, 96 T.C. at 59. Moreover, the validity of claims Legacy paid was established by SRS, an independent third-party administrator, which also determined the validity of claims pursuant to the Discover Re policies. See Harper Grp. v. Commissioner, 96 T.C. at 59. Finally, RAC's subsidiaries did not own stock in, or contribute capital to, Legacy.

II. The Payments to Legacy Were Deductible Insurance Expenses

The Code does not define insurance. The Supreme Court, however, has established two necessary criteria: risk shifting and risk distribution. See Helvering v. Le Gierse, [41-1 ustc ¶10,029]

312 U.S. 531, 539 (1941). In addition, the arrangement must involve insurance risk and meet commonly accepted notions of insurance. See Harper Grp. v. Commissioner, 96 T.C. at 58; AMERCO v. Commissioner, 96 T.C. at 38. These four criteria are not independent or exclusive, but establish a framework for determining "the existence of insurance for Federal tax purposes." See AMERCO v. Commissioner, 96 T.C. at 38. Insurance premiums may be deductible. A taxpayer may not, however, deduct amounts set aside in its own possession to compensate itself for perils which are generally the subject of insurance. See Clougherty Packing Co. v. Commissioner, [Dec. 42,099] 84 T.C. 948, 958 (1985), aff'd, 811 F.2d 1297 (9th Cir. 1987). We consider all of the facts and circumstances to determine whether an arrangement qualifies as insurance. See Harper Grp. v. Commissioner, 96 T.C. at 57. Respondent contends that payments to Legacy represent amounts petitioner set aside to self-insure its risks.

A. The Policies at Issue Involved Insurance Risk

Respondent concedes that petitioner faced insurable risk relating to all three types of risk: workers' compensation, automobile, and general liability. Petitioner entered into contracts with Legacy and Discover Re to address these three types of risk. Thus, insurance risk was present in the arrangement between petitioner and Legacy.

B. Risk Shifting

We must now determine whether the policies at issue shifted risk between RAC's subsidiaries and Legacy. This requires a review of our cases relating to captive insurance arrangements.

1. Precedent Relating to Parent-Subsidiary Arrangements

In 1978, we analyzed parent-subsidiary captive arrangements for the first time. See Carnation Co. v. Commissioner, 71 T.C. 400 (1978), aff'd, 640 F.2d 1010 (9th Cir. 1981). In Carnation, the parties entered into two insurance contracts: an agreement between Carnation and an unrelated insurer, and a reinsurance agreement between the captive and the unrelated insurer. Id. at 402-404. The unrelated insurer expressed concern to Carnation about the captive's financial stability and requested a letter of credit or other guaranty. Id. at 404. Carnation refused to issue a letter of credit or other guaranty but did execute an agreement to provide, upon demand, $2,880,000 of additional capital to the captive. Id. at 402-404. We held, relying on Le Gierse, that the parent-subsidiary arrangement was not insurance because the three agreements (i.e., the two insurance contracts and the agreement to further capitalize the captive), when considered together, were void of insurance risk. Id. at 409. The Court of Appeals for the Ninth Circuit affirmed and concluded that our application of Le Gierse was appropriate given the interdependence of the three agreements. See Carnation Co. v. Commissioner, 640 F.2d at 1013. Furthermore, the Court of Appeals held that "[t]he key was that * * * [the unrelated insurer] refused to enter into the reinsurance contract with * * * [the captive] unless Carnation" executed the capitalization agreement. See id.

In Clougherty, our next opportunity to analyze a parent-subsidiary captive arrangement, the parties entered into two insurance contracts: an agreement between Clougherty and an unrelated insurer, and a reinsurance agreement between the captive and the unrelated insurer. Clougherty Packing Co. v. Commissioner, 84 T.C. at 952. We concluded that "the operative facts in the/17/ instant case * * * [were] indistinguishable from the facts in Carnation", analyzed Clougherty's balance sheet, and held that risk did not shift to the captive:

> We found in Carnation, as we find here, that to the extent the risk was not shifted, insurance does not exist and the payments to that extent are not insurance premiums. The measure of the risk shifted is the percentage of the premium not ceded. This is nothing more than a recharacterization of the payments which petitioner seeks to deduct as insurance premiums.

Id. at 956, 958-959. The Commissioner urged us to adopt his

economic family theory, which posits that the insuring parent corporation and its domestic subsidiaries, and the wholly owned "insurance" subsidiary, though separate corporate entities, represent one economic family with the result that those who bear the ultimate economic burden of loss are the same persons who suffer the loss. To the extent that the risks of loss are not retained in their entirety by * * * or reinsured with * * * insurance companies that are unrelated to the economic family of insureds, there is no risk shifting or risk-distributing, and no insurance, the premiums for which are deductible under section 162 of the Code.

Rev. Rul. 77-316, 1977-2 C.B. 53, 54. In rejecting the Commissioner's economic family theory, we emphasized that "[w]e have done nothing more in Carnation and here but to reclassify, as nondeductible, portions of the payments which the taxpayers deducted as insurance premiums but which were received by the taxpayer's captive insurance subsidiaries." See Clougherty Packing Co. v. Commissioner, 84 T.C. at 960.

The Court of Appeals for the Ninth Circuit affirmed our decision in Clougherty and applied a balance sheet and net worth analysis, pursuant to which a determination of whether risk has shifted depends on whether a covered loss affects the balance sheet and net worth of the insured. See Clougherty Packing Co. v. Commissioner, 811 F.2d at 1305. In defining insurance, the Court of Appeals stated that "a true insurance agreement must remove the risk of loss from the insured party." Id. at 1306. The Court of Appeals elaborated:

> [W]e examine the economic consequences of the captive insurance arrangement to the "insured" party to see if that party has, in fact, shifted the risk. In doing so, we look only to the insured's assets, i.e., those of Clougherty, to determine whether it has divested itself of the adverse economic consequences of a covered workers' compensation claim. Viewing only Clougherty's assets and considering only the effect of a claim on those assets, it is clear that the risk of loss has not been shifted from Clougherty.

Id. at 1305. Furthermore, the Court of Appeals explained that the balance sheet and net worth analysis does not ignore separate corporate existence:

> Moline Properties requires that related corporate entities be afforded separate tax status and treatment. It does not require that the Commissioner, in determining whether a corporation has shifted its risk of loss, ignore the effect of a loss upon one of the corporation's assets merely because that asset happens to be stock in a subsidiary. Because we only consider the effect of a covered claim on Clougherty's assets, our analysis in no way contravenes Moline Properties.

Id. at 1307. Finally, the Court of Appeals concluded that "[t]he parent of a captive insurer retains an economic stake in whether a covered loss occurs. Accordingly, an insurance agreement between parent and captive does not shift the parent's risk of loss and is not an agreement for 'insurance.'" Id.

2. Precedent Relating to Brother-Sister Arrangements

In Humana Inc. & Subs. v. Commissioner, 88 T.C. at 206, we were faced with two distinct issues: the deductibility of premiums paid by a parent to a captive (parent-subsidiary arrangement) and the deductibility of premiums paid by affiliated subsidiaries to a captive (brother-sister arrangement). Humana, Inc. (Humana), operated a hospital network and, in 1976, was unable to renew its existing policies relating to workers' compensation, malpractice, and general liability. Id. at 200. Humana's insurance broker could not obtain comparable coverage and recommended that Humana establish a captive insurance company. Id. Humana subsequently incorporated, and capitalized with $1 million, a Colorado captive. Id. at 201-202. The captive provided coverage relating to Humana and its subsidiaries' workers' compensation, malpractice, and general liability. Id. at 202-204. Humana paid the captive a monthly premium which was allocated among itself and each operating subsidiary. Id. at 203.

We held that the parent-subsidiary premiums were not deductible because Humana did not shift risk to the captive. See id. at 206-207. The brother-sister arrangement, however, presented an issue of first impression. See id. at 208. We rejected the Commissioner's economic family theory and held "that it is more appropriate to examine all of the facts to decide whether or to what extent there has been a shifting of the risk from one entity to the captive insurance company." See id. at 214. We extended our rationale from Carnation and Clougherty (i.e., recharacterizing a captive insurance arrangement as self-insurance) to brothersister arrangements and stated that declining to do so "would exalt form over substance and permit a taxpayer to circumvent our holdings by simple corporate structural changes." See id. at 213. The report on which we relied, prepared by Irving Plotkin, stated: "'A firm placing its risks in a captive insurance company in which it holds a sole or predominant ownership position, is not relieving itself of financial uncertainty.'" Id. at 210 (fn. ref. omitted). In addition, the report stated:

> "True insurance relieves the firm's balance sheet of any potential impact of the financial consequences of the insured peril. For the price of the premiums, the insured rids itself of any economic stake in whether or not the loss occurs. * * * [However] as long as the firm deals with its captive, its balance sheet cannot be protected from the financial vicissitudes of the insured peril."

Humana Inc. & Subs. v. Commissioner, 88 T.C. at 211-212 (alteration in original) (fn. ref. omitted). After quoting extensively from the report and analyzing the facts, "[w]e conclude[d] that there was not the necessary shifting of risk from the operating subsidiaries of Humana Inc. to * * * [the captive] and, therefore, the amounts charged by Humana Inc. to its subsidiaries did not constitute insurance." See id. at 214.

Seven Judges concurred with the opinion of the Court's parent-subsidiary holding but disagreed with the brother-sister holding. See id. at 219 (Korner, J., concurring and dissenting).

They found the opinion of the Court's rationale "disingenuous and entirely unconvincing" and asserted that the opinion of the Court had implicitly adopted the Commissioner's "economic family" theory. Id. at 223. After emphasizing that the subsidiaries had no ownership interest in the captive, paid premiums for their own insurance, and would not be affected (i.e., their balance sheets and net worth) by the payment of an insured claim, the dissent further stated:

> The theory of Helvering v. Le Gierse, 312 U.S. 531 (1941), may have been adequate to sustain the holdings in Carnation and Clougherty, where only a parent and its insurance subsidiary were involved. It cannot be stretched to cover the instant brother-sister situation, where there was nothing—equity ownership or otherwise—to offset the shifting of risk from the hospital subsidiaries to * * * [the captive]. If the majority is to accomplish the fell deed here, "a decent respect to the opinions of mankind requires that they should declare the causes which impel them" to such a result.

Id. at 224 (fn. ref. omitted).

The Court of Appeals for the Sixth Circuit affirmed our decision relating to the parent-subsidiary arrangement, but reversed our decision relating to the brother-sister arrangement./18/ See Humana Inc. & Subs. v. Commissioner, 881 F.2d at 251-252. The Court of Appeals for the Sixth Circuit adopted the Court of Appeals for the Ninth Circuit's balance sheet and net worth analysis and held that the subsidiaries' payments to the captive were deductible. Id. at 252 ("[W]e look solely to the insured's assets, * * * and consider only the effect of a claim on those assets[.]" (citing Clougherty v. Commissioner, 811 F.2d at 1305)). In rejecting our holding relating to the brother-sister arrangement, the Court of Appeals stated that "the tax court incorrectly extended the rationale of Carnation and

Clougherty in holding that the premiums paid by the subsidiaries of Humana Inc. to * * * [the captive], as charged to them by Humana Inc., did not constitute valid insurance agreements" and concluded that "[n]either Carnation nor Clougherty * * * provide a basis for denying the deductions in the brother-sister * * * [arrangement]." Id. at 252-253. In response to our rationalization that "[i]f we decline to extend our holdings in Carnation and Clougherty to the brother-sister factual pattern, we would exalt form over substance and permit a taxpayer to circumvent our holdings by simple corporate structural changes", the Court of Appeals stated:

> Such an argument provides no legal justification for denying the deduction in the brother-sister context. The legal test is whether there has been risk distribution and risk shifting, not whether Humana Inc. is a common parent or whether its affiliates are in a brother-sister relationship to * * * [the captive]. We do not focus on the relationship of the parties per se or the particular structure of the corporation involved. We look to the assets of the insured. * * * If Humana changes its corporate structure and that change involves risk shifting and risk distribution, and that change is for a legitimate business purpose and is not a sham to avoid the payment of taxes, then it is irrelevant whether the changed corporate structure has the side effect of also permitting Humana Inc.'s affiliates to take advantage of the Internal Revenue Code §162(a) (1954) and deduct payments to a captive insurance company under the control of the Humana parent as insurance premiums.

Id. at 255-256.

The Court of Appeals held that "[t]he test to determine whether a transaction under the Internal Revenue Code §162(a)

* * * is legitimate or illegitimate is not a vague and broad 'economic reality' test. The test is whether there is risk shifting and risk distribution." Humana Inc. & Subs. v. Commissioner, 881 F.2d at 255. The Court of Appeals further addressed our analysis and stated:

> The tax court cannot avoid direct confrontation with the separate corporate existence doctrine of Moline Properties by claiming that its decision does not rest on "economic family" principles because it is merely reclassifying or recharacterizing the transaction as nondeductible additions to a reserve for losses. The tax court argues in its opinion that such "recharacterization" does not disregard the separate corporate status of the entities involved, but merely disregards the particular transactions between the entities in order to take into account substance over form and the "economic reality" of the transaction that no risk has shifted.

> The tax court misapplies this substance over form argument. The substance over form or economic reality argument is not a broad legal doctrine designed to distinguish between legitimate and illegitimate transactions and employed at the discretion of the tax court whenever it feels that a taxpayer is taking advantage of the tax laws to produce a favorable result for the taxpayer. * * * The substance over form analysis, rather, is a distinct and limited exception to the general rule under Moline Properties that separate entities must be respected as such for tax purposes. The substance over form doctrine applies to disregard the separate corporate entity where "Congress has evinced an intent to the contrary" * * *

Id. at 254. In short, we do not look to the parent to determine whether premiums paid by the subsidiaries to the captive are deductible. Id. at 252. The policies shifted risk because claims paid by the captive did not affect the net worth of Humana's subsidiaries. See id. at 252-253.

3. Brother-Sister Arrangements May Shift Risk

We find persuasive the Court of Appeals for the Sixth Circuit's critique of our analysis of the brother-sister arrangement in Humana. First, our extension of Carnation and Clougherty to brother-sister arrangements was improper. As the Court of Appeals correctly concluded: " Carnation dealt solely with the parentsubsidiary issue, not the brother-sister issue. Likewise, Clougherty dealt only with the parent-subsidiary issue and not the brother-sister issue. Nothing in either Carnation or Clougherty lends support for denying the deductibility of the payments in the brother-sister context." Id. at 253-254.

Second, the opinion of the Court's extensive reliance on Plotkin's report to analyze the brother-sister arrangement was inappropriate. The report in Humana addressed parent-subsidiary, rather than brother-sister, arrangements. See Humana Inc. & Subs. v. Commissioner, 88 T.C. at 209; see also supra pp. 26-31. In the instant cases, Plotkin explicitly addressed brother-sister arrangements and stated:

Even though the brother, the captive, and the parent are in the same economic family, to the extent that a brother has no ownership interest in the captive, the results of the parent-captive analysis do not apply. It is not the presence or absence of unrelated business, nor the number of other insureds (be they affiliates or non-affiliates), but it is the absence of ownership, the captive's capital, and the number of statistically independent risks (regardless of who owns them) that enables the captive to provide the brother with true insurance as a matter of economics and finance.

We agree. Humana's subsidiaries had no ownership interest in the captive. See Humana Inc. & Subs. v. Commissioner, 88 T.C.

at 201-202. Thus, the parentsubsidiary analysis employed by the opinion of the Court was incorrect.

Third, we did not properly analyze the facts and circumstances. See id. at 214. The balance sheet and net worth analysis provides the proper analytical framework to determine risk shifting in brother-sister arrangements. See Humana Inc. & Subs. v. Commissioner, 881 F.2d at 252; Clougherty Packing Co. v. Commissioner, 811 F.2d at 1305. Instead, we implicitly employed a substanceover-form rationale to recharacterize Humana's subsidiaries' payments as amounts set aside for self-insurance and referenced, but did not apply, the balance sheet and net worth analysis. Indeed, we did not "examine the economic consequences of the captive insurance arrangement to the 'insured' party to see if that party * * * [had], in fact, shifted the risk." See Clougherty v. Commissioner, 811 F.2d at 1305.

4. The Legacy Policies Shifted Risk

In determining whether Legacy's policies shifted risk, we narrow our scrutiny to the arrangement's economic impact on RAC's subsidiaries (i.e., the insured entities). See Humana Inc. & Subs. v. Commissioner, 881 F.2d at 252-253; Clougherty Packing Co. v. Commissioner, 811 F.2d at 1305 ("[W]e examine the economic consequences of the captive insurance arrangement to the 'insured' party to see if that party has, in fact, shifted the risk. In doing so, we look only to the insured's assets"[.]). In direct testimony respondent's expert, however, emphasized that petitioner's "captive program * * * [did] not involve risk shifting that * * * [was] comparable to that provided by a commercial insurance program." We decline his invitation to premise our holding on a specious comparability analysis. Simply put, the risk either was, or was not, shifted.

The policies at issue shifted risk from RAC's insured subsidiaries to Legacy, which was formed for a valid business purpose; was a separate, independent, and viable entity; was financially capable of meeting its obligations; and reimbursed RAC's subsidiaries when they suffered an insurable loss. See

Sears, Roebuck & Co. v. Commissioner, 96 T.C. 61, 100-101 (1991), aff'd in part, rev'd in part, 972 F.2d 858 (7th Cir. 1992); AMERCO v. Commissioner, 96 T.C. at 41. Moreover, a payment from Legacy to RAC's subsidiaries did not reduce the net worth of RAC's subsidiaries because, unlike RAC, the subsidiaries did not own stock in Legacy. Indeed, on cross-examination, respondent's expert conceded that the balance sheets and net worth of RAC's subsidiaries were not affected by a covered loss and that the policies shifted risk:

> [Petitioner's counsel:] But if the loss gets paid, whose balance sheet gets affected in that case?
>
> [Respondent's expert:] What's hanging me up is that I don't know whether—I guess you're right, because * * * [RAC's subsidiary] will treat the payment from—the payment that it expects from Legacy as an asset, so the loss would hit Legacy's [balance sheet].
>
> [Petitioner's counsel:] But it wouldn't hit * * * [RAC's subsidiary's] balance sheet.
>
> [Respondent's expert:] I would think that's right.
> * * *
> [Petitioner's counsel:] Why is that not risk-shifting?
>
> [Respondent's expert:] That's an—why is that not risk-shifting?
>
> [Petitioner's counsel:] Yes. Why is that not risk-shifting? Why hasn't [RAC's subsidiary] shifted its risk to Legacy? Its insurance risk—why hasn't it shifted to Legacy in that scenario?
>
> [Respondent's expert:] I mean, I would say from an accounting perspective, it has managed to have—is it—if we're going to respect all these [corporate] forms, then it will have shifted that risk.

5. The Parental Guaranty Did Not Vitiate Risk Shifting

Legacy, in March 2003, petitioned the BMA and received approval, through December 31, 2003, to treat DTAs as general business assets. On September 17, 2003, RAC issued the parental guaranty to Legacy, which petitioned, and received permission from, the BMA to treat DTAs as general business assets through December 31, 2006. Respondent contends that the parental guaranty abrogated risk shifting between Legacy and RAC's subsidiaries. We disagree. First, and most importantly, the parental guaranty did not affect the balance sheets or net worth of the subsidiaries insured by Legacy. Petitioner's expert, in response to a question the Court posed during cross-examination, convincingly countered respondent's contention:

> [The Court]: * * * [W]hat impact does the corporate structure have on the effect of the parental guarantee?
>
> [Petitioner's expert]: I think it has a great impact on it. None of the subs, as I understand it, are entering in or [are] a part of that guarantee. Only the subs are effectively insureds under the policy. They are the only ones who produce risks that could be covered. The guarantee in no way vitiates the completeness of the transfer of their uncertainty, their risk, to the insuring subsidiary.

Even if one assumes that the guarantee increases the capital that the captive could use to pay losses, none of those payments would go to the detriment of the sub as a separate legal entity.

Second, the cases upon which respondent relies are distinguishable. Respondent cites Malone & Hyde, Inc. v. Commissioner, 62 F.3d 835, 841 (6th Cir. 1995) (holding that a reinsurance arrangement was not bona fide because the captive was undercapitalized and the parent guaranteed the captive's obligations to an unrelated insurer), rev'g T.C. Memo. 1993-585; Carnation Co. v. Commissioner, 71 T.C. at 404, 409 (holding that a reinsurance arrangement lacked insurance risk where the captive was undercapitalized and, at the insistence of an unrelated primary insurer, the parent agreed to provide additional capital); and Kidde Indus., Inc. v. United States, 40 Fed. Cl. 42, 49-50 (1997) (holding that a reinsurance arrangement lacked risk shifting because the parent indemnified the captive's obligation to pay an unrelated primary insurer). Unlike the agreements in these cases, the parental guaranty did not shift the ultimate risk of loss; did not involve an undercapitalized captive; and was not issued to, or requested by, an unrelated insurer. Cf. Malone & Hyde, Inc. v. Commissioner, 62 F.3d at 841-843; Carnation Co. v. Commissioner, 71 T.C. at 404, 409; Kidde Indus., Inc., 40 Fed. Cl. at 49-50.

Third, RAC guaranteed Legacy's "liabilities under the Act [(i.e., the Bermuda Insurance Act and related regulations)]", pursuant to which Legacy was required to maintain "certain solvency and liquidity margins". RAC did not pay any money pursuant to the parental guaranty and Legacy's "liabilities under the Act" did not include Legacy's contractual obligations to RAC's affiliates or obligations to unrelated insurers. For purposes of calculating the minimum solvency margin, Legacy treated a portion of the parental guaranty as a general business asset. See supra pp. 15-16. In sum, by providing the parental guaranty to the BMA, Legacy received permission to treat DTAs as general business assets and ensured its continued compliance with the BMA's solvency requirements./19/ The parental guaranty served no other purpose and was unilaterally revoked by RAC, in 2006, when Legacy met the BMA's solvency requirements without reference to DTAs.

C. The Legacy Policies Distributed Risk

Risk distribution occurs when an insurer pools a large enough collection of unrelated risks (i.e., risks that are generally unaffected by the same event or circumstance). See Humana Inc. & Subs. v. Commissioner, 881 F.2d at 257. "By assuming numerous relatively small, independent risks that occur

in excess of premiums received. And even then, the indemnity or capitalization agreement was coupled with an undercapitalized captive. Accordingly, those cases are distinguishable from the situation presented here.

Malone & Hyde, Inc. v. Commissioner, 62 F.3d 835 (6th Cir. 1995), rev'g T.C. Memo. 1993-585, involved an insurance subsidiary established to provide reinsurance for the parent and its subsidiaries. After incorporating the captive, Malone & Hyde entered into an agreement with a third-party insurer to insure both its own and its subsidiaries' risks. Id. at 836. The third-party insurer then reinsured the first $150,000 of coverage per claim with the captive. Id. Because the captive was thinly capitalized—it had no assets other than $120,000 of paid-in capital—Malone & Hyde executed "hold harmless" agreements in favor of the third-party insurer. Id. These agreements provided that if the captive defaulted on its obligations as reinsurer, then Malone & Hyde would completely shield the third-party insurer from liability. Id. In deciding whether the risk had shifted, the court held that "[w]hen the entire scheme involves either undercapitalization or indemnification of the primary insurer by the taxpayer claiming the deduction, or both, these facts alone disqualify the premium payments from being treated as ordinary and necessary business expenses to the extent such payments are ceded by the primary insurer to the captive insurance subsidiary." Id. at 842-843. In short, Malone & Hyde, Inc. had a thinly capitalized captive insurer and a blanket indemnity. Here, neither of those facts is present.

The facts in Kidde Indus., Inc. are quite similar to those in Malone & Hyde, Inc. Kidde incorporated a captive and entered into an insurance agreement with a third-party insurer who in turn entered into a reinsurance agreement with the captive. Kidde Indus., Inc., 40 Fed. Cl. at 45. As in Malone & Hyde, Inc., the captive was significantly undercapitalized, and Kidde executed an indemnification agreement to provide the third-party insurer with the "level of comfort" needed before it would issue the policies. Id. at 48. Again, the court held that Kidde retained the risk of loss and could not deduct the premiums. Id.

Carnation Co. v. Commissioner, 71 T.C. 400 (1978), aff'd, 640 F.2d 1010 (9th Cir. 1981), involved slightly different facts. A captive reinsured 90% of the third-party insurer's liabilities under Carnation's policy. Id. at 403. As part of this arrangement, the third-party insurer ceded 90% of the premiums to the captive and the captive paid the third-party insurer a 5% commission based on the net premiums ceded. Id. Carnation provided $3 million of capital to the captive—an amount that was well in excess of the total annual premiums paid to the captive— because the third-party insurer had concerns about the captive's capitalization. Id. at 404. The Court held that the reinsurance agreement and the agreement to provide additional capital counteracted each other and voided any insurance risk. Id. at 409. In affirming the Tax Court, the Court of Appeals for the Ninth Circuit held that, in considering whether the risk had shifted, the key was that the thirdparty insurer would not have issued the policies without the capitalization agreement. Carnation Co. v. Commissioner, 640 F.2d at 1013.

Those cases are distinguishable because they all involved undercapitalized captives. As explained previously, the opinion of the Court found that Legacy was adequately capitalized. Further, in each of the three cases above, the parent provided either indemnification or additional capitalization in order to persuade a third-policy insurer to issue insurance policies. Here, Discover Re provided insurance before Legacy's inception and continued providing coverage after Legacy was formed. The parental guaranty was issued to Legacy for the singular purpose of allowing Legacy to treat the DTAs as general business assets. Additionally, the guaranty amounted to only $25 million. This small fraction of the $264 million in premiums for policies written by Legacy during the years in issue does not rise to the level of protection provided by the total indemnities in Malone & Hyde, Inc. and Kidde Indus., Inc.

When we consider the totality of the facts, the parental guaranty appears to have been immaterial. This conclusion is bolstered by the facts that the parental guaranty was unilaterally withdrawn by Rent-A-Center in 2006 and that Rent-A-Center never contributed any funds to Legacy pursuant to that parental guaranty.

III. Consolidated Groups

Judge Lauber's dissent refers to a hodgepodge of facts about how Rent-ACenter operated its consolidated group as evidence that Legacy's status as a separate entity should be disregarded. Examples of the facts cited in that dissent are that Legacy had no employees and that payments between it and other members of the Rent-A-Center consolidated group were handled through journal entries.

In the real world of large corporations, these practices are commonplace. For ease of operations, including running payroll, companies create a staff leasing subsidiary and lease employees companywide. Or they hire outside consultants to handle the operations of a specialty business such as a captive insurer. Legacy, like Humana, hired an outside management company to handle its business operations. Compare op. Ct. p. 6 n.6 (Legacy engaged Aon to provide management services) with Humana Inc. & Subs. v. Commissioner, 88 T.C. at 205 (Humana engaged Marsh & McLennan to provide management services). And it is unrealistic to expect members of a consolidated group to cut checks to each other. Rent-A-Center and Legacy did what is commonplace—they kept track of the flow of funds through journal entries. So long as complete and accurate records are maintained, the commingling of funds is not enough to require the disregarding of a separate business. See, e.g., Kahle v. Commissioner, [Dec. 47,332(M)] T.C. Memo. 1991-203 (finding that the taxpayer "maintained complete and accurate records" notwithstanding the commingling of business and personal funds).

Corporations filing consolidated returns are to be treated as separate entities, unless otherwise mandated. Gottesman & Co. v. Commissioner, 77 T.C. 1149, 1156 (1981). It may be advantageous for a corporation to operate through various subsidiaries for a multitude of reasons. These reasons may include State law implications, creditor demands, or simply convenience, but "so long as that purpose is the equivalent of business activity or is followed by the carrying on of business by the corporation, the corporation remains a separate taxable entity." Moline Props., Inc. v. Commissioner, 319 U.S. 436, 438-439 (1943). Even the consolidated return regulations make clear that an insurance company that is part of a consolidated group is treated separately. See sec. 1.1502-13(e)(2)(ii)(A), Income Tax Regs. ("If a member provides insurance to another member in an intercompany transaction, the transaction is taken into account by both members on a separate entity basis."). Thus, if a corporation gives due regard to the separate corporate structure, we should do the same.

IV. Conclusion

The issue presented in these cases is ultimately a matter of when, not whether, Rent-A-Center is entitled to a deduction relating to workers' compensation, automobile, and general liability losses.//2// Because the IRS has conceded in its rulings that insurance premiums paid between brother-sister corporations may be insurance and the Court determined that, under the facts and circumstances of these cases as found by the Judge who presided at trial, the policies at issue are insurance, Rent-A-Center is entitled to deduct the premiums as reported on its returns. See op. Ct. pp. 21-40.

FOLEY, GUSTAFSON, PARIS, and KERRIGAN, JJ., agree with this concurring opinion.

HALPERN, J., dissenting:

"'The principle of judicial parsimony' (L. Hand, J., in Pressed Steel Car Co. v. Union Pacific Railroad Co., * * * [240 F. 135, 137 (S.D.N.Y. 1917)]), if nothing more, condemns a useless remedy." Sinclair Ref. Co. v. Jenkins Petroleum Process Co., 289 U.S. 689,

694 (1933). While usually invoked by a court to justify a stay in discovery on other issues when one issue is dispositive of a case, 8A Charles Allen Wright, Arthur R. Miller & Richard L. Marcus, Federal Practice and Procedure, sec. 2040, at 198 n.7 (3d ed. 2010), I think the principle should guide us in declining to overrule Humana Inc. & Subs. v. Commissioner, 88 T.C. 197 (1987), aff'd in part, rev'd in part and remanded, 881 F.2d 247 (6th Cir. 1989), to the extent that it holds that a captive insurance arrangement between brother-sister corporations cannot be insurance as a matter of law.

These cases are before the Court Conference for review, see sec. 7460(b), because we perceive that Judge Foley's report is in part overruling Humana, although Judge Foley does not in so many words say so. He says: "We find persuasive the Court of Appeals for the Sixth Circuit's critique of our analysis the brother-sister arrangement in Humana." The Court of Appeals said: "We reverse the tax court on * * * the brother-sister issue." Humana Inc. & Subs v. Commissioner, 881 F.2d at 257. Under our Conference procedures, the Conference may not adopt a report overruling a prior report of the Court absent the affirmative vote of a majority of the Judges entitled to vote on the case. Six of the sixteen Judges entitled to vote on these cases join Judge Foley, for a total of seven clearly affirmative votes. Six Judges voted "no". Three Judges voted "concur in result", and those votes, under our procedures, are counted as affirmative votes. Whether the Court has in fact overruled a portion of Humana undoubtedly will be unclear to many readers of this report. The resulting confusion is unnecessary. Moreover, by putting his report overruling Humana before the Conference, Judge Foley has put before the Conference his subsidiary findings of fact and his ultimate finding that the brother-sister payments were correctly characterized as insurance premiums. That has attracted two side opinions, one characterizing Judge Foley's opinion as "concise" (Judge Buch) and emphasizing evidence in the record that supports his findings and the other characterizing his ultimate findings as "conclusory" (Judge Lauber) and contending "the undisputed facts of the entire record warrant the opposite conclusion * * *, [that] the Rent-A-Center arrangements do not constitute 'insurance' for Federal income tax purposes." Whether I describe Judge Foley's analysis as concise or as conclusory, simply put, there is insufficient depth to it to persuade me to join his findings (i.e., that there is risk shifting, that there is risk distribution, and, in general, that there is a bona fide insurance arrangement). I do agree with Judge Lauber that "[w]hether the facts and circumstances, evaluated in the aggregate, give rise to 'insurance' presents a question of proper characterization. It is thus a mixed question of fact and law." Nevertheless, had Judge Foley steered clear of Humana, I believe that we could have avoided Conference consideration and have left it to the appellate process (if invoked) to determine whether Judge Foley's findings are persuasive.

And I believe that Judge Foley could have steered clear of Humana. As both Judges Buch and Lauber point out, the Commissioner has given up on arguing that captive insurance arrangement between brother-sister corporations cannot be insurance as a matter of law. See, e.g., Rev. Rul. 2001-31, 2001 C.B. 1348. Judge Foley ignores that ruling and its progeny when, pursuant to Rauenhorst v. Commissioner, 119 T.C. 157, 173 (2002), he could have relied on the Commissioner's concessions to steer clear of revisiting Humana. I agree with Judge Foley that Humana is not dispositive of the brother-sister insurance question in these cases, but not because I would overrule Humana on that issue; rather, I see no reason to address Humana in the light of the Commissioner's present administrative position. While I agree with Judge Foley that the facts and circumstances test provides the proper analytical framework, I otherwise dissent from his opinion.

LAUBER, J., agrees with this dissent.

LAUBER, J., dissenting: These cases, like Humana Inc. & Subs. v. Commissioner, 88 T.C. 197 (1987), aff'd in part, rev'd in part and remanded, 881 F.2d 247 (6th Cir. 1989), involve what I will refer to as a "classic" captive insurance company. In these cases, as in Humana, the captive has no outside owners and insures no outside risks. Rather, it is wholly owned by the parent of the affiliated group and it "insures" risks only of the parent and the operating subsidiaries, which stand in a brother-sister relationship to it.

In Humana we held that purported "insurance" premiums paid to a captive by other members of its affiliated group—whether by the parent or by the sister corporations—were not deductible for Federal income tax purposes. An essential requirement of "insurance" is the shifting of risk from insured to insurer. Helvering v. LeGierse, 312 U.S. 531, 539 (1941). We held in Humana that "there was not the necessary shifting of risk" from the operating subsidiaries to the captive, and hence that none of the purported "premiums" constituted amounts paid for "insurance." 88 T.C. at 214. The Court of Appeals for the Sixth Circuit affirmed as to amounts paid to the captive by the parent, but reversed as to amounts paid to the captive by the sister corporations. 881 F.2d at 257.

The opinion of the Court (majority) adopts the reasoning and result of the Sixth Circuit, overrules Humana in part, and holds that amounts charged to the captive's sister corporations constitute deductible "insurance premiums." I dissent both from the majority's decision to overrule Humana and from its holding that amounts charged to the sister corporations constituted payments for "insurance" under the totality of the facts and circumstances.

I. Background

The captive insurance issue has a rich history to which the majority refers only episodically. It has been clear from the outset of our tax law that taxpayers (other than insurance companies) cannot deduct contributions to an insurance reserve. Steere Tank Lines, Inc. v. United States, 577 F.2d 279, 280 (5th Cir. 1978); Spring Canyon Coal Co. v. Commissioner, 43 F.2d 78, 80

(10th Cir. 1930). Thus, if a unitary operating company maintains a reserve for self-insurance, amounts it places in that reserve are not deductible as "insurance premiums."

One strategy by which taxpayers sought to avoid this nondeductibility rule was to place their self-insurance reserve into a captive insurance company. In cases involving "classic" captives—i.e., captives that have no outside owners and insure no outside risks—the courts have uniformly held that this strategy does not work. Employing various legal theories, every court to consider the question has held that amounts paid by a parent to a classic captive do not constitute "insurance premiums."///1///

Insurance and tax advisers soon devised an alternative strategy for avoiding the bar against deduction of contributions to a self-insurance reserve—namely, adoption of or conversion to a holding company structure. In essence, an operating company would drop its self-insurance reserve into a captive; drop its operations into one or more operating subsidiaries; and have the purported "premiums" paid to the captive by the sister companies instead of by the parent. In Humana, we held that this strategy did not work either, reasoning that "we would exalt form over substance and permit a taxpayer to circumvent our holdings [involving parent-captive payments] by simple corporate structural changes." 88 T.C. at 213. In effect, we concluded in Humana that conversion to a holding company structure—without more—should not enable a taxpayer to accomplish indirectly what it cannot accomplish directly, achieving a radically different and more beneficial tax result when there has been absolutely no change in the underlying economic reality.

While the Commissioner had success litigating the parent-captive pattern, he had surprisingly poor luck litigating the brother-sister scenario. The Tenth Circuit, like our Court, agreed that brother-sister payments to a classic captive are not deductible as "insurance premiums."///2/// By contrast, the Sixth Circuit in Humana reversed our holding to this effect.

And after some initial ambivalence, the Court of Federal Claims appears to have concluded that brother-sister "premium" payments are deductible.///3///

The Commissioner had even less success persuading courts to adopt the "single economic family" theory enunciated in Rev. Rul. 77-316, 1977-2 C.B. 53, upon which his litigating position was initially based. That theory was approved by the Tenth Circuit///4/// and found some favor in the Ninth Circuit.///5/// But it was rejected by our Court 6 as well as by the Sixth and Federal Circuits.///7///

Assessing this track record, the Commissioner made a strategic retreat. In 2001 the IRS announced that it "will no longer invoke the economic family theory with respect to captive insurance transactions." Rev. Rul. 2001-31, 2001-1 C.B. 1348, 1348. In 2002 the IRS likewise abandoned its position that there is a per se rule against the deductibility of brother-sister "premiums," concluding that the characterization of such payments as "insurance premiums" should be governed, not by a per se rule, but by the facts and circumstances of the particular case. Rev. Rul. 2002-90, 2002-2 C.B. 985; accord Rev. Rul 2001-31, 2001-1 C.B. at 1348 ("The Service may * * * continue to challenge certain captive insurance transactions based on the facts and circumstances of each case.").

II. Overruling Humana

We decided Humana against a legal backdrop very different from that which we confront today. The Commissioner in Humana urged a per se rule, predicated on his "single economic family" theory, against the deductibility of brother-sister "insurance premiums." The Commissioner has long since abandoned both that per se rule and the theory on which it was based. Given this change in the legal environment, I see no need for the Court to reconsider Humana, which in a practical sense may be water under the bridge.

Respondent's position in the instant cases is consistent with the ruling position the IRS has maintained for the past 12 years—namely, that characterization of intragroup payments as "insurance premiums" should be determined on the basis of the facts and circumstances of the particular case. See Rev. Rul. 2001-31, 2001-1 C.B. at 1348. The majority adopts this approach as the framework for its legal analysis. See op. Ct. p. 22 ("We consider all of the facts and circumstances to determine whether an arrangement qualifies as insurance."). The Court need not overrule Humana to decide (erroneously in my view) that respondent should lose under the facts-and-circumstances approach that respondent is now advancing. In Humana, "we emphasize[d] that our holding * * * [was] based upon the factual pattern presented in * * * [that] case," noting that in other cases "factual patterns may differ." 88 T.C. at 208. That being so, the Court today could rule for petitioners on the basis of what the majority believes to be the controlling "facts and circumstances," distinguishing Humana rather than overruling it. Principles of judicial restraint counsel that courts should decide cases on the narrowest possible ground.

III. The "Facts and Circumstances" Approach

Although I do not believe it necessary or proper to overrule Humana, the continuing vitality of that precedent does not control the outcome. These cases can and should be decided in respondent's favor under the "facts and circumstances" approach that he is currently advancing. In Rev. Rul. 2002-90, 2002-2 C.B. at 985, the IRS concluded that brother-sister payments were correctly characterized as "insurance premiums" where the assumed facts included the following (P = parent and S = captive):

P provides S adequate capital * * *. S charges the 12 [operating] subsidiaries arms-length premiums, which are established according to customary industry rating formulas. * * * There are no parental (or other related party) guarantees of any kind made in favor of S. * * * In all respects, the parties conduct themselves in a manner consistent with the standards applicable to an insurance arrangement between unrelated parties.

The facts of the instant cases, concerning both "risk shifting" and conformity to arm's-length insurance standards, differ substantially from the facts assumed in Rev. Rul. 2002-90, supra. The instant facts also differ substantially from the facts determined in judicial precedents that have characterized intragroup payments as "insurance premiums." Whether the facts and circumstances, evaluated in the aggregate, give rise to "insurance" presents a question of proper characterization. It is thus a mixed question of fact and law.

The majority makes certain findings of basic fact, which I accept for purposes of this dissenting opinion. In many instances, however, the majority makes no findings of basic fact to support its conclusory findings of ultimate fact. In other instances, the majority does not mention facts that tend to undermine its ultimate conclusions. In my view, the undisputed facts of the entire record warrant the opposite conclusion from that reached by the majority and justify a ruling that the Rent-A-Center arrangements do not constitute "insurance" for Federal income tax purposes.

A. Risk Shifting

1. Parental Guaranty

Rent-A-Center, the parent, issued two types of guaranties to Legacy, its captive. First, it guaranteed the multimillion-dollar "deferred tax asset" (DTA) on Legacy's balance sheet, which arose from timing differences between the captive's fiscal year and the parent's calendar year. Normally, a DTA cannot be counted as an "asset" for purposes of the (rather modest) minimum solvency requirements of Bermuda insurance law. The parent's guaranty was essential in order for Legacy to secure an exception from this rule.

Second, the parent subsequently issued an all-purpose guaranty by which it agreed to hold Legacy harmless for its liabilities under the Bermuda Insurance Act up to $25 million. These liabilities necessarily included Legacy's liabilities to pay loss claims of its sister corporations. This all-purpose $25 million guaranty was eliminated at year-end 2006, but it was in existence for the first three tax years at issue.

When approving the brother-sister premiums in Rev. Rul. 2002-90, 2002-2 C.B. at 985, the IRS explicitly excluded from the hypothesized facts the existence of any parental or related-party guaranty executed in favor of the captive. Numerous courts have likewise ruled that the existence of a parental guaranty, indemnification agreement, or similar instrument may negate the existence of "insurance" purportedly supplied by a captive. See, e.g., Malone & Hyde, 62 F.3d 835, 842-843 (6th Cir. 1995) (finding no "insurance" where parent guaranteed captive's liabilities), rev'g T.C. Memo. 1993-585; Humana, 881 F.2d at 254 n.2 (presence of parental indemnification or recapitalization agreement may provide a sufficient basis on which to find no "risk shifting"); Carnation Co., 71 T.C. 400, 402, 409 (1978) (finding no "insurance" where parent agreed to supply captive with additional capital), aff'd, 640 F.2d 1010 (9th Cir. 1981); Kidde Indus., Inc. v. United States, 40 Fed. Cl. 42, 50 (1997) (finding no "insurance" where parent issued indemnification letter).

By guaranteeing Legacy's liabilities, Rent-A-Center agreed to step into Legacy's shoes to pay its affiliates' loss claims. In effect, the parent thus became an "insurer" of its subsidiaries' risks. The majority cites no authority, and I know of none, for the proposition that a holding company can "insure" the risks of its wholly owned subsidiaries. The presence of this parental guaranty argues strongly against the existence of "risk shifting" here.

The majority asserts that Rent-A-Center's parental guaranty "did not vitiate risk shifting" and offers three rationales for this conclusion. See op. Ct. pp. 35-38. None of these rationales is convincing. The majority notes that the parent "did not pay any money pursuant to the parental guaranty" and suggests that the guaranty was really designed only to make sure that Legacy's DTAs were counted in calculating its Bermuda minimum solvency margin. See id. pp. 37-38. The fact that the parent was never required to pay on the guaranty is irrelevant; it is the existence of a parental guaranty that matters in determining whether a captive is truly providing "insurance." And whatever may have prompted the issuance of the guaranty, the fact is that it literally covers all of Legacy's liabilities up to $25 million. The DTAs never got above $9 million during 2003-06. See id. p. 16. Legacy's "liabilities" obviously included Legacy's liability to pay the insurance claims of its sister companies.

The majority contends that the judicial precedents cited above "are distinguishable" because the guaranty issued by Rent-A-Center "did not shift the ultimate risk of loss; did not involve an undercapitalized captive; and was not issued to, or requested by, an unrelated insurer." See op. Ct. pp. 36-37. The majority's first asserted distinction begs the question because it assumes that risk has been shifted to Legacy, which is the proposition that must be proved. The majority's second asserted distinction is a play on words. While Legacy for most of the period at issue was not "undercapitalized" from the standpoint of Bermuda's (modest) minimum solvency rules, it was very poorly capitalized in comparison with real insurance companies. See infra pp. 67-70. Moreover, the Court of Appeals for the Sixth Circuit in Humana indicated that a parental guaranty alone, without regard to the captive's capitalization, can "provide[] a sufficient basis from which to find no risk shifting." 881 F.2d at 245 n.2. The majority's third asserted distinction is a distinction without a difference. While Rent-A-Center's guaranty was not requested by "an unrelated insurer," it was demanded by Legacy's nominal insurance regulator as a condition of meeting Bermuda's minimum solvency requirements.

As the "most important[]" ground for deeming the guaranty irrelevant, the majority asserts that the parental guaranty "did not affect the balance sheets or net worth of the subsidiaries insured by Legacy." See op. Ct. p. 36. The majority here reprises its argument that the "net worth and balance sheet analysis" must be conducted at the level of the operating subsidiaries. See id. pp. 25, 33. Whatever the merit of that argument generally, as applied to the guaranty it clearly proves too much. A parental guaranty of a captive's liabilities will never affect the balance sheet or net worth of the sister company that is allegedly "insured." But the Sixth Circuit, the Federal Circuit, and this Court have all held that the existence of a parental guaranty may negate the existence of "insurance" within an affiliated group.

2. Inadequate Capitalization

When blessing the brother-sister premium payments in Rev. Rul. 2002-90, supra, the Commissioner hypothesized that the parent had supplied the captive with "adequate capital." Numerous judicial opinions have likewise held that risk cannot be "shifted" to a captive unless the captive is sufficiently capitalized to absorb the risk. See, e.g., Beech Aircraft, 797 F.2d at 922 n.1 (no "insurance" where captive was undercapitalized); Carnation Co., 71 T.C. at 409 (same).

The majority bases its conclusion that Legacy was "adequately capitalized" on the fact that Legacy "met Bermuda's minimum statutory requirements" once the parental guaranty of the DTA is counted. See op. Ct. pp. 20-21. The fact that a captive meets the minimum capital requirements of an offshore financial center is not dispositive as to whether the arrangements constitute "insurance" for Federal income tax purposes. Indeed, the Sixth Circuit in Malone & Hyde held that intragroup payments were not "insurance premiums" even though the captive met "the extremely thin minimum capitalization required by Bermuda law." 62 F.3d at 841.

In fact, Legacy's capital structure was extremely questionable during 2003-06. The only way that Legacy was able to meet Bermuda's extremely thin minimum capitalization requirement was by counting as general business assets its DTAs, and those DTAs could be counted only after Rent-A-Center issued its parental guaranty. The DTAs were essentially a bookkeeping entry. Without treating that bookkeeping entry as an "asset,"

Legacy would have been undercapitalized even by Bermuda's lax standards.

The extent of Legacy's undercapitalization is evidenced by its premium-tosurplus ratio, which was wildly out of line with the ratios of real insurance companies. The premium-to-surplus ratio provides a good benchmark of an insurer's ability to absorb risk by drawing on its surplus to pay incurred losses. In this ratio, "premiums written" serves as a proxy for the losses to which the insurer is exposed. Expert testimony in these cases indicated that U.S. property/casualty insurance companies, on average, have something like a 1:1 premium-to-surplus ratio. In other words, their surplus roughly equals the annual premiums for policies they write. By contrast, Legacy's premium-to-surplus ratio—ignoring the parental guaranty of its DTA—was 48:1 in 2003, 19:1 in 2004, 11:1 in 2005, and in excess of 5:1 in 2006 and 2007. In other words, Legacy's surplus covered only 2% of premiums for policies written in 2003 and only 5% of premiums for policies written in 2004, whereas commercial insurance companies have surplus coverage in the range of 100%. Even if we allow the parental guaranty to count toward Legacy's surplus, its premium-to-surplus ratio was never better than 5:1.

Legacy's assets were undiversified and modest. It had a money market fund into which it placed the supposed "premiums" received from its parent. This fund was in no sense "surplus"; it was a mere holding tank for cash used to pay "claims." Apart from this money-market fund, Legacy appears to have had no assets during the tax years at issue except the following: (a) the guaranties issued by its parent; (b) the DTA reflected on its balance sheet; and (c) Rent-A-Center treasury stock that Legacy purchased from its parent. For Federal tax purposes, the parental guaranties cannot count as "assets" in determining whether Legacy was adequately capitalized. They point in the precisely opposite direction.

The DTA and treasury stock have in common several features that make them poor forms of insurance capital. First, neither yields income. The DTA was an accounting entry that by definition cannot yield income, and the Rent-A-Center treasury stock paid no dividends. No true insurance company would invest 100% of its "reserves" in non-income-producing assets. With no potential to earn income, the "reserves" could not grow to afford a cushion against risk.

Moreover, neither the DTA nor the treasury stock was readily convertible into cash. The DTA had no cash value. The treasury stock by its terms could not be sold or alienated, although the parent agreed to buy it back at its issue price. In effect, Legacy relied on the availability of cash from its parent, via repurchase of treasury shares, to pay claims in the event of voluminous losses.///8///

Finally, Legacy's assets were, to a large degree, negatively correlated with its insurance risks. During 2004-06, Legacy purchased $108 million of Rent-ACenter treasury stock, while "insuring" solely Rent-A-Center risks. Thus, if outsized losses occurred, those losses would simultaneously increase Legacy's liabilities and reduce the value of the Rent-A-Center stock that was Legacy's principal asset. No true insurance company invests its reserves in assets that are both undiversified and negatively correlated to the risks that it is insuring.

In sum, when one combines the existence of the parental guaranty, Legacy's extremely weak premium-to-surplus ratio, the speculative nature and poor quality of the assets in Legacy's "insurance reserves," and the fact that Legacy without the parental guaranty would not even have met "the extremely thin minimum capitalization required by Bermuda law," Malone & Hyde, 62 F.3d at 841, the absence of "risk shifting" seems clear. Under the totality of the facts and circumstances, I conclude that there has been no transfer of risk to the captive and hence that the Rent-A-Center arrangements do not constitute "insurance" for Federal income tax purposes.

B. Conformity to Insurance Industry Standards

When blessing the brother-sister premiums in Rev. Rul.

2002-90, supra, the IRS hypothesized that "the parties [had] conduct[ed] themselves in a manner consistent with the standards applicable to an insurance arrangement between unrelated parties." Our Court has similarly ruled that transactions in a captive-insurance context must comport with "commonly accepted notions of insurance." Harper Grp. v. Commissioner, 96 T.C. 45, 58 (1991), aff'd, 979 F.2d 1341 (9th Cir. 1992). Because risk shifting is essential to "insurance," Helvering v. LeGierse, 312 U.S. at 539, the absence of risk shifting alone would dictate that the Rent-A-Center payments are not deductible as "insurance premiums." However, there are a number of respects in which Rent-A-Center, its captive, and the allegedly "insured" subsidiaries did not conduct themselves in a manner consistent with accepted insurance industry norms. These facts provide additional support for concluding that these arrangements did not constitute "insurance."

Several facts discussed above in connection with "risk shifting" show that the Rent-A-Center arrangements do not comport with normal insurance industry practice. These include the facts that Legacy was poorly capitalized; that its premium-to-surplus ratio was way out of line with the ratios of true insurance companies; and that is "reserves" consisted of assets that were non-incomeproducing, illiquid, undiversified, and negatively correlated to the risks it was supposedly "insuring." No true insurance company would act this way.

It appears that Legacy had no actual employees during the tax years at issue. It had no outside directors, and it had no officers apart from people who were also officers of Rent-A-Center, its parent. Legacy's "operations" appear to have been conducted by David Glasgow, an employee of Rent-A-Center, its parent. "Premium payments" and "loss reimbursements" were effected through bookkeeping entries made by accountants at Rent-A-Center's corporate headquarters. Legacy was in practical effect an incorporated pocketbook that served as a repository for what had been, until 2003, Rent-A-Center's self-insurance reserve.

Legacy issued its first two "insurance policies" before receiving a certificate of registration from Bermuda insurance authorities. According to those authorities, Legacy was therefore in violation of Bermuda law and "engaged in the insurance business without a license." (Bermuda evidently agreed to let petitioners fix this problem retroactively.)

For the first three months of its existence, Legacy was in violation of Bermuda's minimum capital rules because the DTA was not cognizable in determining capital adequacy. Only upon the issuance of the parental guaranty in March 2003, and the acceptance of this guaranty by Bermuda authorities, was Legacy able to pass Bermuda's capital adequacy test.

There was no actuarial determination of the premium payable to Legacy by each operating subsidiary based on the specific subsidiary's risk profile. Rather, an outside insurance adviser estimated the future loss exposure of the affiliated group, and Rent-A-Center, the parent, determined an aggregate "premium" using that estimate. The parent paid this "premium" annually to Legacy. The parent's accounting department subsequently charged portions of this "premium" to each subsidiary, in the same manner as self-insurance costs had been charged to those subsidiaries before Legacy was created. In other words, in contrast to the facts assumed in Rev. Rul. 2002-90, supra, there was in these cases no determination of "arms-length premiums * * * established according to customary industry rating formulas." To the contrary, the entire arrangement was orchestrated exactly as it had been orchestrated before 2003, when the Rent-A-Center group maintained a self-insurance reserve for the tranche of risks purportedly "insured" by Legacy.

From Legacy's inception in December 2002 through May 2004, Legacy did not actually pay "loss claims" submitted by the supposed "insureds." Rather, the parent's accounting department netted "loss reimbursements" due to the subsidiaries from

Legacy against "premium payments" due to Legacy from the parent. Beginning in July 2004, the parent withdrew a fixed, preset amount of cash via weekly bank wire from Legacy's money-market account. These weekly withdrawals depleted Legacy's money-market account to near zero just before the next annual "premium" was due. This modus operandi shows that Rent-A-Center regarded Legacy not as an insurer operating at arm's length but as a bank account into which it made deposits and from which it made withdrawals.

These facts, considered in their totality, lead me to disagree with the majority's conclusory assertions that "Legacy entered into bona fide arm's-length contracts with [Rent-A-Center]"; that Legacy "charged actuarially determined premiums"; that Legacy "paid claims from its separately maintained account"; and that Legacy "was adequately capitalized." See op. Ct. pp. 20-21. In my view, the totality of the facts and circumstances could warrant the conclusion that Legacy was a sham. At the very least, the totality of the facts and circumstances makes clear that the arrangements here did not comport with "commonly accepted notions of insurance," Harper Grp., 96 T.C. at 58, and that the Rent-A-Center group of companies did not "conduct themselves in a manner consistent with the standards applicable to an insurance arrangement between unrelated parties," Rev. Rul. 2002-90, 2001-2 C.B. at 985. The departures from accepted insurance industry practice, combined with the absence of risk shifting to the captive from the alleged "insureds," confirms that these arrangements did not constitute "insurance" for Federal income tax purposes.

COLVIN, GALE, KROUPA, and MORRISON, JJ., agree with this dissent.

Footnotes

/1/

Respondent, in his amended answer, asserted an additional $2,603,193 deficiency relating to 2003.

/2/

Unless otherwise indicated, all section references are to the Internal Revenue Code in effect for the years in issue, and all Rule references are to the Tax Court Rules of Practice and Procedure.

/3/

The following insurers provided coverage: U.S. Fidelity & Guarantee Co., Fidelity & Guaranty Insurance Co., Discover Property and Casualty Insurance Co., St. Paul Fire & Marine Co. of Canada, and Fidelity Guaranty Insurance Underwriters Inc.

/4/

SRS was affiliated with the Hartford Insurance Co., a well-established insurer, and did not have a contract with Discover Re.

/5/

RAC contributed $9.9 million of cash and received 120,000 shares of Legacy capital stock with a par value of $1.

/6/

Legacy elected, pursuant to sec. 953(d), to be treated as a domestic corporation for Federal income tax purposes. In addition, Legacy engaged Aon Insurance Managers (Bermuda), Ltd., to monitor Legacy's compliance with Bermudian regulations and to provide management, financial, and administrative services.

/7/

The Bermuda Insurance Act, the Insurance Accounts Regulations, and the Insurance Returns and Solvency Regulations reference "general business", "admitted", and "relevant" assets. See Insurance Act, 1978, sec. 1, Appleby (2008) (Berm.); Insurance Accounts Regulations, 1980, Appleby, Schedule III, Pt. 1, 13 (Berm.); Insurance Returns and Solvency Regulations, 1980, Appleby, Reg. 10(3), 11(4) (Berm.). For purposes of this Opinion, there is no significant difference among these terms.

/8/

From December 31, 2002, through September 12, 2003,

Legacy incurred a $4,861,828 liability relating to claim reimbursements due petitioner. This amount was netted against petitioner's September 12, 2003, premium payment (i.e., petitioner paid a net premium of $37,938,472 rather than the $42,800,300 gross premium).

/9/

Each premium was generally paid in September of the year following the year in which the policy became effective. Use of the recurring item exception allowed petitioner to claim a premium deduction relating to the year in which the policy became effective, rather than the following year when the premium was actually paid. See sec. 461(h)(3)(A)(iii). On August 28, 2007, petitioner filed Form 3115, Application for Change in Accounting Method, requesting permission to revoke its use of the recurring item exception.

/10/

See infra pp. 15-16.

/11/

See infra pp. 15-16.

/12/

See supra pp. 9-10.

/13/

See supra p. 11.

/14/

Premium-to-surplus ratio is one measure of an insurer's economic performance. On Legacy's reports and statements, Arthur Morris referred to Legacy's premium-to-surplus ratio as the "premium to statutory capital & surplus ratio". For purposes of this Opinion, there is no significant difference between these terms.

/15/

Net underwriting income equals gross premiums earned minus underwriting expenses.

/16/

A class 4 insurance company may carry on insurance business, including excess liability business or property catastrophe reinsurance business. See Insurance Act, 1978, sec. 4E.

/17/

Our Opinion emphasized that the "operative" facts related to the "interdependence of all of the agreements" as confirmed by the "execution dates". See Clougherty Packing Co. v. Commissioner, 84 T.C. 948, 957 (1985), aff'd, 811 F.2d 1297 (9th Cir. 1987).

/18/

We need not defer to the Court of Appeals for the Sixth Circuit's holding because this matter is appealable to the Court of Appeals for the Fifth Circuit, which has not addressed this issue. See Golsen v. Commissioner, 54 T.C. 742, 757 (1970), aff'd, 445 F.2d 985 (10th Cir. 1971).

/19/

Legacy used a portion of the parental guaranty as a general business asset. See supra pp. 15-16. Legacy's DTAs always exceeded the amount of the parental guaranty treated as a general business asset. See supra pp. 15-16.

//1//

Legacy's premiums attributable to workers' compensation liability were $28,586,597 in 2003; $35,392,000 in 2004; $36,463,579 in 2005; $39,086,374 in 2006; and $45,425,032 in 2007.

//2//

If the Court had determined that the policies were not insurance, then Rent-A-Center would nevertheless have been entitled to deduct the losses as they were paid or incurred. See sec. 162. By forming Legacy and giving due regard to its separate structure, Rent-A-Center achieved some acceleration of deductions relating to losses that would otherwise be deductible, along with other nontax benefits. See op. Ct. pp. 17-18.

///1///

See Beech Aircraft Corp. v. United States, 797 F.2d 920 (10th Cir. 1986); Stearns-Roger Corp. v. United States, 774 F.2d 414,

415-416 (10th Cir. 1985); Humana Inc. & Subs. v. Commissioner, 88 T.C. 197, 207 (1987), aff'd in part, rev'd in part and remanded, 881 F.2d 247 (6th Cir. 1989); Clougherty Packing Co. v. Commissioner, 84 T.C. 948 (1985), aff'd, 811 F.2d 1297, 1307 (9th Cir. 1987); Carnation Co. v. Commissioner, 71 T.C. 400 (1978), aff'd, 640 F.2d 1010, 1013 (9th Cir. 1981). On the other hand, the courts have held that parent-captive payments may constitute "insurance premiums" where the captive has a sufficient percentage of outside owners or insures a sufficient percentage of outside risks. See, e.g., Sears, Roebuck & Co. v. Commissioner, 96 T.C. 61 (1991) (approximately 99.75% of insured risks were outside risks), supplemented by 96 T.C. 671 (1991), aff'd in part and rev'd in part, 972 F.2d 858 (7th Cir. 1992); Harper Grp. v. Commissioner, 96 T.C. 45 (1991) (approximately 30% of insured risks were outside risks), aff'd, 979 F.2d 1341 (9th Cir. 1992); AMERCO v. Commissioner, 96 T.C. 18 (1991) (between 52% and 74% of insured risks were outside risks), aff'd, 979 F.2d 162 (9th Cir. 1992).

///2///

See Beech Aircraft Corp., 797 F.2d at 922; Stearns-Roger Corp., 774 F.2d at 415-416.

///3///

Compare Mobil Oil Corp. v. United States, 8 Cl. Ct. 555, 566 (1985) ("[B]y deducting the premiums on its tax returns, [the affiliated group] achieved indirectly that which it could not do directly. It is well settled that tax consequences must turn upon the economic substance of a transaction[.]"), with Kidde Indus., Inc. v. United States, 40 Fed. Cl. 42 (1997) (brother-sister payments deductible for years for which parent did not provide indemnity agreement). See generally Ocean Drilling & Exploration Co. v. United States, 988 F.2d 1135, 1153 (Fed. Cir. 1993) (1991) (brother-sister payments deductible where captive insured significant outside risks).

///4///

See Beech Aircraft Corp., 797 F.2d 920; Stearns-Roger Corp.,

774 F.2d at 415-416. See generally Humana, 881 F.2d at 251 ("Stearns-Roger, Mobil Oil, and Beech Aircraft * * * each explicitly or implicitly adopted the economic family concept.").

///5///

See Clougherty Packing, 811 F.2d at 1304 ("[W]e seriously doubt that the use of an economic family concept in defining insurance runs afoul of the Supreme Court's holding in Moline Properties."); id. at 1305 (finding "considerable merit in the Commissioner's [economic family] argument" but finding it unnecessary to rely on that theory); Carnation Co., 640 F.2d at 1013.

///6///

See Humana, 88 T.C. at 214 (rejecting the Commissioner's "economic family" concept); Clougherty Packing, 84 T.C. at 956 (same); Carnation Co., 71 T.C. at 413 (same).

///7///

See Malone & Hyde, Inc. v. Commissioner, 62 F.3d 835 (6th Cir. 1995) (rejecting "economic family" theory but ruling against deductibility of payments to captive based on facts and circumstances), rev'g T.C. Memo. 1993-585; Ocean Drilling & Exploration Co., 988 F.2d at 1150-1151; Humana, 881 F.2d at 251.

///8///

Because Legacy "insured" losses only below a defined threshold, there was a cap on the size of any individual loss that it might have to pay. See op. Ct. p. 8. However, the number of individual loss events within that tranche could exceed expectations.

SECURITAS HOLDINGS, INC. V. COMMISSIONER

Securitas Holdings, Inc. v. Commissioner, T.C. Memo. 2014-225
(2014)

MEMORANDUM FINDINGS OF FACT AND OPINION

BUCH, Judge: Respondent issued a notice of deficiency determining deficiencies of $13,801,906 for 2003 and $16,496,539 for 2004. The deficiencies largely stem from respondent's partial disallowance of deductions for interest expenses and deductions for insurance expenses related to a captive insurance arrangement. The sole issue remaining for us to decide is whether petitioner is entitled to deduct premiums paid through the captive insurance arrangement established by its parent corporation. Respondent does not dispute that the arrangement involved insurable risks, and we hold that the captive arrangement shifted risks, distributed risks, and constituted insurance in the commonly accepted sense. Therefore, the arrangement is insurance for Federal tax purposes, and petitioner is entitled to the deduction under section 162/1/ for insurance expenses.

FINDINGS OF FACT

I. Parent-Subsidiary Structure

Securitas AB is a public Swedish company. Beginning in the late 1980s and continuing through the 1990s Securitas AB expanded its business outside of Sweden by acquiring other companies throughout Europe. Securitas AB first entered the U.S. security services market in 1999 when it established

Securitas Holdings, Inc. (SHI). SHI is the parent company of an affiliated group of U.S. corporations (SHI Group or petitioner). During 2003 and 2004, the years in issue, SHI had no employees, owned no vehicles, and did not provide any security services itself. The SHI Group used the accrual method of accounting throughout the years in issue.

In 1999 SHI acquired Pinkerton's, Inc. (Pinkerton's), a Delaware corporation, and its subsidiaries. Before its acquisition Pinkerton's was a publicly traded company that provided various security services and had approximately 48,000 employees in over 250 offices worldwide. In 2000 and 2001 SHI acquired several additional security companies, including Burns International Services Corp. (Burns), also a Delaware corporation, and its subsidiaries. Like Pinkerton's, Burns was a publicly traded company that provided various security services and had approximately 75,000 employees in 300 offices in North America, South America, and Europe.

According to Securitas AB's 2003 annual report, Securitas AB and its subsidiaries (Securitas AB Group) accounted for 8% of the total world market for security services. During 2003 and 2004 the Securitas AB Group employed over 200,000 people in 20 countries, mostly in North America and Europe.

II. Services

In 2003 and 2004 the Securitas AB Group and the SHI Group provided guarding services, alarm systems services, and cash handling services. Guarding services include providing uniformed security officers to maintain a secure environment for clients as well as consulting and investigation services. In 2003 and 2004 the SHI subsidiaries providing guarding services had approximately 101,080 and 91,170 employees, respectively. These subsidiaries also operated 2,250 and 2,495 vehicles, respectively. In mid-2003 many of the SHI subsidiaries providing guarding services were consolidated into a newly formed corporation and subsidiary of SHI, Securitas Security Services USA, Inc. (SSUSA).

Alarm systems services include the installation of alarm systems and alarm-to-response solutions. Pinkerton's Systems Integration, Inc., an SHI subsidiary, provided alarm systems services. This company was later renamed Securitas Security Systems USA, Inc., and employed approximately 270 people during 2003 and 2004.

Cash handling services include cash transport, cash processing, and ATM services. Loomis, Fargo & Co. (Loomis), an SHI subsidiary, provided cash handling services and had approximately 7,122 employees in 2003 and 7,481 employees in 2004.

III. Protectors

Protectors Insurance Co. of Vermont (Protectors) was incorporated in Vermont in 1986 as a licensed captive insurance company. As a result of various acquisitions, the SHI Group acquired Protectors in early 2000, and Protectors became a direct, wholly owned subsidiary of SHI in January 2003. Between November 1, 1996, and December 30, 2002, Protectors did not write new or renewal coverage, and its operations consisted solely of the runoff of previously written coverage.

Protectors had no employees during 2003 and 2004. Protectors maintained separate books and records, maintained a separate bank account for its operations, prepared financial statements, and held annual meetings of its board of directors. Throughout 2003 and 2004 none of the U.S. operating subsidiaries of SHI or the non-U.S. operating subsidiaries of Securitas AB owned any interest in Protectors, and it was managed by a company that was unrelated by ownership to SHI.

During 2003 and 2004 Protectors was subject to regulation as a captive insurance company in the State of Vermont and paid premium taxes to the State of Vermont. In June 2003 Protectors requested permission from the Vermont Department of Banking, Insurance, Securities & Health Care Administration (Vermont regulators) to lend all but $1 million of its capital to SHI. The Vermont regulators approved this request. Further, in early 2004 the Vermont regulators allowed the SHI Group to avoid contributing additional capital to Protectors as a result of Protectors' issuing an insurance policy for 2004 to Loomis. The Vermont regulators also waived the premium taxes with respect to the policy.

IV. Securitas Group Reinsurance Limited

In late 2002 Securitas AB informed the Irish Department of Enterprise, Trade, and Employment that it intended to establish a new captive reinsurance company in Ireland called Securitas Group Reinsurance Ltd. (SGRL) and that it intended SGRL to be fully operational before the end of 2002. The Irish authorities responded that they had no objection, and SGRL was incorporated under the laws of Ireland.

Beginning in December 2002 and continuing through 2004, SGRL operated as a wholly owned subsidiary of Securitas AB, and it was subject to regulation as a reinsurance company in Ireland. SGRL's total shareholders' funds were $51,456,000 at the end of 2003 and $77,497,000 at the end of 2004. During 2003 and 2004 none of the U.S. operating subsidiaries of SHI and none of the non-U.S. operating subsidiaries of Securitas AB owned any interest in SGRL. SGRL maintained separate books and records, maintained a separate bank account for its operations, prepared financial statements, and held meetings of its board of directors.

V. Implementation of the Captive Insurance Program

After wages, the cost of risk is the second largest cost for the Securitas AB Group. The operating subsidiaries of the SHI Group had exposure to various insurable risks, including: workers' compensation, automobile, employment practices, general, and fidelity liabilities. In 2002, 2003, and 2004 the SHI Group obtained insurance coverage from third-party insurers. These third-party policies had deductibles or self-insured retentions which were the responsibility of the SHI Group subsidiaries.

Several events converged in the early 2000s causing the

insurance market to harden and causing insurance rates to increase. In response to the increase, the Securitas AB Group tried to control risks and to obtain more favorable insurance rates. As part of this effort, the Securitas AB Group decided to implement a captive insurance program to insure the risks within the deductible layers of the existing third-party policies. A captive insurance program was attractive to the Securitas AB Group for a variety of reasons, including that the cost of adopting the program was less than the cost of reducing deductibles and purchasing insurance from third parties. The captive program also allowed Securitas AB to centralize risks. Further, it allowed the subsidiaries to know their cost of risk in advance. In the years since its implementation, the captive insurance program has provided more cost-effective insurance coverage than would have otherwise been available.

It was part of the implementation that Securitas AB formed SGRL in 2002. Because SGRL was a reinsurance company and could not issue policies directly, Protectors provided insurance for U.S. subsidiaries, and XL Insurance Co. Ltd. (XL Insurance), a United Kingdom company, provided insurance to the non-U.S. subsidiaries.

VI. Insurance Coverages for U.S. Subsidiaries

In December 2002 Protectors issued a loss portfolio transfer policy to SHI to cover the unresolved or unreported losses for the insurable risks of most of the SHI Group's operating subsidiaries up to the deductibles or self-insured retentions of the third-party policies. Protectors also issued a similar policy to Loomis in December 2003.

For 2003 Protectors issued prospective insurance policies to cover the insurable risks of most of the SHI Group's operating subsidiaries up to the deductible or self-insured retentions of the third-party policies. For 2004 Protectors issued similar policies except that the policies each had a $15,000 deductible, making the subsidiaries responsible for losses up to that amount. The insurance policies identified the insured, contained an effective period, specified the covered risks, identified a premium amount, and were signed by an authorized representative./2/

A. Parental Guaranty

In 2000 the SHI Group acquired Centaur Insurance Co. (Centaur) as part of the larger acquisition of Burns. Centaur is an Illinois insurance company that had been in rehabilitation proceedings since 1987. Centaur has claimed to be tax exempt under section 501(c)(15) since 1990 because it has received no premium income.

While preparing to implement the captive insurance program, the SHI Group learned that reactivation of Protectors could adversely affect Centaur's tax-exempt status. The premium test under section 501(c)(15) limits the amount of premiums that can make up gross receipts for an insurance company that seeks tax-exempt status. The premium test is applied on a controlled group basis, and Protectors and Centaur were part of the same controlled group during 2002, 2003, and 2004.

In late 2002 the SHI Group considered selling Centaur's stock to a non-U.S. affiliated company in order to remove Centaur from the U.S. controlled group. In early December 2002 the SHI Group chose to have SHI execute a parental guaranty guaranteeing the performance of Protectors, as opposed to selling Centaur's stock. Before the end of 2002 SHI executed a parental guaranty guaranteeing the performance of Protectors with respect to the 2002 loss portfolio transfer policy written by Protectors to the SHI Group's subsidiaries. SHI also executed an amended and restated guaranty guaranteeing the performance of Protectors with respect to any and all agreements that were effective on or after November 25, 2002, that were issued by Protectors regarding risks retained by the SHI Group's operating subsidiaries. The amended and restated guaranty replaced the first guaranty. The amended and restated guaranty was in effect during 2003 and 2004. As a result of the amended and restated guaranty, it was the SHI Group's position that Protectors did not qualify as an insurance company for Federal income tax purposes during 2002, 2003, and 2004. The intended effect of this position was to remove Protectors from the premium test under section 501(c)(15) and, by extension, to preserve Centaur's tax-exempt status. There is no evidence in the record to suggest that any amount was ever paid out under the guaranty.

In 2003 the SHI Group continued to pursue the possibility of selling Centaur's stock. However, the SHI Group did not sell the stock during 2003 or 2004.

B. Reinsurance

All of the insurable risks covered under the two loss protection policies and the prospective insurance policies were reinsured with SGRL. In 2003 SGRL received premiums from over 25 separate entities. In 2004 SGRL received premiums from over 45 separate entities. Like the policies that Protectors issued, the reinsurance policies identified the insured, contained an effective period, specified the covered risks, identified a premium amount, and were signed by an authorized representative./3/

No guaranty was ever provided to SGRL by any party for any of the risks reinsured under the agreement with Protectors. Additionally, neither the insurance policies that Protectors issued nor the policies that SGRL issued contained a cut-through provision that would allow the insured the right to seek claims payment directly from the reinsurer on the primary insurer's failure to meet its obligations fully or on time.

C. Premiums to SHI Group Subsidiaries

During the years in issue outside actuaries reviewed the premiums and determined they were reasonable./4/ From January to July 1, 2003, Pinkerton's paid the 2003 premiums on behalf of the other SHI Group subsidiaries. From July 1, 2003, to the end of 2003, after the merger of many of the subsidiaries into SSUSA, SSUSA paid the premiums on behalf of the other SHI Group subsidiaries. Pinkerton's, and later SSUSA, recorded general ledger accounts payable to SGRL for the amounts of the premiums. These accounts payable were booked pro rata on a monthly basis, except for the one for the first quarter of 2003, which was booked at the end of March. Pinkerton's and SSUSA paid claims that were covered under the Protectors policies and recorded general ledger accounts receivable from SGRL for those amounts. Pinkerton's and SSUSA also paid administrative fees relating to the Protectors policies and recorded general ledger accounts receivable from SGRL for those amounts. These amounts were reversed that same year when it was determined that administrative fees had not been taken into account when setting the premiums. In July and August 2003 the excess of the accounts payable over the accounts receivable was paid by wire transfer from Pinkerton's/SSUSA to Protectors. Protectors then paid that amount to SGRL, minus a $225,000 ceding commission that Protectors retained. Of the 2003 premiums, $56,242,080 was paid and deducted for Federal income tax purposes in 2003 and $5,144,918 was paid and deducted for Federal income tax purposes in 2004.

The $16 million premium for the 2003 Protectors policy insuring Loomis was paid to Protectors in 2003 by Loomis. Protectors then paid that amount to SGRL, minus a $50,000 ceding commission.

During 2003 SSUSA allocated the premiums among the subsidiaries as follows:

Entity	Petitioner's premium allocation per entity	Each entity's percentage of the total premium payable to Protectors
Pinkerton's	$8,658,886	11.189
Pinkerton Management	2,204	.003
Guardian Uniforms	254,446	.329
Renaissance Center	131,956	.171
Pinkerton Protection Svcs	242,031	.313
Pinkerton Government Svcs	2,617,868	3.382
Burns	19,489,689	25.185
Burns International Security Services of Florida	1,279,162	1.653
Hall Security	65,706	.085
SSUSA	28,645,052	37.015
Loomis	16,000,000	20.675
Total	77,387,000	

SSUSA paid the 2004 premiums in a similar manner. SSUSA paid the premiums on behalf of the other subsidiaries and recorded general ledger accounts payable to SGRL. The accounts payable were booked pro rata on a monthly basis. Throughout the year SSUSA paid claims and administrative fees that were covered by the policies and recorded general ledger accounts receivable for those amounts. Again, the accounts receivable were booked pro rata on a monthly basis. In July, October, and December 2004 the excess of the accounts payable over the accounts receivable was paid by wire transfer from SSUSA to Protectors. Protectors then paid the amount to SGRL, minus a $225,000 ceding commission that Protectors retained. Of the 2004 premiums, $51,592,517 was paid and deducted for Federal income tax purposes in 2004 and $1,132,573 was paid and deducted for Federal income tax purposes in 2005.

The $4,258,100 premium for the 2004 Protectors policy insuring Loomis was paid to Protectors in 2004 by Loomis. Protectors then paid this amount over to SGRL, minus a $25,000 ceding commission.

During 2004 the premiums were allocated among the subsidiaries as follows:

Entity	Petitioner's premium allocation per entity	Each entity's percentage of the total premium payable to Protectors
SSUSA	$50,342,514	88.346
Renaissance Center	85,112	.149
Pinkerton Government Svcs	2,297,464	4.032
Loomis	4,258,100	7.472
Total	$56,983,190	

VII. Insurance Coverages for Non-U.S. Subsidiaries

During 2003 and 2004 XL Insurance Co. Ltd. (XL Insurance) issued insurance policies to cover general liability insurance risks for the non-U.S. subsidiaries of Securitas AB. XL Insurance was unrelated by ownership to the entities in the Securitas AB Group. Like the Protectors policies, the XL Insurance policies provided only the first layer of coverage. In 2003 and 2004 XL

Insurance reinsured a portion of its risk under the insurance policies with SGRL. The premiums for the 2003 and 2004 reinsurance agreements totaled $9,103,733, which XL Insurance paid to SGRL. During these years no subsidiary was allocated more than 50% of the premiums.

VIII. Notice of Deficiency

On July 1, 2010, the IRS issued a notice of deficiency to the SHI Group for its 2003 and 2004 taxable years. In the notice the IRS disallowed portions of the SHI Group's deductions for interest expenses and insurance premiums and made other computational adjustments. The adjustments resulted in tax increases of $13,801,906 for 2003 and $16,496,539 for 2004.

Because the parties stipulated the interest expense deductions, the only issue remaining is whether the SHI Group is entitled to deduct insurance premiums paid. Of the $72,242,080 deduction amount claimed on its 2003 return, the IRS disallowed deductions of $47,729,741 and allowed deductions of $24,512,339. The amount allowed consists of $8,512,339 in actual paid claims and expenses and the $16 million premium paid for the Loomis loss protection policy./5/ Of the $61,394,596 deduction amount claimed on its 2004 return, the IRS disallowed deductions of $41,270,724 and allowed deductions of $20,123,872. The amount allowed consists of $15,466,711 in actual paid claims and expenses and $4,657,161 in premiums that Loomis paid.

The SHI Group, while maintaining its principal place of business in California, timely petitioned.

OPINION

I. Insurance Premium Deduction

Section 162(a) permits a deduction for "all the ordinary and necessary expenses paid or incurred during the taxable year in carrying on any trade or business". Insurance premiums may be deductible business expenses./6/ Although insurance premiums may be deductible, amounts placed in reserve as self- insurance are not./7/ Such amounts can be deducted only at the time that the loss for which the reserve was established is actually incurred./8/

Neither the Code nor the regulations define "insurance". However, the Supreme Court has stated that "[h]istorically and commonly insurance involves risk-shifting and risk-distributing."/9/ Over time, courts have looked primarily to four criteria in deciding whether an arrangement constitutes insurance for Federal income tax purposes: (1) the arrangement must involve insurable risks; (2) the arrangement must shift the risk of loss to the insurer; (3) the insurer must distribute the risks among its policyholders; and (4) the arrangement must be insurance in the commonly accepted sense./10/ Although these criteria are not independent or exclusive, they establish a framework for determining whether insurance exists under the Federal tax law./11/

Respondent does not dispute that the arrangement here involved insurable risks.

A. Risk Shifting

In order for an arrangement to be considered insurance, it must shift risk of loss from the insured to the insurer./12/ "From the insured's perspective, insurance is protection from financial loss provided by the insurer upon payment of a premium, i.e., it is a risk-transfer device."/13/ Risk shifting transfers the threat of an economic loss from the insured to the insurer because "[i]f the insured has shifted its risk to the insurer, then a loss by or a claim against the insured does not affect it because the loss is offset by the proceeds of an insurance payment."/14/ When evaluating whether risk shifting occurred, we consider separate but related insurance contracts, such as insurance and reinsurance, together./15/

In brother-sister corporation arrangements, such as the arrangement before us, we look to what has become known as the balance sheet and net worth analysis to determine whether risk has been shifted./16/ Under the balance sheet and net worth analysis, we examine the economic consequences of the captive insurance arrangement to determine whether the insured party has shifted the risk./17/ In doing so, we look only at the insured's assets to determine whether the insured "divested itself of the adverse economic consequences" of a claim covered by the insurance policy./18/ Additionally, we generally afford related corporate entities separate tax status and treatment./19/

Respondent argues that the guaranty from SHI to Protectors prevents risk from shifting from the SHI Group subsidiaries to SGRL because SHI bore the ultimate risk of loss. In making this argument, respondent relies on three cases, Malone & Hyde, Inc. v. Commissioner, 62 F.3d 835 (6th Cir. 1995), rev'g, T.C. Memo. 1993-585, Kidde Indus., Inc. v. United States, 40 Fed. Cl. 42 (1997), and Hospital Corp. of Am. v. Commissioner, T.C. Memo. 1997-482. We recently addressed Malone & Hyde and Kidde in the opinion of the Court and the concurring opinion in Rent-A-Center, Inc. v. Commissioner, 142 T.C. ___, ___ (slip op. at 36-37) (Jan. 14, 2014). In that case, we distinguished the facts of Malone & Hyde and Kidde on the basis that they all involved undercapitalized captives where the parent corporation provided indemnification or additional capitalization in order to persuade a third-policy insurer to issue policies./20/ We did not address Hospital Corp.

A close examination of the facts of Hospital Corp. reveals that it is wholly consistent with our conclusion both here and in Rent-A-Center. In Hospital Corp., various subsidiaries obtained most of their primary insurance through a captive insurance company. Workers' compensation liabilities were handled differently. The subsidiaries of Hospital Corporation obtained primary insurance for those liabilities with a third party, and the captive insurance company provided reinsurance. When the third-party insurer became insolvent, the parent corporation agreed to indemnify it. Later, the parent agreed to indemnify another third-party insurer as a condition of the agreement that it would take over the risks of the insolvent insurer (but only as to the liabilities of the insolvent insurer). We held that there was no risk shifting as to the workers' compensation liability. This falls squarely within our analysis in Rent-A-Center, where we distinguished a line of cases, stating that the parental guaranty at issue in Rent-A-Center did not shift the ultimate risk of loss; did not involve an undercapitalized captive; and was not issued to, or requested by, an unrelated insurer./21/ The indemnity agreement at issue in Hospital Corp. was issued to an unrelated insurer because of the insolvency of the primary insurer. That is very different from the facts before us here, where indemnity was not provided to a third-party insurer and where the captive insurer is sufficiently capitalized.

Respondent argues that the presence of the parental guaranty mitigates risk shifting because of the theoretical possibility that SHI may have to pay in accordance with the guaranty. However, this is the case whenever a guaranty from the parent is involved, and we have previously held that the existence of a parental guaranty by itself is not enough to justify disregarding the captive insurance arrangement./22/ The guaranty was provided only to preserve the tax-exempt status of Centaur and here, as in Rent-A-Center, no amount was paid out under the guaranty. Accordingly, we must decide whether something else was present to vitiate risk shifting.

Although respondent argues that Protectors was undercapitalized, we do not agree. After consulting with the Vermont regulators, Protectors decided to maintain a premium-to-surplus ratio of 7.5. to 1.0. At times, the SHI Group would have to provide additional capital or seek permission to avoid going above the 7.5 to 1.0 ratio. SHI Group's expert, Ann Conway, stated that the industry standard net premium-to-surplus ratio for long-tail casualty exposures,/23/ which constitute most of the exposures here, is 4.0 to 1.0. Respondent's argument is that Protectors was undercapitalized because it did not maintain a premium-to-surplus ratio of 4.0 to 1.0 or lower. However, respondent fails to take into account the fact that Protectors' risks were reinsured. Because Protectors reinsured

100% of its risks through SGRL, Protectors' net premium-to-surplus ratio was 0 to 1, which falls below the industry standard. Ms. Conway testified that SGRL was adequately capitalized, and respondent did not refute this assertion. Considering the insurance and reinsurance contracts together, we find that Protectors was adequately capitalized for its role as a primary insurer that reinsured all of its risks with SGRL.

Respondent further argues that the SHI Group financial arrangement resulted in SHI maintaining the risk of loss. Respondent maintains that Pinkerton's and SSUSA paid the claims of the operating subsidiaries and then sought reimbursement directly from SGRL, thus effectively eliminating Protectors from the captive arrangement. Because, in respondent's view, Protectors did not pay the claims as required, SGRL's legal obligation to reimburse Protectors did not arise, and Protectors' failure to pay the claims meant that SHI remained responsible. Again, we previously addressed a similar point and stated that "it is unrealistic to expect members of a consolidated group to cut checks to each other" and using journal entries to keep track of the flow of funds is "commonplace"./24/ Pinkerton's and SSUSA kept records showing the amounts payable to and receivable from SGRL, and the parties have stipulated that the amount due to SGRL was first transferred to Protectors and then to SGRL. Respondent has not alleged, and we do not find, that the journal entries were inaccurate or incomplete. Accordingly, we do not agree that the SHI Group's manner of paying the claims and premiums prevented the risk from shifting.

On the basis of the foregoing and evaluating the captive arrangement as a whole, we find that the arrangement adequately shifted risk. The balance sheet and net worth analysis indicates that the captive insurance arrangement has shifted any economic consequence of a risk from the SHI Group subsidiaries to Protectors and then to SGRL.

B. Risk Distribution

We evaluate risk distribution through the actions of the insurer. The insurer achieves risk distribution when it pools a large enough collection of unrelated risks, those that are not generally affected by the same circumstance or event. 25 "Distributing risk allows the insurer to reduce the possibility that a single costly claim will exceed the amount taken in as a premium * * * [because] [b]y assuming numerous relatively small, independent risks that occur randomly over time, the insurer smoothes out losses to match more closely its receipt of premiums."/26/ Risk distribution incorporates the law of large numbers which has been described as follows: "'As the size of the pool increases, the chance that the loss per policy during any given period will deviate from the expected loss by a given amount (or proportion) declines.'"/27/

Protectors, and ultimately SGRL, insured five types of risks: workers' compensation, automobile, employment practice, general, and fidelity liabilities. During the years in issue the Securitas AB Group employed over 200,000 people in 20 countries, and the SHI Group, alone, employed approximately 100,000 people each year and operated over 2,250 vehicles. In 2003 SGRL received premiums from over 25 separate entities. In 2004 SGRL received premiums from over 45 separate entities. However, respondent argues that there is not adequate risk distribution because most of the premiums paid to SGRL were attributable to Protectors, and after mid-2003 most of those premiums were attributable to SSUSA.

Risk distribution is viewed from the insurer's perspective. As a result of the large number of employees, offices, vehicles, and services provided by the U.S. and non-U.S. operating subsidiaries, SGRL was exposed to a large pool of statistically independent risk exposures. This does not change merely because multiple companies merged into one. The risks associated with those companies did not vanish once they all fell under the same umbrella. As the SHI Group's expert, Dr. Neil Doherty, explained in his expert report: "It is the pooling of exposures that brings about the risk distribution—who owns the exposures is not crucial." We agree and find that by insuring the various risks of U.S. and non-U.S. subsidiaries, the captive arrangement achieved risk distribution.

C. Insurance in the Commonly Accepted Sense

The final factor that we look to is whether the captive arrangement constitutes insurance in the commonly accepted sense. Previously, this Court has looked to factors such as whether: (1) the insurer was organized, operated, and regulated as an insurance company; (2) the insurer was adequately capitalized; (3) the insurance policies were valid and binding; (4) the premiums were reasonable; and (5) the premiums were paid and the losses were satisfied./28/

Protectors and SGRL were both organized, operated, and regulated as insurance companies. Protectors was subject to regulation under the laws of Vermont, kept its own books and records, maintained separate bank accounts, prepared financial statements, and held meetings of its board of directors. Similarly, SGRL was regulated under the laws of Ireland and also kept its own books and records, maintained separate bank accounts, prepared financial statements, and held meetings of its board of directors.

As stated above, Protectors was adequately capitalized. Further, Ms. Conway testified that SGRL was adequately capitalized on the basis of her finding that SGRL's financial ratio met or exceeded industry standards. Respondent did not challenge Ms. Conway's assertion, and we agree with it as well.

The insurance and reinsurance policies issued by Protectors and SGRL were valid and binding. Each insurance policy identified the insured, contained an effective period for the policy, specified what was covered by the policy, stated the premium amount, and was signed by an authorized representative of the company.

The premiums set by Protectors and SGRL were reasonable. They were reviewed by outside actuaries and determined to be within the range of reasonable premiums. Additionally, respondent does not challenge the reasonableness of the premium amounts.

Finally, the premiums were paid, and the losses were satisfied. The SHI Group subsidiaries kept ledger entries corresponding to the accounts payable and receivable. These amounts were booked pro rata on a monthly basis. During each year, the subsidiaries would pay Protectors the amounts due, which Protectors would then pay to SGRL after subtracting its ceding commission. Considering all the facts and circumstances, we find that the captive arrangement constituted insurance in the commonly accepted sense.

II. Conclusion

We find that the captive arrangement is insurance for Federal tax purposes. The captive arrangement shifted risk from the SHI Group to Protectors and ultimately to SGRL. Further, the captive arrangement distributed risk by insuring a large pool of differing risks. Lastly, the captive arrangement constitutes insurance in the commonly accepted sense. Accordingly, the premiums paid by the SHI Group are deductible under section 162 as insurance expenses.

To reflect the foregoing and the concessions of the parties,

Decision will be entered for petitioner.

Footnotes

/1/

Unless otherwise indicated, all section references are to the Internal Revenue Code (Code) in effect for the years in issue, and all Rule references are to the Tax Court Rules of Practice and Procedure. All monetary amounts are rounded to the nearest dollar.

/2/

Some of the policies were signed after the policy's effective date. There is no explanation for this in the record, and neither party argues that this renders the policies ineffective.

/3/

Again, some of the policies were signed after the policy's effective date. There is no explanation for this in the record, and neither party argues that this renders the policies ineffective.

/4/

Respondent does not challenge the reasonableness of the premiums.

/5/

Although the insurance transaction involving Loomis appears strikingly similar to the transaction involving the rest of the SHI Group subsidiaries, respondent could provide no explanation at trial regarding why the premiums paid by Loomis were allowed and the other premiums were not.

/6/

Sec. 1.162-1(a), Income Tax Regs.

/7/

Steere Tank Lines, Inc. v. United States, 577 F.2d 279, 280 (5th Cir. 1978); Spring Canyon Coal Co. v. Commissioner, 43 F.2d 78, 80 (10th Cir. 1930), aff'g, 13 B.T.A. 189 (1928).

/8/

United States v. General Dynamics Corp., 481 U.S. 239, 243-245 (1987).

/9/

Helvering v. Le Gierse, 312 U.S. 531, 539 (1941).

/10/

Harper Grp. v. Commissioner, 96 T.C. 45, 58 (1991), aff'd, 979 F.2d 1341 (9th Cir. 1992); AMERCO v. Commissioner, 96 T.C. 18, 38 (1991), aff'd, 979 F.2d 162 (9th Cir. 1992).

/11/

AMERCO v. Commissioner, 96 T.C. at 38.

/12/

Clougherty Packing Co. v. Commissioner, 811 F.2d 1297, 1300 (9th Cir. 1987), aff'g, 84 T.C. 948 (1985).

/13/

Harper Grp. v. Commissioner, 96 T.C. at 57.

/14/

Clougherty Packing Co. v. Commissioner, 811 F.2d at 1300.

/15/

Helvering v. Le Gierse, 312 U.S. at 540-542; Carnation Co. v. Commissioner, 71 T.C. 400, 408-409 (1978), aff'd, 640 F.2d 1010 (9th Cir. 1981).

/16/

Rent-A-Center, Inc. v. Commissioner, 142 T.C. ___, ___ (slip op. at 33) (Jan. 14, 2014).

/17/

Clougherty Packing Co. v. Commissioner, 811 F.2d at 1305.

/18/

Clougherty Packing Co. v. Commissioner, 811 F.2d at 1305.

/19/

Clougherty Packing Co. v. Commissioner, 811 F.2d at 1307 (citing Moline Props., Inc. v. Commissioner, 319 U.S. 436 (1943)); see also Rent-A-Center, Inc., 142 T.C. at ___ (slip. op. at 17).

/20/

Rent-A-Center, Inc. v. Commissioner, 142 T.C. at ___ (slip op. at 36-37); see also id. at ___ (slip op. at 45-47) (Buch, J., concurring).

/21/

Rent-A-Center, Inc. v. Commissioner, 142 T.C. at ___ (slip op. at 37).

/22/

Rent-A-Center, Inc. v. Commissioner, 142 T.C. at ___ (slip op. at 35-38).

/23/

Policies relating to workers' compensation, automobile liability, and general liability are typically referred to as long-tail coverage because "claims may involve damages that are not readily observable or injuries that are difficult to ascertain." Acuity, A Mut. Ins. Co., & Subs. v. Commissioner, T.C. Memo. 2013-209, at *8-*9.

/24/

Rent-A-Center, Inc. v. Commissioner, 142 T.C. at ___ (slip op.

at 49) (Buch, J., concurring) (citing Kahle v. Commissioner, T.C. Memo. 1991-203).

/25/

Rent-A-Center, Inc. v. Commissioner, 142 T.C. at ___ (slip op. at 38).

/26/

Clougherty Packing Co. v. Commissioner, 811 F.2d at 1300.

/27/

AMERCO v. Commissioner, 96 T.C. at 33 n.14 (quoting expert witness).

/28/

See Rent-A-Center, Inc. v. Commissioner, 142 T.C. at ___ (slip op. at 39); Harper Grp. v. Commissioner, 96 T.C. at 60.

REVENUE RULING 77-316

Revenue Ruling 77-316, 1977-2 CB 53 (January 1, 1977)

Advice has been requested whether, under each of the three situations described below, amounts paid as insurance premiums by a domestic parent corporation and its domestic subsidiaries to a wholly owned foreign "insurance" subsidiary of the parent are deductible as ordinary and necessary business expenses under section 162 of the Internal Revenue Code of 1954. Advice has also been requested whether deductions for losses that are incurred by the domestic parent and its domestic subsidiaries and that are otherwise allowable under section 165(a), will be reduced by amounts received from the "insurance" subsidiary with respect to risks retained by the "insurance" subsidiary. In addition, advice has been requested whether the wholly owned foreign "insurance" subsidiary in each situation described below qualifies as an insurance company for Federal income tax purposes.

Situation 1

During the taxable year domestic corporation X and its domestic subsidiaries entered into a contract for fire and other casualty insurance with S1, a newly organized wholly owned foreign "insurance" subsidiary of X. S1 was organized to insure properties and other casualty risks of X and its domestic subsidiaries. X and its domestic subsidiaries paid amounts as casualty insurance premiums directly to S1. Such amounts reflect commercial rates for the insurance involved. S1 has not accepted risks from parties other than X and its domestic subsidiaries.

Situation 2

The facts are the same as set forth in Situation 1 except that domestic corporation Y and its domestic subsidiaries paid amounts as casualty insurance premiums to M, an unrelated domestic insurance company. This insurance was placed with M under a contractual arrangement that provided that M would immediately transfer 95 percent of the risks under reinsurance agreements to S2, the wholly owned foreign "insurance" subsidiary of Y. However, the contractual arrangement for reinsurance did not relieve M of its liability as the primary insurer of Y and its domestic subsidiaries; nor was there any collateral agreement between M and Y, or any of Y's subsidiaries, to reimburse M in the event that S2 could not meet its reinsurance obligations.

Situation 3

The facts are the same as set forth in Situation 1 except that domestic corporation Z and its domestic subsidiaries paid amounts as casualty insurance premiums directly to Z's wholly-owned foreign "insurance" subsidiary, S3. Contemporaneous with the acceptance of this insurance risk, and pursuant to a contractual obligation to Z and its domestic subsidiaries, S3 transferred 90 percent of the risk through reinsurance agreements to an unrelated insurance company, W.

Section 162(a) of the Code provides, in part, that there shall be allowed as a deduction all the ordinary and necessary expenses paid or incurred during the taxable year in carrying on any trade or business.

Section 1.162-1(a) of the Income Tax Regulations provides, in part, that among the items included in business expenses are insurance premiums against fire, storms, theft, accident, or other similar losses in the case of a business.

Historically, insurance involves risk-shifting and risk-distributing, and the sharing and distribution of the insurance risk by all the parties insured is essential to the concept of true insurance. See Helvering v. Le Gierse, 312 U.S. 531 (1941); Commissioner v. Treganowan, 183 F. 2d 188 (2d Cir. 1950); and Rev. Rul. 60-275, 1960-2 C.B. 43. Thus, when there is no economic shift or distribution of the risk "insured," the contract is not one of insurance, and the premiums therefor are not deductible under section 1.162-1(a) of the regulations.

Also, both the Internal Revenue Service and the courts have long held that amounts set aside by a taxpayer as a reserve for self-insurance, though equal to commercial insurance premiums, are not deductible for Federal income tax purposes as "ordinary and necessary expenses paid or incurred during the taxable year." See Rev. Rul. 60-275, Rev. Rul. 57-485, 1957-2 C.B. 117, and Pan American Hide Co. v. Commissioner, 1 B.T.A. 1249 (1925). Even where a self-insurance fund is administered by an independent agent, such fact does not make payments to such fund deductible. See Spring Canyon Coal Company v. Commissioners, 43 F. 2d 78 (10th Cir. 1930), cert. denied, 284 U.S. 654 (1930).

Under the three situations described, there is no economic shifting or distributing of risks of loss with respect to the risks carried or retained by the wholly owned foreign subsidiaries, S1, S2, and S3, respectively. In each situation described, the insuring parent corporation and its domestic subsidiaries, and the wholly owned "insurance" subsidiary, though separate corporate entities, represent one economic family with the result that those who bear the ultimate economic burden of loss are the same persons who suffer the loss. To the extent that the risks of loss are not retained in their entirety by (as in Situation 2) or reinsured with (as in Situation 3) insurance companies that are unrelated to the economic family of insureds, there is no risk-shifting or risk-distributing, and no insurance, the premiums for which are deductible under section 162 of the Code.

Thus, the amounts paid by X, Y, and Z, and their domestic subsidiaries, and retained by S1 (100 percent), S2 (95 percent), and S3 (10 percent), respectively, are not deductible under section 162 of the Code as "ordinary and necessary expenses paid or incurred during the taxable year." Because such amounts remain within the economic family and under the practical control of the respective parent in each situation, there has been no amount "paid or incurred." See Rev. Rul. 60-275, and Rev. Rul. 69-512, 1969-2 C.B. 24.

However, in Situation 2, to the extent the unrelated insurer, M, retains the risks (5 percent) that are not reinsured by S2, and in Situation 3, to the extent S3 transfers the risks (90 percent) through reinsurance agreements to W, the unrelated reinsurer, that portion of the premiums paid by Y and Z and their domestic subsidiaries to cover these risks are deductible under section 162 of the Code. Since these amounts are not withdrawable by either Y and its domestic subsidiaries or Z and its domestic subsidiaries, they have been "paid or incurred" within the meaning of section 162. Furthermore, the requisite shifting and distribution of the risks has occurred to the extent the unrelated insurers, M and W, respectively, bear the risks of loss.

Amounts paid as so-called insurance premiums by X, Y, and Z, and their domestic subsidiaries, with respect to risks remaining with S1, S2, and S3, respectively, with not constitute taxable income to S1, S2, and S3 under section 61 of the Code as nothing has occurred other than a movement of an asset (cash) within each family of related corporations. Instead such amounts will be considered contributions of capital under section 118.

Because the parent through its control of the corporate family members (its domestic subsidiaries and its wholly owned foreign subsidiary) has control over the movement of assets within the family, the payments of so-called "insurance" premiums made by the domestic subsidiaries of X, Y, and Z to S1, S2, and S3, respectively, to the extent of available earnings and profits, are viewed first as a distribution of dividends under section 301 of the Code from such subsidiaries (equal to premiums paid that end up in the foreign "insurance" subsidiary) to their respective parents and then as a contribution of capital by the parents to the respective foreign subsidiaries. Compare Rev. Rul. 69-630, 1969-2 C.B. 112, discussing the treatment of a "bargain sale" between two corporate entities controlled by the same shareholders.

Furthermore, any proceeds paid by S1, S2, and S3 to their respective parents or the parents' domestic subsidiaries with respect to risks of loss retained by S1, S2, and S3 are viewed, to the extent of available earnings and profits, as distributions under section 301 of the Code of the respective parent. Specifically, proceeds paid by S1, S2, and S3 to domestic subsidiaries of their respective parents are viewed, to the extent of available earnings and profits, as distributions under section 301 to the respective parent followed by a contribution of capital from the respective parent to the domestic subsidiary.

The preceding analysis recognizes S1, S2, and S3 as independent corporate entities in view of their business activities (Moline Properties v. Commissioner, 319 U.S. 436 (1943), 1943 C.B. 1011), but also examines the economic reality of each situation described. It is concluded that the "insurance agreement" with respect to the risks retained by S1, S2, and S3 is designed to obtain a deduction by indirect means that would be denied if sought directly.

The second issue relates to whether any loss otherwise allowable to X, Y, and Z and their respective domestic subsidiaries under section 165 of the Code would be reduced by the proceeds received from S1, S2, and S3 to the extent such payments are with respect to risks retained by S1, S2, and S3. Section 165(a) provides as a general rule that there shall be allowed as a deduction any loss sustained during the taxable year and not compensated for by insurance or otherwise.

Consistent with the reasons given above in denying the deduction of the amounts paid as insurance premiums by X, Y, and Z and their respective domestic subsidiaries, any benefits paid by S1, S2, and S3 to their respective parents and affiliates could not qualify as compensation by insurance or otherwise to the extent they result from the risks remaining with S1, S2, and S3. Accordingly, X and its domestic subsidiaries in Situation 1 are entitled to a deduction under section 165(a) of the Code for any losses sustained during the taxable year, since the losses are not compensated by insurance or otherwise. Y and its domestic subsidiaries in Situation 2 are entitled to a deduction for losses sustained during the taxable year to the extent not compensated for by insurance (that is, not compensated by insurance relating to risks assumed by M). Z and its domestic subsidiaries in Situation 3 are entitled to a deduction for losses sustained during the taxable year to the extent not compensated for by insurance (that is, not compensated by insurance relating to risks reinsured by W).

The final issue is whether S1, S2, or S3 qualifies as an insurance company for Federal income tax purposes. Section 1.831-3(a) of the regulations (applicable generally to stock casualty insurance companies) provides, in part, that the term "insurance companies" means only those companies that qualify as insurance companies under the definition provided by section 1.801-1(b), predecessor to section 1.801-3(a).

Section 1.801-3(a) of the regulations defines an insurance company for purposes of subchapter L as follows:

> The term "insurance company" means a company whose primary and predominant business activity during the taxable year is the issuing of insurance or annuity contracts or the reinsuring of risks underwritten by insurance companies. Thus, though its name, charter powers, and subjection to State insurance laws are significant in determining the business which a company is authorized and intends to carry on, it is the character of the business actually done in the taxable year which determines whether a company is taxable as an insurance company under the Internal Revenue Code.

The question, therefore, is whether S1, S2, and S3 are primarily and predominantly engaged in the insurance business, either by virtue of their assuming a portion of the risks of their respective parents and the parents' domestic subsidiaries, or on the basis of the business it transfers for reinsurance with unrelated insurance companies. Since the arrangement whereby S1, S2, and S3 assume a portion of the risks of their respective corporate families is not insurance under the standards set forth in Le Gierse, such an arrangement does not constitute the issuing of insurance or annuity contracts or the reinsuring of risks underwritten by insurance companies as stated in section 1.801-3(a)(1) of the regulations. Also, S3 is not engaged in the business of insurance by transferring the risks of its parent corporation and affiliates to an unrelated insurance company because, under a reinsurance agreement, there will be no shifting to or assumption by S3 of any risk constituting insurance. See Rev. Rul. 56-106, 1956-1 C.B. 313, for the proposition that an insurance company that disposes of its insurance business under a reinsurance agreement ceases to be an insurance company on the effective date of the agreement and thereafter becomes taxable as an ordinary corporation.

Accordingly, S1, S2, and S3, as described above, are not insurance companies within the definition of section 1.801-3(a)(1) of the regulations because their primary and predominant business activity is not the issuing of insurance and annuity contracts or the reinsuring of risks underwritten by other insurance companies.

REVENUE RULING 2001-31

Revenue Ruling 2001-31, 2001-1 CB 1348 (June 4, 2001)

In Rev. Rul. 77-316, 1977-2 C.B. 53, three situations were presented in which a taxpayer attempted to seek insurance coverage for itself and its operating subsidiaries through the taxpayer's wholly-owned captive insurance subsidiary. The ruling explained that the taxpayer, its non-insurance subsidiaries, and its captive insurance subsidiary represented one "economic family" for purposes of analyzing whether transactions involved sufficient risk shifting and risk distribution to constitute insurance for federal income tax purposes. See Helvering v. Le Gierse, 312 U.S. 531 (1941). The ruling concluded that the transactions were not insurance to the extent that risk was retained within that economic family. Therefore, the premiums paid by the taxpayer and its non-insurance subsidiaries to the captive insurer were not deductible.

No court, in addressing a captive insurance transaction, has fully accepted the economic family theory set forth in Rev. Rul. 77-316. See, e.g., Humana, Inc. v. Commissioner, 881 F.2d 247 (6th Cir. 1989); Clougherty Packing Co. v. Commissioner, 811 F.2d 1297 (9th Cir. 1987) (employing a balance sheet test, rather than the economic family theory, to conclude that transaction between parent and subsidiary was not insurance); Kidde Industries, Inc. v. United States, 40 Fed. Cl. 42 (1997). Accordingly, the Internal Revenue Service will no longer invoke the economic family theory with respect to captive insurance transactions.

The Service may, however, continue to challenge certain captive insurance transactions based on the facts and circumstances of each case. See, e.g., Malone & Hyde v. Commissioner, 62 F.3d 835 (6th Cir. 1995) (concluding that brother-sister transactions were not insurance because the taxpayer guaranteed the captive's performance and the captive was thinly capitalized and loosely regulated); Clougherty Packing Co. v. Commissioner (concluding that a transaction between parent and subsidiary was not insurance).

EFFECT ON OTHER DOCUMENTS

Rev. Rul. 77-316, 1977-2 C.B. 53; Rev. Rul. 78-277, 1978-2 C.B. 268; Rev. Rul. 88-72, 1988-2 C.B. 31; and Rev. Rul. 89-61, 1989-1 C.B. 75, are obsoleted.

Rev. Rul. 78-338, 1978-2 C.B. 107; Rev. Rul. 80-120, 1980-1 C.B. 41; Rev. Rul. 92-93, 1992-2 C.B. 45; and Rev. Proc. 2000-3, 2000-1 I.R.B. 103, are modified.

REVENUE RULING 2002-89

Revenue Ruling 2002-89, 2002-2 CB 984 (December 10, 2002)

ISSUE

Are the amounts paid by a domestic parent corporation to its wholly owned insurance subsidiary deductible as "insurance premiums" under § 162 of the Internal Revenue Code?

FACTS

Situation 1. P, a domestic corporation, enters into an annual arrangement with its wholly owned domestic subsidiary S whereby S "insures" the professional liability risks of P either directly or as a reinsurer of these risks. S is regulated as an insurance company in each state where S does business.

The amounts P pays to S under the arrangement are established according to customary industry rating formulas. In all respects, the parties conduct themselves consistently with the standards applicable to an insurance arrangement between unrelated parties.

In implementing the arrangement, S may perform all necessary administrative tasks, or it may outsource those tasks at prevailing commercial market rates. P does not provide any guarantee of S's performance, and all funds and business records of P and S are separately maintained. S does not loan any funds to P.

In addition to the arrangement with P, S enters into insurance contracts whereby S serves as a direct insurer or a reinsurer of the professional liability risks of entities unrelated to P or S. The risks of unrelated entities and those of P are homogeneous. The amounts S receives from

these unrelated entities under these insurance contracts likewise are established according to customary industry rating formulas.

The premiums S earns from the arrangement with P constitute 90% of S's total premiums earned during the taxable year on both a gross and net basis. The liability coverage S provides to P accounts for 90% of the total risks borne by S.

Situation 2. Situation 2 is the same as Situation 1 except that the premiums S earns from the arrangement with P constitute less than 50% of S's total premiums earned during the taxable year on both a gross and net basis. The liability coverage S provides to P accounts for less that 50% of the total risks borne by S.

LAW AND ANALYSIS

Section 162(a) of the Code provides, in part, that there shall be allowed as a deduction all the ordinary and necessary expenses paid or incurred during the taxable year in carrying on any trade or business.

Section 1.162–1(a) of the Income Tax Regulations provides, in part, that among the items included in business expenses are insurance premiums against fire, storms, theft, accident, or other similar losses in the case of a business.

Neither the Code nor the regulations define the terms "insurance" or "insurance contract." The United States Supreme Court, however, has explained that in order for an arrangement to constitute insurance for federal income tax purposes, both risk shifting and risk distribution must be present. Helvering v. LeGierse, 312 U.S. 531 (1941).

Risk shifting occurs if a person facing the possibility of an economic loss transfers some or all of the financial consequences of the potential loss to the insurer, such that a loss by the insured does not affect the insured because the loss is offset by the insurance payment. Risk distribution incorporates the statistical phenomenon known as the law of large numbers. Distributing risk allows the insurer to reduce the possibility that a single costly claim will exceed the amount taken in as premiums and set aside for the payment of such a claim. By assuming numerous relatively small, independent risks that occur randomly over time, the insurer smooths out losses to match more closely its receipt of premiums. Clougherty Packing Co. v. Commissioner, 811 F.2d 1297, 1300 (9th Cir. 1987). Risk distribution necessarily entails a pooling of premiums, so that a potential insured is not in significant part paying for its own risks. See Humana, Inc. v. Commissioner, 881 F.2d 247, 257 (6th Cir. 1989).

No court has held that a transaction between a parent and its wholly-owned subsidiary satisfies the requirements of risk shifting and risk distribution if only the risks of the parent are "insured." See Stearns-Roger Corp. v. United States, 774 F.2d 414 (10th Cir. 1985); Carnation Co. v. Commissioner, 640 F.2d 1010 (9th Cir. 1981), cert. denied 454 U.S. 965 (1981). However, courts have held that an arrangement between a parent and its subsidiary can constitute insurance because the parent's premiums are pooled with those of unrelated parties if (i) insurance risk is present, (ii) risk is shifted and distributed, and (iii) the transaction is of the type that is insurance in the commonly accepted sense. See, e.g., Ocean Drilling & Exploration Co. v. United States, 988 F.2d 1135 (Fed. Cir. 1993); AMERCO, Inc. v. Commissioner, 979 F.2d 162 (9th Cir. 1992).

S is regulated as an insurance company in each state in which it transacts business, and the arrangements between P and S and between S and entities unrelated to P or S are established and conducted consistently with the standards applicable to an insurance arrangement. P does not guarantee S's performance and S does not make any loans to P; P's and S's funds and records are separately maintained. The narrow question presented in Situation 1 and Situation 2 is whether S underwrites sufficient risks of unrelated parties that the arrangement between P and S constitutes insurance for federal income tax purposes.

In Situation 1, the premiums that S earns from its arrangement with P constitute 90% of its total premiums earned during the taxable year on both a gross and a net basis. The liability coverage S provides to P accounts for 90% of the total risks borne by S. No court has treated such an arrangement between a parent and its whollyowned subsidiary as insurance. To the contrary, the arrangement lacks the requisite risk shifting and risk distribution to constitute insurance for federal income tax purposes.

In Situation 2, the premiums that S earns from its arrangement with P constitute less than 50% of the total premiums S earned during the taxable year on both a gross and a net basis. The liability coverage S provides to P accounts for less than 50% of the total risks borne by S. The premiums and risks of P are thus pooled with those of the unrelated insureds. The requisite risk shifting and risk distribution to constitute insurance for federal income tax purposes are present. The arrangement is insurance in the commonly accepted sense.

HOLDINGS

In Situation 1, the arrangement between P and S does not constitute insurance for federal income tax purposes, and amounts paid by P to S pursuant to that arrangement are not deductible as "insurance premiums" under § 162.

In Situation 2, the arrangement between P and S constitutes insurance for federal income tax purposes, and the amounts paid by P to S pursuant to that arrangement are deductible as "insurance premiums" under § 162.

EFFECT ON OTHER DOCUMENTS

Rev. Rul. 2001–31, 2001–1 C.B. 1348, is amplified.

REVENUE RULING 2002-90

Revenue Ruling 2002-90, 2002-2 CB 985 (December 10, 2002)

ISSUE

Are the amounts paid for professional liability coverage by domestic operating subsidiaries to an insurance subsidiary of a common parent deductible as "insurance premiums" under § 162 of the Internal Revenue Code?

FACTS

P, a domestic holding company, owns all of the stock of 12 domestic subsidiaries that provide professional services. Each subsidiary in the P group has a geographic territory comprised of a state in which the subsidiary provides professional services. The subsidiaries in the P group operate on a decentralized basis. The services provided by the employees of each subsidiary are performed under the general guidance of a supervisory professional for a particular facility of the subsidiary. The general categories of the professional services rendered by each of the subsidiaries are the same throughout the P group. Together the 12 subsidiaries have a significant volume of independent, homogeneous risks.

P, for a valid non-tax business purpose, forms S as a wholly-owned insurance subsidiary under the laws of State C. P provides S adequate capital and S is fully licensed in State C and in the 11 other states where the respective operating subsidiaries conduct their professional service businesses. S directly insures the professional liability risks of the 12 operating subsidiaries in the

P group. S charges the 12 subsidiaries arms-length premiums, which are established according to customary industry rating formulas. None of the operating subsidiaries have liability coverage for less than 5%, nor more than 15%, of the total risk insured by S. S retains the risks that it insures from the 12 operating subsidiaries. There are no parental (or other related party) guarantees of any kind made in favor of S. S does not loan any funds to P or to the 12 operating subsidiaries. In all respects, the parties conduct themselves in a manner consistent with the standards applicable to an insurance arrangement between unrelated parties. S does not provide coverage to any entity other than the 12 operating subsidiaries.

LAW AND ANALYSIS

Section 162(a) of the Code provides, in part, that there shall be allowed as a deduction all the ordinary and necessary expenses paid or incurred during the taxable year in carrying on any trade or business.

Section 1.162–1(a) of the Income Tax Regulations provides, in part, that among the items included in business expenses are insurance premiums against fire, storms, theft, accident, or other similar losses in the case of a business.

Neither the Code nor the regulations define the terms "insurance" or "insurance contract." The United States Supreme Court, however, has explained that in order for an arrangement to constitute "insurance" for federal income tax purposes, both risk shifting and risk distribution must be present. Helvering v. LeGierse, 312 U.S. 531 (1941).

Risk shifting occurs if a person facing the possibility of an economic loss transfers some or all of the financial consequences of the potential loss to the insurer, such that a loss by the insured does not affect the insured because the loss is offset by the insurance payment. Risk distribution incorporates the statistical phenomenon known as the law of large numbers. Distributing risk allows the insurer to reduce the possibility that a single costly claim will exceed the amount taken in as premiums and set aside for the payment of such a claim. By assuming numerous relatively small, independent risks that occur randomly over time, the insurer smooths out losses to match more closely its receipt of premiums. Clougherty Packing Co. v. Commissioner, 811 F.2d 1297, 1300 (9th Cir. 1987). Risk distribution necessarily entails a pooling of premiums, so that a potential insured is not in significant part paying for its own risks. See Humana Inc. v. Commissioner, 881 F.2d 247, 257 (6th Cir. 1989).

In Humana, the United States Court of Appeals for the Sixth Circuit held that arrangements between a parent corporation and its insurance company subsidiary did not constitute insurance for federal income tax purposes. The court also held, however, that arrangements between the insurance company subsidiary and several dozen other subsidiaries of the parent (operating an even larger number of hospitals) qualified as insurance for federal income tax purposes because the requisite risk shifting and risk distribution were present. But see Malone & Hyde, Inc. v. Commissioner, 62 F.3d 835 (6th Cir. 1995) (concluding the lack of a business purpose, the undercapitalization of the offshore captive insurance subsidiary and the existence of related party guarantees established that the substance of the transaction did not support the taxpayer's characterization of the transaction as insurance). In Kidde Industries, Inc. v. United States, 40 Fed. Cl. 42 (1997), the United States Court of Federal Claims concluded that an arrangement between the captive insurance subsidiary and each of the 100 operating subsidiaries of the same parent constituted insurance for federal income tax purposes. As in Humana, the insurer in Kidde insured only entities within its affiliated group during the taxable years at issue.

In the present case, the professional liability risks of 12 operating subsidiaries are shifted to S. Further, the premiums of the operating subsidiaries, determined at armslength, are pooled such that a loss by one operating subsidiary is borne, in substantial part, by the premiums paid by others. The 12 operating subsidiaries and S conduct themselves in all respects as would unrelated parties to a traditional insurance relationship, and S is regulated as an insurance company in each state where it does business. The narrow question presented is whether P's common ownership of the 12 operating subsidiaries and S affects the conclusion that the arrangements at issue are insurance for federal income tax purposes. Under the facts presented, we conclude the arrangements between S and each of the 12 operating subsidiaries of S' s parent constitute insurance for federal income tax purposes.

HOLDING

The amounts paid for professional liability coverage by the 12 domestic operating subsidiaries to S are "insurance premiums" deductible under § 162.

EFFECT ON OTHER DOCUMENTS

Rev. Rul. 2001–31, 2001–1 C.B. 1348, is amplified.

REVENUE RULING 2002-91

Revenue Ruling 2002-91, 2002-2 CB 991 (December 30, 2002)

ISSUE

Whether a "group captive" formed by a relatively small group of unrelated businesses involved in a highly concentrated industry to provide insurance coverage is an insurance company within the meaning of §831 of the Internal Revenue Code under the circumstances described below.

FACTS

X is one of a small group of unrelated businesses involved in one highly concentrated industry. Businesses involved in this industry face significant liability hazards. X and the other businesses involved in this industry are required by regulators to maintain adequate liability insurance coverage in order to continue to operate. Businesses that participate in this industry have sustained significant losses due to the occurrence of unusually severe loss events. As a result, affordable insurance coverage for businesses that participate in this industry is not available from commercial insurance companies.

X and a significant number of the businesses involved in this industry (Members) form a so-called "group captive" (GC) to provide insurance coverage for stated liability risks. GC provides insurance only to X and the other Members. The business operations of GC are separate from the business operation of each Member. GC is adequately capitalized.

No Member owns more than 15% of GC, and no Member has

more than 15% of the vote on any corporate governance issue. In addition, no Member's individual risk insured by GC exceeds 15% of the total risk insured by GC. Thus, no one member controls GC.

GC issues insurance contracts and charges premiums for the insurance coverage provided under the contracts. GC uses recognized actuarial techniques, based, in part, on commercial rates for similar coverage, to determine the premiums to be charged to an individual Member.

GC pools all the premiums it receives in its general funds and pays claims out of those funds. GC investigates any claim made by a Member to determine the validity of the claim prior to making any payment on that claim. GC conducts no other business than the issuing and administering of insurance contracts.

No Member has any obligation to pay GC additional premiums if that Member's actual losses during any period of coverage exceed the premiums paid by that Member. No Member will be entitled to a refund of premiums paid if that Member's actual losses are lower than the premiums paid for coverage during any period. Premiums paid by any Member may be used to satisfy claims of the other Members. No Member that terminates its insurance coverage or sells its ownership interest in GC is required to make additional premium or capital payments to GC to cover losses in excess of its premiums paid. Moreover, no Member that terminates its coverage or disposes of its ownership interest in GC is entitled to a refund of premiums paid in excess of insured losses.

LAW AND ANALYSIS

Section 162(a) of the Code provides, in part, that there shall be allowed as a deduction all the ordinary and necessary expenses paid or incurred during the taxable year in carrying on any trade or business.

Section 1.162-1(a) of the Income Tax Regulations provides, in part, that among the items included in business expenses are insurance premiums against fire, storms, theft, accident, or other similar losses in the case of a business.

Section 831(a) of the Code provides that taxes computed under section 11 are imposed for each tax year on the taxable income of every insurance company other than a life insurance company.

Section 1.801-3(a) provides that an insurance company is "a company whose primary and predominant business activity is the issuing of insurance or annuity contracts or the reinsuring of risks underwritten by insurance companies."

Neither the Code nor the regulations define the terms "insurance" or "insurance contract." The United States Supreme Court, however, has explained that in order for an arrangement to constitute insurance for federal income tax purposes, both risk shifting and risk distribution must be present. *Helvering v. LeGierse*, 312 U.S. 531 (1941).

Risk shifting occurs if a person facing the possibility of an economic loss transfers some or all of the financial consequences of the potential loss to the insurer, such that a loss by the insured does not affect the insured because the loss is offset by the insurance payment. Risk distribution incorporates the statistical phenomenon known as the law of large numbers. Distributing risk allows the insurer to reduce the possibility that a single costly claim will exceed the amount taken in as premiums and set aside for the payment of such a claim. By assuming numerous relatively small, independent risks that occur randomly over time, the insurer smooths out losses to match more closely its receipt of premiums. *Clougherty Packing Co. v. Commissioner*, 811 F.2d 1297, 1300 (9th Cir. 1987). Risk distribution necessarily entails a pooling of premiums, so that a potential insured is not in significant part paying for its own risks. *See Humana, Inc. v. Commissioner*, 881 F.2d 247, 257 (6th Cir. 1989).

No court has held that a transaction between a parent and its wholly-owned subsidiary satisfies the requirements of risk shifting and risk distribution if only the risks of the parent are "insured." *See Stearns-Roger Corp. v. United States*, 774 F.2d 414

(10th Cir. 1985); *Carnation Co. v. Commissioner*, 640 F.2d 1010 (9th Cir. 1981), *cert. denied*, 454 U.S. 965 (1981). However, courts have held that an arrangement between a parent and its subsidiary can constitute insurance because the parent's premiums are pooled with those of unrelated parties if (i) insurance risk is present, (ii) risk is shifted and distributed, and (iii) the transaction is of the type that is insurance in the commonly accepted sense. *See, e.g., Ocean Drilling & Exploration Co. v. United States*, 988 F.2d 1135 (Fed. Cir. 1993); *AMERCO, Inc. v. Commissioner*, 979 F.2d 162 (9th Cir. 1992).

Additional factors to be considered in determining whether a captive insurance transaction is insurance include: whether the parties that insured with the captive truly face hazards; whether premiums charged by the captive are based on commercial rates; whether the validity of claims was established before payments are made; and whether the captive's business operations and assets are kept separate from the business operations and assets of its shareholders. *Ocean Drilling & Exploration Co.* at 1151.

In Rev. Rul. 2001-31, 2001-26 I.R.B. 1348, the Service stated that it will not invoke the economic family theory in Rev. Rul. 77-316 with respect to captive insurance arrangements. Rev. Rul. 2001-31 provides, however, that the Service may continue to challenge certain captive insurance transactions based on the facts and circumstances of each case.

Rev. Rul. 78-338, 1978-2 C.B.107, presented a situation in which 31 unrelated corporations created a group captive insurance company to provide those corporations with insurance that was not otherwise available. In that ruling, none of the unrelated corporations held a controlling interest in the group captive. In addition, no individual corporation's risk exceeded 5 percent of the total risks insured by the group captive. The Service concluded that because the corporations that owned, and were insured by, the group captive were not economically related, the economic risk of loss could be shifted and distributed among the shareholders that comprised the insured group.

X and the other Members face true insurable hazards. X and the other Members are required to maintain general liability insurance coverage in order to continue to operate in their industry. X and the other Members are unable to obtain affordable insurance from unrelated commercial insurers due to the occurrence of unusually severe loss events. Notwithstanding the fact that the group of Members is small, there is a real possibility that a Member will sustain a loss in excess of the premiums it paid. No individual Member will be reimbursed for premiums paid in excess of losses sustained by that Member. Finally, X and the other Members are unrelated. Therefore, the contracts issued by GC to X and the other Members are insurance contracts for federal income tax purposes, and the premiums paid by the Members are deductible under §162.

GC is an entity separate from its owners. GC is adequately capitalized. GC issues insurance contracts, charges premiums, and pays claims after investigating the validity of the claim. GC will not engage in any business activities other than issuing and administering insurance contracts. Premiums charged by GC will be actuarially determined using recognized actuarial techniques, and will be based, in part, on commercial rates. As GC 's only business activity is the business of insurance, it is taxed as an insurance company.

HOLDING

The arrangement between *X* and *GC* constitutes insurance for federal income tax purposes, and the amounts paid as "insurance premiums" by *X* to *GC* pursuant to that arrangement are deductible as ordinary and necessary business expenses. *GC* is in the business of issuing insurance and will be treated as an insurance company taxable under §831.

REVENUE RULING 2005-40

Revenue Ruling 2005-40, I.R.B. 2005-27 (June 17, 2005)

ISSUE

Do the arrangements described below constitute insurance for federal income tax purposes? If so, are amounts paid to the issuer deductible as insurance premiums and does the issuer qualify as an insurance company?

FACTS

Situation 1. X, a domestic corporation, operates a courier transport business covering a large portion of the United States. X owns and operates a large fleet of automotive vehicles representing a significant volume of independent, homogeneous risks. For valid, non-tax business purposes, X entered into an arrangement with Y, an unrelated domestic corporation, whereby in exchange for an agreed amount of "premiums," Y "insures" X against the risk of loss arising out of the operation of its fleet in the conduct of its courier business.

The amount of "premiums" under the arrangement is determined at arm's length according to customary insurance industry rating formulas. Y possesses adequate capital to fulfill its obligations to X under the agreement, and in all respects operates in accordance with the applicable requirements of state law. There are no guarantees of any kind in favor of Y with respect to the agreement, nor are any of the "premiums" paid by X to Y in turn loaned back to X. X has no obligation to pay Y additional premiums if X 's actual losses during any period of coverage exceed the "premiums" paid by X. X will not be entitled to any refund of "premiums" paid if X 's actual losses are lower than the "premiums" paid during any period. In all respects, the parties conduct themselves consistent with the standards applicable to an insurance arrangement between unrelated parties, except that Y does not "insure" any entity other than X.

Situation 2. The facts are the same as in Situation 1 except that, in addition to its arrangement with X, Y enters into an arrangement with Z, a domestic corporation unrelated to X or Y, whereby in exchange for an agreed amount of "premiums," Y also "insures" Z against the risk of loss arising out of the operation of its own fleet in connection with the conduct of a courier business substantially similar to that of X. The amounts Y earns from its arrangements with Z constitute 10% of Y 's total amounts earned during the taxable year on both a gross and net basis. The arrangement with Z accounts for 10% of the total risks borne by Y.

Situation 3. X, a domestic corporation, operates a courier transport business covering a large portion of the United States. X conducts the courier transport business through 12 limited liability companies (LLCs) of which it is the single member. The LLCs are disregarded as entities separate from X under the provisions of §301.7701-3 of the Procedure and Administration Regulations. The LLCs own and operate a large fleet of automotive vehicles, collectively representing a significant volume of independent, homogeneous risks. For valid, non-tax business purposes, the LLCs entered into arrangements with Y, an unrelated domestic corporation, whereby in exchange for an agreed amount of "premiums," Y "insures" the LLCs against the risk of loss arising out of the operation of the fleet in the conduct of their courier business. None of the LLCs account for less than 5%, or more than 15%, of the total risk assumed by Y under the agreements.

The amount of "premiums" under the arrangement is determined at arm's length according to customary insurance industry rating formulas. Y possesses adequate capital to fulfill its obligations to the LLCs under the agreement, and in all respects operates in accordance with the licensing and other requirements of state law. There are no guarantees of any kind in favor of Y with respect to the agreements, nor are any of the "premiums" paid by the LLCs to Y in turn loaned back to X or to the LLCs. No LLC has any obligation to pay Y additional premiums if that LLC's actual losses during the arrangement exceed the "premiums" paid by that LLC. No LLC will be entitled to a refund of "premiums" paid if that LLC's actual losses are lower than the "premiums" paid during any period. Y retains the risks that it assumes under the agreement. In all respects, the parties conduct themselves consistent with the standards applicable to an insurance arrangement between unrelated parties, except that Y does not "insure" any entity other than the LLCs.

Situation 4. The facts are the same as in Situation 3, except that each of the 12 LLCs elects pursuant to §301.7701-3(a) to be classified as an association.

LAW

Section 831(a) of the Internal Revenue Code provides that taxes, computed as provided in §11, are imposed for each taxable year on the taxable income of each insurance company other than a life insurance company. Section 831(c) provides that, for purposes of §831, the term "insurance company" has the meaning given to such term by §816(a). Under §816(a), the term "insurance company" means any company more than half of the business of which during the taxable year is the issuing of insurance or annuity contracts or the reinsuring of risks underwritten by insurance companies.

Section 162(a) provides, in part, that there shall be allowed as a deduction all the ordinary and necessary expenses paid or incurred during the taxable year in carrying on any trade or business. Section 1.162-1(a) of the Income Tax Regulations provides, in part, that among the items included in business expenses are insurance premiums against fire, storms, theft, accident, or other similar losses in the case of a business.

Neither the Code nor the regulations define the terms "insurance" or "insurance contract." The United States Supreme Court, however, has explained that in order for an arrangement to constitute insurance for federal income tax purposes, both risk shifting and risk distribution must be present. Helvering v. Le Gierse, 312 U.S. 531 (1941).

The risk transferred must be risk of economic loss. Allied Fidelity Corp. v. Commissioner, 572 F.2d 1190, 1193 (7th Cir.), cert. denied, 439 U.S. 835 (1978). The risk must contemplate the fortuitous occurrence of a stated contingency, Commissioner v. Treganowan, 183 F.2d 288, 290-91 (2d Cir.), cert. denied, 340 U.S. 853 (1950), and must not be merely an investment or business risk. Le Gierse, at 542; Rev. Rul. 89-96, 1989-2 C.B. 114.

Risk shifting occurs if a person facing the possibility of an economic loss transfers some or all of the financial consequences of the potential loss to the insurer, such that a loss by the insured does not affect the insured because the loss is offset by a payment from the insurer. Risk distribution incorporates the statistical phenomenon known as the law of large numbers. Distributing risk allows the insurer to reduce the possibility that a single costly claim will exceed the amount taken in as premiums and set aside for the payment of such a claim. By assuming numerous relatively small, independent risks that occur randomly over time, the insurer smooths out losses to match more closely its receipt of premiums. Clougherty Packing Co. v. Commissioner, 811 F.2d 1297, 1300 (9th Cir. 1987).

Courts have recognized that risk distribution necessarily entails a pooling of premiums, so that a potential insured is not in significant part paying for its own risks. Humana, Inc. v. Commissioner, 881 F.2d 247, 257 (6th Cir. 1989). See also Ocean Drilling & Exploration Co. v. United States, 988 F.2d 1135, 1153 (Fed. Cir. 1993) ("Risk distribution involves spreading the risk of loss among policyholders."); Beech Aircraft Corp. v. United

States, 797 F.2d 920, 922 (10th Cir. 1986) (" '[R]isk distributing' means that the party assuming the risk distributes his potential liability, in part, among others."); Treganowan, at 291 (quoting Note, The New York Stock Exchange Gratuity Fund: Insurance that Isn't Insurance, 59 Yale L. J. 780, 784 (1950)) (" 'By diffusing the risks through a mass of separate risk shifting contracts, the insurer casts his lot with the law of averages. The process of risk distribution, therefore, is the very essence of insurance.' "); Crawford Fitting Co. v. United States, 606 F.Supp. 136, 147 (N.D. Ohio 1985) ("[T]he court finds…that various nonaffiliated persons or entities facing risks similar but independent of those faced by plaintiff were named insureds under the policy, enabling the distribution of the risk thereunder."); AMERCO and Subsidiaries v. Commissioner, 96 T.C. 18, 41 (1991), aff'd, 979 F.2d 162 (9th Cir. 1992) ("The concept of risk-distributing emphasizes the pooling aspect of insurance: that it is the nature of an insurance contract to be part of a larger collection of coverages, combined to distribute risk between insureds.").

ANALYSIS

In order to determine the nature of an arrangement for federal income tax purposes, it is necessary to consider all the facts and circumstances in a particular case, including not only the terms of the arrangement, but also the entire course of conduct of the parties. Thus, an arrangement that purports to be an insurance contract but lacks the requisite risk distribution may instead be characterized as a deposit arrangement, a loan, a contribution to capital (to the extent of net value, if any), an indemnity arrangement that is not an insurance contract, or otherwise, based on the substance of the arrangement between the parties. The proper characterization of the arrangement may determine whether the issuer qualifies as an insurance company and whether amounts paid under the arrangement may be deductible.

In Situation 1, Y enters into an "insurance" arrangement with X. The arrangement with X represents Y 's only such agreement.

Although the arrangement may shift the risks of X to Y, those risks are not, in turn, distributed among other insureds or policyholders. Therefore, the arrangement between X and Y does not constitute insurance for federal income tax purposes.

In Situation 2, the fact that Y also enters into an arrangement with Z does not change the conclusion that the arrangement between X and Y lacks the requisite risk distribution to constitute insurance. Y 's contract with Z represents only 10% of the total amounts earned by Y, and 10% of total risks assumed, under all its arrangements. This creates an insufficient pool of other premiums to distribute X 's risk. See Rev. Rul. 2002-89, 2002-2 C.B. 984 (concluding that risks from unrelated parties representing 10% of total risks borne by subsidiary are insufficient to qualify arrangement between parent and subsidiary as insurance).

In Situation 3, Y contracts only with 12 single member LLCs through which X conducts a courier transport business. The LLCs are disregarded as entities separate from X pursuant to §301.7701-3. Section 301.7701-2(a) provides that if an entity is disregarded, its activities are treated in the same manner as a sole proprietorship, branch or division of the owner. Applying this rule in Situation 3, Y has entered into an "insurance" arrangement only with X. Therefore, for the reasons set forth in Situation 1 above, the arrangement between X and Y does not constitute insurance for federal income tax purposes.

In Situation 4, the 12 LLCs are not disregarded as entities separate from X, but instead are classified as associations for federal income tax purposes. The arrangements between Y and each LLC thus shift a risk of loss from each LLC to Y. The risks of the LLCs are distributed among the various other LLCs that are insured under similar arrangements. Therefore the arrangements between the 12 LLCs and Y constitute insurance for federal income tax purposes. See Rev. Rul. 2002-90, 2002-2 C.B. 985 (similar arrangements between affiliated entities constituted insurance). Because the arrangements with the 12

LLCs represent Y 's only business, and those arrangements are insurance contracts for federal income tax purposes, Y is an insurance company within the meaning of §§831(c) and 816(a). In addition, the 12 LLCs may be entitled to deduct amounts paid under those arrangements as insurance premiums under §162 if the requirements for deduction are otherwise satisfied.

HOLDINGS

In Situations 1, 2 and 3, the arrangements do not constitute insurance for federal income tax purposes.

In Situation 4, the arrangements constitute insurance for federal income tax purposes and the issuer qualifies as an insurance company. The amounts paid to the issuer may be deductible as insurance premiums under §162 if the requirements for deduction are otherwise satisfied.

REVENUE RULING 2008-8

Revenue Ruling 2008-8, I.R.B. 2008-5 (January 15, 2008)
Revised January 17, 2008

ISSUES

Under the facts described below, do the arrangements entered into between X and Cell X, and between the subsidiaries of Y and Cell Y, of Protected Cell Company constitute insurance for federal income tax purposes? If so, are amounts paid by X to Cell X and by the subsidiaries of Y to Cell Y deductible as "insurance premiums" under §162 of the Internal Revenue Code?

FACTS

Protected Cell Company is a legal entity formed by Sponsor under the laws of Jurisdiction A. Pursuant to the laws of Jurisdiction A, Protected Cell Company has established multiple accounts, or cells, each of which has its own name and is identified with a specific participant, but is not treated as a legal entity distinct from Protected Cell Company. Sponsor owns all the common stock of Protected Cell Company. All of the non-voting preferred stock associated with each cell is owned by that cell's participant or participants. The terms "common stock" and "preferred stock" as used in the Protected Cell Company and cell instruments do not necessarily reflect the federal income tax status of those instruments.

Each cell is funded by its participant's capital contribution (the amount paid by the participant for the preferred stock associated with its cell) and by "premiums" collected with respect to contracts to which the cell is a party. Each cell is required to pay out claims with respect to contracts to which it is a party. The income, expense, assets, liabilities, and capital of each cell are accounted for separately from the income, expense, assets, liabilities, and capital of any other cell and of Protected Cell Company generally. The assets of each cell are statutorily protected from the creditors of any other cell and from the creditors of Protected Cell Company. Protected Cell Company maintains non-cellular assets and capital representing the minimum amount of capital necessary to maintain its charter. Each cell may make distributions with respect to the class of stock that corresponds to that cell, regardless of whether distributions are made with respect to any other class of stock. In the event a participant ceases its participation in Protected Cell Company, the participant is entitled to a return of the assets of the cell in which it participated, subject to any outstanding obligations of that cell.

A company like Protected Cell Company is sometimes referred to as a protected cell company, a segregated account company or segregated portfolio company.

Situation 1

X, a domestic corporation, owns all the preferred stock issued with respect to Cell X. Each year, X enters into a 1-year contract, or arrangement, whereby Cell X "insures" the professional liability risks of X, either directly or as a reinsurer of those risks. The amounts X pays as "premiums" under the annual arrangement are established according to customary industry rating formulas. In all respects, X and Cell X conduct themselves consistently with the standards applicable to an insurance arrangement between unrelated parties. In implementing the arrangement, Cell X may perform any necessary administrative tasks, or it may outsource those tasks at prevailing commercial market rates. X does not provide any guarantee of Cell X 's performance, and all funds and business records of X and Cell X are separately maintained. Cell X does not loan any funds to X.

Cell X does not enter into any arrangements with entities other than X. Taking into account the total assets of Cell X, both from capital contributions and from amounts received pursuant to the annual arrangement with X, Cell X is adequately capitalized relative to the risks assumed under that arrangement.

Situation 2

The facts are the same as in Situation 1, except that Y, a domestic corporation, owns all the preferred stock issued with respect to Cell Y. Y also owns all of the stock of 12 domestic subsidiaries that provide professional services. Each subsidiary in the Y group has a geographic territory comprised of a state in which the subsidiary provides professional services. The subsidiaries of Y operate on a decentralized basis. The services provided by the employees of each subsidiary are performed under the general guidance of a supervisory professional for a particular facility of the subsidiary. The general categories of the professional services rendered by each of the subsidiaries are the same throughout the Y group. Together the 12 subsidiaries have a significant volume of independent, homogeneous risks.

Each year, each subsidiary of Y enters into a 1-year contract, or arrangement, with Cell Y whereby Cell Y "insures" the professional liability risks of that subsidiary, either directly or as a reinsurer of those risks. The amounts charged each subsidiary as "premiums" under the annual arrangements are established according to customary industry rating formulas. None of the subsidiaries have liability coverage for less than 5% nor more than 15% of the total risk insured by Cell Y. Cell Y retains the risk that it insures from the subsidiaries. In all respects, Y, Cell Y, and each subsidiary, conduct themselves consistently with the standards applicable to an insurance arrangement between unrelated parties. In implementing the arrangement, Cell Y may perform all necessary administrative tasks, or it may outsource those tasks at prevailing commercial market rates. Neither Y nor any subsidiary of Y guarantees Cell Y 's performance, and all funds and business records of Y, Cell Y, and each subsidiary, are separately maintained. Cell Y does not loan any funds to Y or to any subsidiary of Y. Cell Y does not enter into any arrangements with entities other than Y or its subsidiaries. Taking into account the total assets of Cell Y, both from capital contributions from Y and from amounts received pursuant to the annual arrangements with the subsidiaries of Y, Cell Y is adequately capitalized relative to the risks assumed under those arrangements.

LAW

Section 162(a) of the Code provides, in part, that there shall be allowed as a deduction all the ordinary and necessary expenses paid or incurred during the taxable year in carrying on any trade or business. Section 1.162-1(a) of the Income Tax Regulations provides, in part, that among the items included in business expenses are insurance premiums against fire, storms, theft, accident or other similar losses in the case of a business.

Neither the Code nor the regulations define the terms insurance or insurance contract. The United States Supreme Court, however, has explained that in order for an arrangement to constitute insurance for federal income tax purposes, both risk shifting and risk distribution must be present. Helvering v. LeGierse, 312 U.S. 531 (1941).

Risk shifting occurs if a person facing the possibility of an economic loss transfers some or all of the financial consequences of the potential loss to the insurer, such that a loss by the insured does not affect the insured because the loss is offset by the insurance payment. Risk distribution occurs when the party assuming the risk distributes its potential liability among others, at least in part. Beech Aircraft Corp. v. United States, 797 F.2d 920, 922 (10th Cir. 1986). Risk distribution "emphasizes the broader, social aspect of insurance as a method or dispelling the danger of a potential loss by spreading its cost throughout a group", Commissioner v. Treganowan, 183 F.2d 288, 291 (2d Cir. 1950), and "involves spreading the risk of loss among policyholders." Ocean Drilling & Exploration Co. v. United States, 24 Cl.Ct. 714, 731 (1991) aff'd per curiam, 988 F.2d 1135

(Fed. Cir. 1993). Risk distribution necessarily entails a pooling of premiums, so that a potential insured is not in significant part paying for its own risks. See Humana, Inc. v. Commissioner, 881 F.2d 247, 257 (6th Cir. 1989).

A transaction between a parent and its wholly-owned subsidiary does not satisfy the requirements of risk shifting and risk distribution if only the risks of the parent are insured. See Stearns-Roger Corp. v. United States, 774 F.2d 414 (10th Cir. 1985); Carnation Co. v. Commissioner, 640 F.2d 1010 (9th Cir. 1981), cert. denied 454 U.S. 965 (1981). However, courts have held that an arrangement between a parent and its subsidiary can constitute insurance when the parent's premiums are pooled with those of unrelated parties if (i) insurance risk is present, (ii) risk is shifted and distributed, and (iii) the transaction is of the type that is insurance in the commonly accepted sense. See, e.g., Ocean Drilling & Exploration Co.; AMERCO, Inc. v. Commissioner, 979 F.2d 162 (9th Cir. 1992); Rev. Rul. 2002-89, 2002-2 C.B. 984. An arrangement between an insurance subsidiary and other subsidiaries of the same parent may qualify as insurance for federal income tax purposes, even if there are no insured policyholders outside the affiliated group, provided the requisite risk shifting and risk distribution are present. See, e.g., Humana, Inc. v. Commissioner, 881 F.2d 247 (6th Cir. 1989); Kidde Industries v. U.S., 40 Fed. Cl. (1997); Rev. Rul. 2002-90, 2002-2 C.B. 985.

The qualification of an arrangement as an insurance contract does not depend on the regulatory status of the issuer. See, e.g., Commissioner v. Treganowan, 183 F.2d 288 (2d Cir. 1950) (arrangement with stock exchange "gratuity fund" treated as life insurance because the requisite risk shifting and risk distribution were present). See also Rev. Rul. 83-172, 1983-2 C.B. 107 (group issuing workmen's compensation insurance taxable as an insurance company even though not recognized as an insurance company under state law); Rev. Rul. 83-132, 1983-2 C.B. 270 (non-corporate business entity taxable as an insurance company if it is primarily engaged in the business of issuing insurance contracts). The same principles apply to determine the insurance contract status of an arrangement involving a cell of a protected cell company as apply to determine the status of an arrangement with any other issuer.

ANALYSIS

In order to determine the nature of an arrangement for federal income tax purposes, it is necessary to consider all the facts and circumstances in a particular case, including not only the terms of the arrangement, but also the entire course of conduct of the parties. Thus, an arrangement that purports to be an insurance contract but lacks the requisite risk distribution may instead be characterized as a deposit arrangement, a loan, a contribution to capital (to the extent of net value, if any) an indemnity arrangement that is not an insurance contract, or otherwise, based on the substance of the arrangement between the parties. The proper characterization of the arrangement may determine whether the issuer qualifies as an insurance company and whether amounts paid under the arrangement may be deductible.

Under the facts presented, all the income, expense, assets, liabilities and capital of Cell X are separately accounted for and, upon liquidation, become the property of X, who is the sole shareholder with respect to Cell X. The amounts X pays as premiums under the 1-year agreement to "insure" its professional liability risks are held by Cell X, together with any capital and surplus, for the satisfaction of X 's claims. The premiums that Cell X earns from its arrangement with X constitute 100% of its total premiums earned during the taxable year; the liability coverage Cell X provides to X accounts for all the risks borne by Cell X. In the event of a claim, payment will be made to X out of X 's own premiums and contributions to the capital of Cell X; no amount may be paid out of any other cell in satisfaction of any claims by X. The arrangement between X and Cell X is akin to an arrangement between a parent and its wholly-owned subsidiary, which, in the absence of unrelated risk, lacks the requisite risk shifting and risk distribution to constitute insurance. Because Cell X does not enter into arrangements with any policyholders other than X, the arrangement between X and Cell X is not an insurance contract for federal income tax purposes, and X may not deduct amounts paid pursuant to the arrangement as "insurance premiums" under §162. See Rev. Rul. 2005-40, 2005-2 C.B. 4 (arrangement lacks necessary risk distribution, and therefore does not qualify as insurance, if the issuer of the arrangement contracts with only a single policyholder); Rev. Rul. 2002-89, 2002-2 C.B. 984 (amounts paid by a domestic parent corporation to its wholly owned insurance subsidiary are not deductible as insurance premiums if the parent's premiums are not sufficiently pooled with those of unrelated parties).

All the income, expense, assets, liabilities and capital of Cell Y likewise are separately accounted for, and upon liquidation, become the property of Y, who is the sole shareholder with respect to Cell Y. Under the arrangements between the 12 subsidiaries of Y and Cell Y, the subsidiaries shift to Cell Y their professional liability risks in exchange for premiums that are determined at arms-length. Those premiums are pooled such that a loss by one subsidiary is not in substantial part, paid from its own premiums. The subsidiaries of Y and Cell Y conduct themselves in all respects as would unrelated parties to a traditional insurance relationship. Had the subsidiaries of Y entered into identical arrangements with a sibling corporation that was regulated as an insurance company, the arrangements would constitute insurance and amounts paid pursuant to the arrangements would be deductible as insurance premiums under §162. See Rev. Rul. 2002-90, 2002-2 C.B. 985. The fact that the subsidiaries' risks were instead shifted to a cell of a protected cell company, and distributed within that cell, does not change this result. Accordingly, the arrangements between Cell Y and each subsidiary of Y are insurance contracts for federal income tax purposes; amounts paid pursuant to those arrangements are insurance premiums, deductible under §162 if the requirements for deduction are otherwise satisfied.

HOLDINGS

In Situation 1, the annual arrangement between Cell X and X does not constitute insurance for federal income tax purposes. In Situation 2, the arrangements between Cell Y and each subsidiary of Y do constitute insurance for federal income tax purposes; amounts paid pursuant to those arrangements are deductible as insurance premiums under §162 if the requirements for deduction are otherwise satisfied.

ADDITIONAL GUIDANCE

The Internal Revenue Service and the Treasury Department are aware that further guidance may be needed in this area. Notice 2008-19, this Bulletin, requests comments on further guidance that addresses when a cell of a Protected Cell Company is treated as an insurance company for federal income tax purposes.

REVENUE RULING 2009-26

Revenue Ruling 2009-26, I.R.B. 2009-38 (September 1, 2009)

In the situations described below, is Z's agreement with IC Y treated as "reinsuring risks" underwritten by insurance companies for purposes of determining whether Z is an insurance company within the meaning of § 831(c)?

FACTS

Situation 1. IC Y and Z are stock corporations that are licensed and regulated as insurance companies in all jurisdictions in which they do business. IC Y is an insurance company for federal income tax purposes, subject to tax under § 831(a).

For valid, non-tax business purposes, IC Y entered into a contract, or treaty, with Z at the beginning of Year 1. Under the contract, IC Y agreed to pay to Z 90 percent of all the premiums received with regard to all the insurance contracts issued by IC Y in the commercial multiple peril line of business in a 10-state region. In exchange, Z agreed to indemnify IC Y for 90 percent of all the losses under those contracts. IC Y remained directly liable to its policyholders. A contract of this type is sometimes referred to as indemnity reinsurance.

During Year 1, insurance contracts that IC Y entered into with 10,000 unrelated policyholders were subject to the contract between IC Y and Z. Z possessed adequate capital to fulfill its obligations under the contract, and in all respects operated at arms-length in its transaction with IC Y and in accordance with the applicable requirements of state law. The contract with IC Y was Z's only business during Year 1.

Situation 2. The facts are the same as in Situation 1, except that the contract between IC Y and Z covered only the risks of X, a policyholder of IC Y unrelated to Z. In addition, Z assumed risks of policyholders unrelated to X but in the same line of business through contracts with other insurance companies. The contracts with IC Y and with other insurance companies were Z's only business during Year 1. Had Z assumed these risks by entering into contracts with each of the original policyholders (including X) directly, those contracts would have qualified as insurance contracts for federal income tax purposes, and Z would have qualified as an insurance company for federal income tax purposes. See, e.g., Rev. Ruls. 2005-40, 2005-2 C.B. 4; 2002-91, 2002-2 C.B. 991; 2002-90, 2002-2 C.B. 985; and 2002-89, 2002-2 C.B. 984.

LAW

Section 831(a) of the Internal Revenue Code provides that taxes, computed as provided in § 11, are imposed for each taxable year on the taxable income of each insurance company other than a life insurance company. Section 831(c) provides that, for purposes of § 831, the term "insurance company" has the meaning given to such term by § 816(a). Under § 816(a), the term "insurance company" means "any company more than half the business of which during the taxable year is the issuing of insurance or annuity contracts or the reinsuring of risks underwritten by insurance companies."

Neither the Code nor the regulations define the terms "insurance" or "insurance contract." The Supreme Court of the United States has explained that in order for an arrangement to constitute insurance for federal income tax purposes, both risk shifting and risk distribution must be present. Helvering v. Le Gierse, 312 U.S. 531 (1941). The risk transferred must be risk of economic loss. Allied Fidelity Corp. v. Commissioner, 572 F.2d 1190, 1193 (7th Cir. 1978). The risk must contemplate the fortuitous occurrence of a stated contingency, Commissioner v. Treganowan, 183 F.2d 288, 290-91 (2d Cir. 1950), and must not be merely an investment or business risk. Rev. Rul. 2007-47, 2007-2 C.B. 127. In addition, the arrangement must constitute insurance in the commonly accepted sense. See, e.g., Ocean Drilling & Exploration Co. v. U.S., 988 F.2d 1135, 1153 (Fed. Cir. 1993); AMERCO, Inc. v. Commissioner, 979 F.2d 162 (9th Cir. 1992).

Risk shifting occurs if a person facing the possibility of an economic loss transfers some or all of the financial consequences of the potential loss to the insurer, such that a loss by the insured does not affect the insured because the loss is offset by a payment from the insurer. Risk distribution incorporates the statistical phenomenon known as the law of large numbers. Distributing risk allows the insurer to reduce the possibility that a single costly claim will exceed the amount taken in as premiums and set aside for the payment of such a claim. By assuming numerous relatively small, independent risks that occur randomly over time, the insurer smooths out losses to match more closely its receipt of premiums. Clougherty Packing Co. v. Commissioner, 811 F.2d 1297, 1300 (9th Cir. 1987).

Courts have recognized that risk distribution necessarily entails a pooling of premiums, so that a potential insured is not in significant part paying for its own risks. Humana, Inc. v. Commissioner, 881 F.2d 247, 257 (6th Cir. 1989). See also Ocean Drilling & Exploration Co., 988 F.2d at 1153 ("Risk distribution involves spreading the risk of loss among policyholders."); Beech Aircraft Corp. v. U.S., 797 F.2d 920, 922 (10th Cir. 1986) ("'[R]isk distributing means that the party assuming the risk distributes his potential liability, in part, among others.") Thus, purported insurance arrangements that involve an issuer who contracts with only one policyholder do not qualify as insurance contracts for federal income tax purposes. Rev. Rul. 2005-40.

The Code and administrative guidance treat reinsurance in a manner similar to insurance for many purposes. For example, gross premiums of both life and non-life insurance companies include not only premiums on direct business, but also gross premiums in respect of assumed liabilities under contracts issued by another company. Section 803(b)(1)(E); Rev. Rul. 77-453, 1977-2 C.B. 236. Consistently, both life insurance reserves under § 807 and discounted unpaid losses under § 846 include not only reserves and losses on direct business, but also reserves and losses on liabilities assumed under contracts issued by another company. Furthermore, a contract that reinsures another contract is treated in the same manner as the reinsured contract under § 848(e)(5) for purposes of computing the amount of specified policy acquisition expenses that must be capitalized and amortized as deferred acquisition costs (DAC) under § 848. Most importantly, both direct insurance and reinsurance business may qualify a taxpayer as an insurance company under § 816(a) or § 831(c), as applicable. But see § 845 (granting the Secretary explicit authority to reallocate, recharacterize, or make other adjustments with respect to certain reinsurance arrangements, but not referring to direct insurance).

Courts have generally analogized reinsurance to insurance, as well. For example, in Ocean Drilling & Exploration Co., 988 F.2d at 1153 n.25, the court noted that "[d]irect insurance and reinsurance are both considered insurance," and in Cologne Life Reinsurance Co. v. Commissioner, 80 T.C. 859, 862 (1983), acq, 1985-2 C.B. viii, the court noted that "[u]nder [part I of subchapter L], the issuance of indemnity life reinsurance is treated generally as the issuance of life insurance", except where specified otherwise.

In Alinco Life Insurance Co. v. United States, 373 F.2d 336 (Ct.Cl. 1967), a large finance company formed a wholly-owed subsidiary corporation (Alinco), which qualified as a life insurance company under the laws of Indiana. Customers of the finance company (borrowers) purchased credit life insurance from an unrelated insurance company, which in turn reinsured a fixed proportion of those contracts with Alinco. Even though

Alinco reinsured risks underwritten by only one insurance company, those risks aggregated nearly one billion dollars of business, with a large number of customers, for which Alinco was required by the state insurance department to maintain reserves. Interpreting regulatory language that was identical to what now appears in § 816(a), the court concluded that Alinco was in the business of "reinsuring risks" underwritten by insurance companies.

In the context of captive insurance, courts have likewise looked through a fronting arrangement to analyze whether the requirements of risk shifting and risk distribution were met. See, e.g., Carnation Co. v. Commissioner, 71 T.C. 400 (1978), aff'd, 640 F.2d 1010 (9th Cir. 1981) (concluding that premiums paid by taxpayer to an unrelated insurer were not deductible to the extent risks under the contract were in turn reinsured with taxpayer's wholly-owned subsidiary); Kidde Industries, Inc. v. United States, 40 Fed. Cl. 42 (1997).

ANALYSIS

Situation 1

In Situation 1, the contracts issued by IC Y to 10,000 unrelated policyholders involved commercial multiple peril risks, which are insurance risks. The contracts shifted those insurance risks from those policyholders to IC Y, and distributed those risks such that a loss by one policyholder was not borne, in substantial part, by the premiums paid by that policyholder. The contracts were insurance in the commonly accepted sense. The contracts thus were insurance contracts for federal income tax purposes.

The contract, or treaty, between IC Y and Z in turn shifted 90 percent of the risks under those insurance contracts from IC Y, an insurance company, to Z. As in Alinco Life, the transaction shifted insurance risks which were funded by reserves and constituted reinsurance in the commonly accepted sense. As to Z, the risks of each original policyholder were still distributed such that a loss by one such policyholder was not borne, in substantial part, by the premiums paid by that policyholder.

Hence, by entering into its arrangement with IC Y, Z was "reinsuring risks" within the meaning of §§ 816(a) and 831(c).

Because, under the arrangement with IC Y, Z was treated as "reinsuring risks" underwritten by an insurance company, and the arrangement represented more than half the business of Z for Year 1, Z qualified as an insurance company within the meaning of § 831(c), even though the contract with IC Y was Z's only business for the year.

Situation 2

In Situation 2, the facts are the same as in Situation 1, except that the arrangement between IC Y and Z shifted to Z only the risks of X, a policyholder of IC Y unrelated to Z. Z assumed additional risks of the same line under contracts with other insurance companies in the same line of business.

The risks assumed by Z under the arrangements with IC Y and with other insurance companies were insurance risks. Those risks were shifted from the original policyholders (including X) to the primary insurers (including IC Y), and in turn to Z. As to Z, the risks of each original policyholder (including X) were distributed such that a loss by one policyholder was not borne, in substantial part, by the premiums paid by that policyholder. Hence, by entering into its arrangements with the primary insurers (including IC Y), Z was "reinsuring risks" underwritten by insurance companies within the meaning of §§ 816(a) and 831(c).

Because under the arrangements with the primary insurers (including IC Y) Z is treated as "reinsuring risks" underwritten by insurance companies, and those arrangements represented more than half the business of Z for Year 1, Z qualified as an insurance company within the meaning of § 831(c).

HOLDINGS

In Situation 1, Z's agreement with IC Y is treated as "reinsuring risks" underwritten by an insurance company because, even though the agreement was Z's only business during Year 1, the requirement of risk distribution was still met from the standpoint of Z as to each original policyholder. Accordingly, Z was an insurance company within the meaning of § 831(c).

In Situation 2, Z's agreement with IC Y is treated as" reinsuring risks" underwritten by insurance companies because, even though the agreement covered only the risks of a single policyholder, Z assumed sufficient risks under agreements with other insurance companies in Year 1 such that requirement of risk distribution was met from the standpoint of Z as to each original policyholder. Accordingly, Z was an insurance company within the meaning of § 831(c).

REVENUE RULING 2014-15

Revenue Ruling 2014-15, I.R.B. 2014-22 (May 8, 2014)

ISSUE

Does the arrangement described below constitute insurance within the meaning of subchapter L of the Internal Revenue Code? If so, does the issuer qualify as an insurance company?

FACTS

X, a domestic corporation whose stock is widely held, provides health benefits within certain limits to a large group of named retired employees and their dependents, even though it is not legally obligated to do so, and may cancel the coverage at any time. X maintains a single-employer voluntary employees' beneficiary association that satisfies the requirements of §501(c)(9) (VEBA) and makes a contribution to the VEBA to provide the health benefits. X deducts the contribution in accordance with, and to the extent permitted by, §§419 and 419A of the Code. X has complied with, and will continue to comply with, all requirements of the Employment Retirement Income Security Act of 1974, as amended (ERISA).

In connection with the provision of health benefits to retirees and their dependents and as an alternative to providing the benefits on a self-insured basis, the VEBA enters into Contract A with an unrelated commercial insurance company, IC. IC's participation in the arrangement is a condition of an exemption from the Department of Labor from certain of the prohibited transaction provisions of ERISA.

IC is taxable as a life insurance company under §801 of the Code. Contract A provides noncancellable accident and health coverage. Under Contract A, IC will issue quarterly reimbursements to the VEBA for medical claims that are incurred by the covered retirees and their dependents and paid by the VEBA. Contract A is regulated by the relevant State insurance commissioner as an accident and health insurance contract. At the time that Contract A goes into effect, neither X nor the VEBA have any commitment or obligation to offer health benefits to the covered retirees and their dependents, and both X and the VEBA may cancel any provided coverage at any time.

In an effort to keep the premium payment under Contract A affordable, IC then enters into Contract B with X's wholly owned subsidiary, S1, under which S1 receives a premium and reinsures 100 percent of IC's liabilities under Contract A. Contract B constitutes S1's sole business. S1 is regulated as an insurance company under state law, and Contract B is regulated as insurance. The amount of premium under Contract B is determined at arm's length in accordance with applicable insurance industry standards. S1 possesses adequate capital to fulfill its obligations to IC under Contract B. There are no guarantees that the VEBA or X will reimburse S1 with respect to its obligations under Contract B, nor is any of the premium received by S1 for Contract B loaned back to the VEBA or X. In all respects, the parties conduct themselves consistent with the standards applicable to an insurance arrangement between unrelated parties, except that S1 does not reinsure any other insurance contracts.

LAW

Subchapter L of the Code sets forth the regime for taxing insurance companies. In particular, §801(a) provides that a life insurance company must pay tax on its life insurance company taxable income, which is defined in §801(b) to mean life insurance gross income less life insurance deductions. Section 816(a), in part, defines a life insurance company as an insurance company that has life insurance reserves and unearned premiums and unpaid losses on noncancellable life, accident, or health policies comprising more than 50 percent of total reserves. Under §816(a), the term "insurance company" means any company more than half of the business of which during the taxable year is the issuing of insurance or annuity contracts or the reinsuring of risks underwritten by insurance companies. Section 831(c) applies the same definition of "insurance company" to determine whether a taxpayer is an insurance company other than a life insurance company and therefore subject to tax under §831(a).

Neither the Code nor the regulations define the terms "insurance" or "insurance contract." The United States Supreme Court, however, has explained that for an arrangement to constitute insurance for federal income tax purposes, both risk shifting and risk distribution must be present. Helvering v. Le Gierse, 312 U.S. 531, 539 (1941).

The risk transferred must be risk of economic loss. Allied Fidelity Corp. v. Commissioner, 572 F.2d 1190, 1193 (7th Cir. 1978), cert. denied, 439 U.S. 835 (1978). The risk must contemplate the fortuitous occurrence of a stated contingency, Commissioner v. Treganowan, 183 F.2d 288, 290-91 (2d Cir. 1950), cert. denied, 340 U.S. 853 (1950), and must not be merely an investment or business risk. Le Gierse, 312 U.S. at 542; Rev. Rul. 89-96, 1989-2 C.B. 114.

Risk shifting occurs if a person facing the possibility of an economic loss transfers some or all of the financial consequences of the potential loss to the insurer, such that a loss by the insured does not affect the insured because the loss is offset by a payment from the insurer. Clougherty Packing Co. v. Commissioner, 811 F.2d 1297, 1300 (9th Cir. 1987). Risk distribution incorporates the statistical phenomenon known as the law of large numbers. Id. Distributing risk allows the insurer to reduce the possibility that a single costly claim will exceed the amount taken in as premiums and set aside for the payment of such a claim. Id.

By assuming numerous, relatively small, independent risks that occur randomly over time, the insurer smoothes out losses to match more closely its receipt of premiums. Id.

Courts have recognized that risk distribution necessarily entails a pooling of premiums, so that a potential insured is not in significant part paying for its own risks. Ocean Drilling & Exploration Co. v. United States, 988 F.2d 1135, 1153 (Fed. Cir. 1993) ("Risk distribution involves spreading the risk of loss among policyholders."); see also Beech Aircraft Corp. v. United States, 797 F.2d 920, 922 (10th Cir. 1986) ("[R]isk distributing' means that the party assuming the risk distributes his potential liability, in part, among others."); Crawford Fitting Co. v. United States, 606 F.Supp. 136, 147 (N.D. Ohio 1985) ("[T]he court finds…that various nonaffiliated persons or entities facing risks similar but independent of those faced by plaintiff were named insureds under the policy, enabling the distribution of risk thereunder."); AMERCO and Subsidiaries v. Commissioner, 96 T.C. 18, 41 (1991), aff'd, 979 F.2d 162 (9th Cir. 1992) ("The concept of risk-distributing emphasizes the pooling aspect of insurance: that it is the nature of an insurance contract to be part of a larger collection of coverages, combined to distribute risk between insureds."). Accordingly, Rev. Rul. 2005-40, 2005-2 C.B. 4, concludes that an arrangement under which an issuer contracts to indemnify the risks of a single policyholder does not qualify as insurance for federal income tax purposes because those risks are not, in turn, distributed among other insureds or policyholders. Similarly, Rev. Rul. 2002-89, 2002-C.B. 984, concludes that the requirements of risk shifting and risk distribution are not satisfied when a wholly owned subsidiary's agreement to indemnify the risks of its parent represents 90% of the subsidiary's business.

In Rev. Rul. 92-93, 1992-2 C.B. 45, modified by Rev. Rul. 2001-31, 2001-1 C.B. 1348, a parent corporation carried insurance on its employees' lives under a group-term life insurance contract purchased from its wholly owned insurance subsidiary. In concluding that the value of insurance was includible in the employees' gross income, the revenue ruling stated:

> Although [parent corporation] purchased the group-term life insurance contract covering its employees from its wholly owned insurance subsidiary, S1, this fact does not cause the arrangement to be "self-insurance" because the economic risk of loss being insured shifted to S1 is not a risk of [parent corporation]....This insurance on the employees' lives is an economic benefit to the employees since it relieves them of the expense of providing life insurance for themselves.

Revenue Ruling 92-93 states that "[t]he holdings of this revenue ruling also apply to accident and health insurance." See also Rev. Rul. 92-94, 1992-2 C.B. 144.

ANALYSIS

To determine the nature of an arrangement for federal income tax purposes, it is necessary to consider all the facts and circumstances of a particular case, including the risks being shifted and distributed. The proper characterization of an arrangement may determine whether the issuer qualifies as an insurance company for federal income tax purposes and whether amounts paid under such arrangement may be deductible.

In the situation above, the risks being indemnified are the covered retirees' and their dependents' risks of incurring medical expenses during retirement due to accident and health contingencies. Although the VEBA entered into Contract A, the covered retirees' health insurance is an economic benefit to the retirees since it relieves them of the expense of purchasing health insurance for themselves and their dependents. Furthermore, at the time that Contract A goes into effect, neither X nor the VEBA have any commitment or obligation to offer health benefits to the covered retirees and their dependants, and both X and the VEBA may cancel any provided coverage at any time.

Consequently, the risks that are shifted in the situation above are those of the covered retirees and their dependents and not risks of the VEBA or X. These risks are reinsured by S1 under Contract B. The risks under Contract B are distributed among this large group of covered individuals, and the analyses of Rev. Rul. 2002-89 and Rev. Rul. 2005-40 are inapplicable. Accordingly, the risks under Contract B are insurance risks, and Contract B constitutes insurance for federal income tax purposes.

HOLDING

In the situation above, S1 is regulated as an insurance company under state law. Contract B constitutes insurance. Because Contract B is more than half of the business done by S1 during this year, S1 qualifies as an insurance company under Subchapter L for this taxable year.

This revenue ruling does not address whether the health benefits are provided through a self-insured medical reimbursement plan for purposes of the nondiscrimination rules under §105(h) (see Treas. Reg. §1.105-11(b)(1)(iii)).

This ruling also does not address the deductibility of a contribution by X to the VEBA under §§419 and 419A; whether S1, or any account held by IC or S1, with respect to Contract A or Contract B is a welfare benefit fund (as defined in §419(e)); or the application of §419A(g). Furthermore, because the arrangement described in this revenue ruling provides welfare benefits through a VEBA, this ruling does not address certain issues that would arise if an employer provided welfare benefits other than through a VEBA, including whether an entity (or any account held by any person) that is part of such an arrangement is a welfare benefit fund or, if not, whether the arrangement is a plan deferring the receipt of compensation for purposes of §§404(a)(5) and 404(b).

EFFECT ON OTHER REVENUE RULINGS

Rev. Rul. 2002-89 and Rev. Rul. 2005-40 are distinguished.

PROPOSED TREASURY REGULATIONS § 301.7701-1(A)(5)

Proposed Treasury Regulations § 301.7701-1(a)(5)

Internal Revenue Service (September 14, 2010)

AGENCY: Internal Revenue Service (IRS), Treasury.

ACTION: Notice of proposed rulemaking.

SUMMARY: This document contains proposed regulations regarding the classification for Federal tax purposes of a series of a domestic series limited liability company (LLC), a cell of a domestic cell company, or a foreign series or cell that conducts an insurance business. The proposed regulations provide that, whether or not a series of a domestic series LLC, a cell of a domestic cell company, or a foreign series or cell that conducts an insurance business is a juridical person for local law purposes, for Federal tax purposes it is treated as an entity formed under local law. Classification of a series or cell that is treated as a separate entity for Federal tax purposes generally is determined under the same rules that govern the classification of other types of separate entities. The proposed regulations provide examples illustrating the application of the rule. The proposed regulations will affect domestic series LLCs; domestic cell companies; foreign series, or cells that conduct insurance businesses; and their owners.

DATES: Written or electronic comments and requests for a public hearing must be received by December 13, 2010.

ADDRESSES: Send submissions to: CC:PA:LPD:PR

(REG-119921-09), Room 5203, Internal Revenue Service, PO Box 7604, Ben Franklin Station, Washington, DC 20044. Submissions may be hand-delivered Monday through Friday between the hours of 8 a.m. and 4 p.m. to CC:PA:LPD:PR (REG-119921-09), Courier's Desk, Internal Revenue Service, 1111 Constitution Avenue, NW, Washington, DC, or sent electronically, via the Federal eRulemaking portal at www.regulations.gov (IRS REG-119921-09).

FOR FURTHER INFORMATION CONTACT: Concerning the proposed regulations, Joy Spies, (202) 622-3050; concerning submissions of comments, Oluwafunmilayo (Funmi) Taylor, (202) 622-7180 (not toll-free numbers).

SUPPLEMENTARY INFORMATION:

Background

1. Introduction

A number of states have enacted statutes providing for the creation of entities that may establish series, including limited liability companies (series LLCs). In general, series LLC statutes provide that a limited liability company may establish separate series. Although series of a series LLC generally are not treated as separate entities for state law purposes and, thus, cannot have members, each series has "associated" with it specified members, assets, rights, obligations, and investment objectives or business purposes. Members' association with one or more particular series is comparable to direct ownership by the members in such series, in that their rights, duties, and powers with respect to the series are direct and specifically identified. If the conditions enumerated in the relevant statute are satisfied, the debts, liabilities, and obligations of one series generally are enforceable only against the assets of that series and not against assets of other series or of the series LLC.

Certain jurisdictions have enacted statutes providing for entities similar to the series LLC. For example, certain statutes provide for the chartering of a legal entity (or the establishment of cells) under a structure commonly known as a protected cell company, segregated account company or segregated portfolio company (cell company). A cell company may establish multiple accounts, or cells, each of which has its own name and is identified with a specific participant, but generally is not treated under local law as a legal entity distinct from the cell company. The assets of each cell are statutorily protected from the creditors of any other cell and from the creditors of the cell company.

Under current law, there is little specific guidance regarding whether for Federal tax purposes a series (or cell) is treated as an entity separate from other series or the series LLC (or other cells or the cell company, as the case may be), or whether the company and all of its series (or cells) should be treated as a single entity.

Notice 2008-19 (2008-5 IRB 366) requested comments on proposed guidance concerning issues that arise if arrangements entered into by a cell constitute insurance for Federal income tax purposes. The notice also requested comments on the need for guidance concerning similar segregated arrangements that do not involve insurance. The IRS received a number of comments requesting guidance for similar arrangements not involving insurance, including series LLCs and cell companies. These comments generally recommended that series and cells should be treated as separate entities for Federal tax purposes if they are established under a statute with provisions similar to the series LLC statutes currently in effect in several states. The IRS and Treasury Department generally agree with these comments. See §601.601(d)(2)(ii)(b).

2. Entity Classification for Federal Tax Purposes

A. Regulatory framework

Sections 301.7701-1 through 301.7701-4 of the Procedure and Administration Regulations provide the framework for determining an organization's entity classification for Federal tax purposes. Classification of an organization depends on whether the organization is treated as: (i) a separate entity under §301.7701-1, (ii) a "business entity" within the meaning of

§301.7701-2(a) or a trust under §301.7701-4, and (iii) an "eligible entity" under §301.7701-3.

Section 301.7701-1(a)(1) provides that the determination of whether an entity is separate from its owners for Federal tax purposes is a matter of Federal tax law and does not depend on whether the organization is recognized as an entity under local law. Section 301.7701-1(a)(2) provides that a joint venture or other contractual arrangement may create a separate entity for Federal tax purposes if the participants carry on a trade, business, financial operation, or venture and divide the profits therefrom. However, a joint undertaking merely to share expenses does not create a separate entity for Federal tax purposes, nor does mere co-ownership of property where activities are limited to keeping property maintained, in repair, and rented or leased. Id.

Section 301.7701-1(b) provides that the tax classification of an organization recognized as a separate entity for tax purposes generally is determined under §§301.7701-2, 301.7701-3, and 301.7701-4. Thus, for example, an organization recognized as an entity that does not have associates or an objective to carry on a business may be classified as a trust under §301.7701-4.

Section 301.7701-2(a) provides that a business entity is any entity recognized for Federal tax purposes (including an entity with a single owner that may be disregarded as an entity separate from its owner under §301.7701-3) that is not properly classified as a trust or otherwise subject to special treatment under the Internal Revenue Code (Code). A business entity with two or more members is classified for Federal tax purposes as a corporation or a partnership. See §301.7701-2(a). A business entity with one owner is classified as a corporation or is disregarded. See §301.7701-2(a). If the entity is disregarded, its activities are treated in the same manner as a sole proprietorship, branch, or division of the owner. However, §301.7701-2(c)(2)(iv) and (v) provides for an otherwise disregarded entity to be treated as a corporation for certain Federal employment tax and excise tax purposes.

Section 301.7701-3(a) generally provides that an eligible entity, which is a business entity that is not a corporation under §301.7701-2(b), may elect its classification for Federal tax purposes.

B. Separate entity classification

The threshold question for determining the tax classification of a series of a series LLC or a cell of a cell company is whether an individual series or cell should be considered an entity for Federal tax purposes. The determination of whether an organization is an entity separate from its owners for Federal tax purposes is a matter of Federal tax law and does not depend on whether the organization is recognized as an entity under local law. Section 301.7701-1(a)(1). In Moline Properties, Inc. v. Commissioner, 319 U.S. 436 (1943), the Supreme Court noted that, so long as a corporation was formed for a purpose that is the equivalent of business activity or the corporation actually carries on a business, the corporation remains a taxable entity separate from its shareholders. Although entities that are recognized under local law generally are also recognized for Federal tax purposes, a state law entity may be disregarded if it lacks business purpose or any business activity other than tax avoidance. See Bertoli v. Commissioner, 103 T.C. 501 (1994); Aldon Homes, Inc. v. Commissioner, 33 T.C. 582 (1959).

The Supreme Court in Commissioner v. Culbertson, 337 U.S. 733 (1949), and Commissioner v. Tower, 327 U.S. 280 (1946), set forth the basic standard for determining whether a partnership will be respected for Federal tax purposes. In general, a partnership will be respected if, considering all the facts, the parties in good faith and acting with a business purpose intended to join together to conduct an enterprise and share in its profits and losses. This determination is made considering not only the stated intent of the parties, but also the terms of their agreement and their conduct. Madison Gas & Elec. Co. v. Commissioner, 633 F.2d 512, 514 (7th Cir. 1980); Luna v. Commissioner, 42 T.C. 1067, 1077-78 (1964).

Conversely, under certain circumstances, arrangements that are not recognized as entities under state law may be treated as separate entities for Federal tax purposes. Section 301.7701-1(a)(2). For example, courts have found entities for tax purposes in some co-ownership situations where the co-owners agree to restrict their ability to sell, lease or encumber their interests, waive their rights to partition property, or allow certain management decisions to be made other than by unanimous agreement among co-owners. Bergford v. Commissioner, 12 F.3d 166 (9th Cir. 1993); Bussing v. Commissioner, 89 T.C. 1050 (1987); Alhouse v. Commissioner, T.C. Memo. 1991-652. However, the Internal Revenue Service (IRS) has ruled that a co-ownership does not rise to the level of an entity for Federal tax purposes if the owner employs an agent whose activities are limited to collecting rents, paying property taxes, insurance premiums, repair and maintenance expenses, and providing tenants with customary services. Rev. Rul. 75-374 (1975-2 CB 261). See also Rev. Rul. 79-77 (1979-1 CB 448), (see §601.601(d)(2)(ii)(b)).

Rev. Proc. 2002-22 (2002-1 CB 733), (see §601.601(d)(2)(ii)(b)), specifies the conditions under which the IRS will consider a request for a private letter ruling that an undivided fractional interest in rental real property is not an interest in a business entity under §301.7701-2(a). A number of factors must be present to obtain a ruling under the revenue procedure, including a limit on the number of co-owners, a requirement that the co-owners not treat the co-ownership as an entity (that is, that the co-ownership may not file a partnership or corporate tax return, conduct business under a common name, execute an agreement identifying any or all of the co-owners as partners, shareholders, or members of a business entity, or otherwise hold itself out as a partnership or other form of business entity), and a requirement that certain rights with respect to the property (including the power to make certain management decisions) must be retained by co-owners. The revenue procedure provides that an organization that is an entity for state law purposes may not be characterized as a co-ownership under the guidance in the revenue procedure.

The courts and the IRS have addressed the Federal tax classification of investment trusts with assets divided among a number of series. In National Securities Series-Industrial Stocks Series v. Commissioner, 13 T.C. 884 (1949), acq., 1950-1 CB 4, several series that differed only in the nature of their assets were created within a statutory open-end investment trust. Each series regularly issued certificates representing shares in the property held in trust and regularly redeemed the certificates solely from the assets and earnings of the individual series. The Tax Court stated that each series of the trust was taxable as a separate regulated investment company. See also Rev. Rul. 55-416 (1955-1 CB 416), (see §601.601(d)(2)(ii)(b)). But see Union Trusteed Funds v. Commissioner, 8 T.C. 1133 (1947), (series funds organized by a state law corporation could not be treated as if each fund were a separate corporation).

In 1986, Congress added section 851(g) to the Code. Section 851(g) contains a special rule for series funds and provides that, in the case of a regulated investment company (within the meaning of section 851(a)) with more than one fund, each fund generally is treated as a separate corporation. For these purposes, a fund is a segregated portfolio of assets the beneficial interests in which are owned by holders of interests in the regulated investment company that are preferred over other classes or series with respect to these assets.

C. Insurance company classification

Section 7701(a)(3) and §301.7701-2(b)(4) provide that an arrangement that qualifies as an insurance company is a corporation for Federal income tax purposes. Sections 816(a) and 831(c) define an insurance company as any company more than half the business of which during the taxable year is the issuing of insurance or annuity contracts or the reinsuring of risks underwritten by insurance companies. See also

§1.801-3(a)(1), ("[T]hough its name, charter powers, and subjection to State insurance laws are significant in determining the business which a company is authorized and intends to carry on, it is the character of the business actually done in the taxable year which determines whether a company is taxable as an insurance company under the Internal Revenue Code."). Thus, an insurance company includes an arrangement that conducts insurance business, whether or not the arrangement is a state law entity.

3. Overview of Series LLC Statutes and Cell Company Statutes

A. Domestic statutes

Although §301.7701-1(a)(1) provides that state classification of an entity is not controlling for Federal tax purposes, the characteristics of series LLCs and cell companies under their governing statutes are an important factor in analyzing whether series and cells generally should be treated as separate entities for Federal tax purposes.

Series LLC statutes have been enacted in Delaware, Illinois, Iowa, Nevada, Oklahoma, Tennessee, Texas, Utah and Puerto Rico. Delaware enacted the first series LLC statute in 1996. Del. Code Ann. Tit. 6, section 18-215 (the Delaware statute). Statutes enacted subsequently by other states are similar, but not identical, to the Delaware statute. All of the statutes provide a significant degree of separateness for individual series within a series LLC, but none provides series with all of the attributes of a typical state law entity, such as an ordinary limited liability company. Individual series generally are not treated as separate entities for state law purposes. However, in certain states (currently Illinois and Iowa), a series is treated as a separate entity to the extent provided in the series LLC's articles of organization.

The Delaware statute provides that a limited liability company may establish, or provide for the establishment of, one or more designated series of members, managers, LLC interests or assets. Under the Delaware statute, any such series may have separate rights, powers, or duties with respect to specified property or obligations of the LLC or profits and losses associated with specified property or obligations, and any such series may have a separate business purpose or investment objective. Additionally, the Delaware statute provides that the debts, liabilities, obligations, and expenses of a particular series are enforceable against the assets of that series only, and not against the assets of the series LLC generally or any other series of the LLC, and, unless the LLC agreement provides otherwise, none of the debts, liabilities, obligations, and expenses of the series LLC generally or of any other series of the series LLC are enforceable against the assets of the series, provided that the following requirements are met: (1) the LLC agreement establishes or provides for the establishment of one or more series; (2) records maintained for any such series account for the assets of the series separately from the other assets of the series LLC, or of any other series of the series LLC; (3) the LLC agreement so provides; and (4) notice of the limitation on liabilities of a series is set forth in the series LLC's certificate of formation.

Unless otherwise provided in the LLC agreement, a series established under Delaware law has the power and capacity to, in its own name, contract, hold title to assets, grant liens and security interests, and sue and be sued. A series may be managed by the members of the series or by a manager. Any event that causes a manager to cease to be a manager with respect to a series will not, in itself, cause the manager to cease to be a manager of the LLC or of any other series of the LLC.

Under the Delaware statute, unless the LLC agreement provides otherwise, any event that causes a member to cease to be associated with a series will not, in itself, cause the member to cease to be associated with any other series or with the LLC, or cause termination of the series, even if there are no remaining members of the series. Additionally, the Delaware statute allows a series to be terminated and its affairs wound up without causing the dissolution of the LLC. However, all series of the

LLC terminate when the LLC dissolves. Finally, under the Delaware statute, a series generally may not make a distribution to the extent that the distribution will cause the liabilities of the series to exceed the fair market value of the series' assets.

The series LLC statutes of Illinois, 805 ILCS 180/37-40 (the Illinois statute), and Iowa, I.C.A. §489.1201 (the Iowa statute) provide that a series with limited liability will be treated as a separate entity to the extent set forth in the articles of organization. The Illinois statute provides that the LLC and any of its series may elect to consolidate their operations as a single taxpayer to the extent permitted under applicable law, elect to work cooperatively, elect to contract jointly, or elect to be treated as a single business for purposes of qualification to do business in Illinois or any other state.

In addition, under the Illinois statute, a series' existence begins upon filing of a certificate of designation with the Illinois secretary of state. A certificate of designation must be filed for each series that is to have limited liability. The name of a series with limited liability must contain the entire name of the LLC and be distinguishable from the names of the other series of the LLC. If different from the LLC, the certificate of designation for each series must list the names of the members if the series is member-managed or the names of the managers if the series is manager-managed. The Iowa and Illinois statutes both provide that, unless modified by the series LLC provisions, the provisions generally applicable to LLCs and their managers, members, and transferees are applicable to each series.

Some states have enacted series provisions outside of LLC statutes. For example, Delaware has enacted series limited partnership provisions (6 Del. C. §17-218). In addition, Delaware's statutory trust statute permits a statutory trust to establish series (12 Del. C. §3804). Both of these statutes contain provisions that are nearly identical to the corresponding provisions of the Delaware series LLC statute with respect to the ability of the limited partnership or trust to create or establish separate series with the same liability protection enjoyed by series of a Delaware series LLC.

All of the series LLC statutes contain provisions that grant series certain attributes of separate entities. For example, individual series may have separate business purposes, investment objectives, members, and managers. Assets of a particular series are not subject to the claims of creditors of other series of the series LLC or of the series LLC itself, provided that certain record-keeping and notice requirements are observed. Finally, most series LLC statutes provide that an event that causes a member to cease to be associated with a series does not cause the member to cease to be associated with the series LLC or any other series of the series LLC.

However, all of the state statutes limit the powers of series of series LLCs. For example, a series of a series LLC may not convert into another type of entity, merge with another entity, or domesticate in another state independent from the series LLC. Several of the series LLC statutes do not expressly address a series' ability to sue or be sued, hold title to property, or contract in its own name. Ordinary LLCs and series LLCs generally may exercise these rights. Additionally, most of the series LLC statutes provide that the dissolution of a series LLC will cause the termination of each of its series.

B. Statutes with respect to insurance

The insurance codes of a number of states include statutes that provide for the chartering of a legal entity commonly known as a protected cell company, segregated account company, or segregated portfolio company. See, for example, Vt. Stat. Ann. tit. 8, chap.141, §§ 6031-6038 (sponsored captive insurance companies and protected cells of such companies); S.C. Code Ann. tit. 38, chap. 10, §§ 38-10-10 through 39-10-80 (protected cell insurance companies). Under those statutes, as under the series LLC statutes described above, the assets of each cell are segregated from the assets of any other cell. The cell may issue insurance or annuity contracts, reinsure such contracts, or facilitate the securitization of obligations of a sponsoring insurance company. Rev. Rul. 2008-8 (2008-1 CB 340), (see §601.601(d)(2)(ii)(b)), analyzes whether an arrangement entered into between a protected cell and its owner possesses the requisite risk shifting and risk distribution to qualify as insurance for Federal income tax purposes. Under certain domestic insurance codes, the sponsor may be organized under a corporate or unincorporated entity statute.

Series or cell company statutes in a number of foreign jurisdictions allow series or cells to engage in insurance businesses. See, for example, The Companies (Guernsey) Law, 2008 Part XXVII (Protected Cell Companies), Part XXVIII (Incorporated Cell Companies); The Companies (Jersey) law, 1991, Part 18D; Companies Law, Part XIV (2009 Revision) (Cayman Isl.) (Segregated Portfolio Companies); and Segregated Accounts Companies Act (2000) (Bermuda).

Explanation of Provisions

1. In General

The proposed regulations provide that, for Federal tax purposes, a domestic series, whether or not a juridical person for local law purposes, is treated as an entity formed under local law.

With one exception, the proposed regulations do not apply to series or cells organized or established under the laws of a foreign jurisdiction. The one exception is that the proposed regulations apply to a foreign series that engages in an insurance business.

Whether a series that is treated as a local law entity under the proposed regulations is recognized as a separate entity for Federal tax purposes is determined under §301.7701-1 and general tax principles. The proposed regulations further provide that the classification of a series that is recognized as a separate entity for Federal tax purposes is determined under §301.7701-1(b), which provides the rules for classifying organizations that are recognized as entities for Federal tax purposes.

The proposed regulations define a series organization as a juridical entity that establishes and maintains, or under which is established and maintained, a series. A series organization includes a series limited liability company, series partnership, series trust, protected cell company, segregated cell company, segregated portfolio company, or segregated account company.

The proposed regulations define a series statute as a statute of a State or foreign jurisdiction that explicitly provides for the organization or establishment of a series of a juridical person and explicitly permits (1) members or participants of a series organization to have rights, powers, or duties with respect to the series; (2) a series to have separate rights, powers, or duties with respect to specified property or obligations; and (3) the segregation of assets and liabilities such that none of the debts and liabilities of the series organization (other than liabilities to the State or foreign jurisdiction related to the organization or operation of the series organization, such as franchise fees or administrative costs) or of any other series of the series organization are enforceable against the assets of a particular series of the series organization. For purposes of this definition, a "participant" of a series organization includes an officer or director of the series organization who has no ownership interest in the series or series organization, but has rights, powers, or duties with respect to the series.

The proposed regulations define a series as a segregated group of assets and liabilities that is established pursuant to a series statute by agreement of a series organization. A series includes a cell, segregated account, or segregated portfolio, including a cell, segregated account, or segregated portfolio that is formed under the insurance code of a jurisdiction or is engaged in an insurance business. However, the term "series" does not include a segregated asset account of a life insurance company, which consists of all assets the investment return and market value of which must be allocated in an identical manner to any variable life insurance or annuity contract invested in any of the assets.

See §1.817-5(e). Such an account is accorded special treatment under subchapter L. See generally section 817(a) through (c).

Certain series statutes provide that the series liability limitation provisions do not apply if the series organization or series does not maintain records adequately accounting for the assets associated with each series separately from the assets of the series organization or any other series of the series organization. The IRS and the Treasury Department considered whether a failure to elect or qualify for the liability limitations under the series statute should affect whether a series is a separate entity for Federal tax purposes. However, limitations on liability of owners of an entity for debts and obligations of the entity and the rights of creditors to hold owners liable for debts and obligations of the entity generally do not alter the characterization of the entity for Federal tax purposes. Therefore, the proposed regulations provide that an election, agreement, or other arrangement that permits debts and liabilities of other series or the series organization to be enforceable against the assets of a particular series, or a failure to comply with the record keeping requirements for the limitation on liability available under the relevant series statute, will not prevent a series from meeting the definition of "series" in the proposed regulations. For example, a series generally will not cease to be an entity under the proposed regulations simply because it guarantees the debt of another series within the series organization.

The proposed regulations treat a series as created or organized under the laws of the same jurisdiction in which the series is established. Because a series may not be a separate juridical entity for local law purposes, this rule provides the means for establishing the jurisdiction of the series for Federal tax purposes.

Under §301.7701-1(b), §301.7701-2(b) applies to a series that is recognized as a separate entity for Federal tax purposes. Therefore, a series that is itself described in §301.7701-2(b)(1) through (8) would be classified as a corporation regardless of the classification of the series organization.

The proposed regulations also provide that, for Federal tax purposes, ownership of interests in a series and of the assets associated with a series is determined under general tax principles. A series organization is not treated as the owner of a series or of the assets associated with a series merely because the series organization holds legal title to the assets associated with the series. For example, if a series organization holds legal title to assets associated with a series because the statute under which the series organization was organized does not expressly permit a series to hold assets in its own name, the series will be treated as the owner of the assets for Federal tax purposes if it bears the economic benefits and burdens of the assets under general Federal tax principles. Similarly, for Federal tax purposes, the obligor for the liability of a series is determined under general tax principles.

In general, the same legal principles that apply to determine who owns interests in other types of entities apply to determine the ownership of interests in series and series organizations. These principles generally look to who bears the economic benefits and burdens of ownership. See, for example, Rev. Rul. 55-39 (1955-1 CB 403), (see §601.601(d)(2)(ii)(b)). Furthermore, common law principles apply to the determination of whether a person is a partner in a series that is classified as a partnership for Federal tax purposes under §301.7701-3. See, for example, Commissioner v. Culbertson, 337 U.S. 733 (1949); Commissioner v. Tower, 327 U.S. 280 (1946).

The IRS and the Treasury Department considered other approaches to the classification of series for Federal tax purposes. In particular, the IRS and the Treasury Department considered whether series should be disregarded as entities separate from the series organization for Federal tax purposes. This approach would be supported by the fact that series are not generally considered entities for local law purposes (except, for example, potentially under the statutes of Illinois and Iowa, where a series may be treated as a separate entity to the extent set forth in the articles of organization). Additionally, while the statutes enabling series organizations grant series significant autonomy, under no current statute do series possess all of the attributes of independence that entities recognized under local law generally possess. For example, series generally cannot convert into another type of entity, merge with another entity, or domesticate in another jurisdiction independent of the series organization. In addition, the dissolution of a series organization generally will terminate all of its series.

The IRS and the Treasury Department believe that, notwithstanding that series differ in some respects from more traditional local law entities, domestic series generally should be treated for Federal tax purposes as entities formed under local law. Because Federal tax law, and not local law, governs the question of whether an organization is an entity for Federal tax purposes, it is not dispositive that domestic series generally are not considered entities for local law purposes. Additionally, the IRS and the Treasury Department believe that, overall, the factors supporting separate entity status for series outweigh the factors in favor of disregarding series as entities separate from the series organization and other series of the series organization. Specifically, managers and equity holders are "associated with" a series, and their rights, duties, and powers with respect to the series are direct and specifically identified. Also, individual series may (but generally are not required to) have separate business purposes and investment objectives. The IRS and the Treasury Department believe these factors are sufficient to treat domestic series as entities formed under local law.

Although some statutes creating series organizations permit an individual series to enter into contracts, sue, be sued, and/ or hold property in its own name, the IRS and the Treasury Department do not believe that the failure of a statute to explicitly provide these rights should alter the treatment of a domestic series as an entity formed under local law. These attributes primarily involve procedural formalities and do not appear to affect the substantive economic rights of series or their creditors with respect to their property and liabilities. Even in jurisdictions where series may not possess these attributes, the statutory liability shields would still apply to the assets of a particular series, provided the statutory requirements are satisfied.

Furthermore, the rule provided in the proposed regulations would provide greater certainty to both taxpayers and the IRS regarding the tax status of domestic series and foreign series that conduct insurance businesses. In effect, taxpayers that establish domestic series are placed in the same position as persons that file a certificate of organization for a state law entity. The IRS and the Treasury Department believe that the approach of the proposed regulations is straightforward and administrable, and is preferable to engaging in a case by case determination of the status of each series that would require a detailed examination of the terms of the relevant statute. Finally, the IRS and the Treasury Department believe that a rule generally treating domestic series as local law entities would be consistent with taxpayers' current ability to create similar structures using multiple local law entities that can elect their Federal tax classification pursuant to §301.7701-3.

The IRS and the Treasury Department believe that domestic series should be classified as separate local law entities based on the characteristics granted to them under the various series statutes. However, except as specifically stated in the proposed regulations, a particular series need not actually possess all of the attributes that its enabling statute permits it to possess. The IRS and the Treasury Department believe that a domestic series should be treated as a separate local law entity even if its business purpose, investment objective, or ownership overlaps with that of other series or the series organization itself. Separate state law entities may have common or overlapping business purposes, investment objectives and ownership, but generally are still treated as separate local law entities for Federal tax purposes.

The proposed regulations do not address the entity status for Federal tax purposes of a series organization. Specifically, the proposed regulations do not address whether a series organization is recognized as a separate entity for Federal tax purposes if it has no assets and engages in no activities independent of its series.

Until further guidance is issued, the entity status of a foreign series that does not conduct an insurance business will be determined under applicable law. Foreign series raise novel Federal income tax issues that continue to be considered and addressed by the IRS and the Treasury Department.

2. Classification of a Series that is Treated as a Separate Entity for Federal Tax Purposes

If a domestic series or a foreign series engaged in an insurance business is treated as a separate entity for Federal tax purposes, then §301.7701-1(b) applies to determine the proper tax classification of the series. However, the proposed regulations do not provide how a series should be treated for Federal employment tax purposes. If a domestic series is treated as a separate entity for Federal tax purposes, then the series generally is subject to the same treatment as any other entity for Federal tax purposes. For example, a series that is treated as a separate entity for Federal tax purposes may make any Federal tax elections it is otherwise eligible to make independently of other series or the series organization itself, and regardless of whether other series (or the series organization) do not make certain elections or make different elections.

3. Entity Status of Series Organizations

The proposed regulations do not address the entity status or filing requirements of series organizations for Federal tax purposes. A series organization generally is an entity for local law purposes. An organization that is an entity for local law purposes generally is treated as an entity for Federal tax purposes. However, an organization characterized as an entity for Federal income tax purposes may not have an income or information tax filing obligation. For example, §301.6031(a)-(1)(a)(3)(i) provides that a partnership with no income, deductions, or credits for Federal income tax purposes for a taxable year is not required to file a partnership return for that year. Generally, filing fees of a series organization paid by series of the series organization would be treated as expenses of the series and not as expenses of the series organization. Thus, a series organization characterized as a partnership for Federal tax purposes that does not have income, deductions, or credits for a taxable year need not file a partnership return for the year.

4. Continuing Applicability of Tax Law Authority to Series

Notwithstanding that a domestic series or a foreign series engaged in an insurance business is treated as an entity formed under local law under the proposed regulations, the Commissioner may under applicable law, including common law tax principles, characterize a series or a portion of a series other than as a separate entity for Federal tax purposes. Series covered by the proposed regulations are subject to applicable law to the same extent as other entities. Thus, a series may be disregarded under applicable law even if it satisfies the requirements of the proposed regulations to be treated as an entity formed under local law. For example, if a series has no business purpose or business activity other than tax avoidance, it may be disregarded under appropriate circumstances. See Bertoli v. Commissioner, 103 T.C. 501 (1994); Aldon Homes, Inc. v. Commissioner, 33 T.C. 582 (1959). Furthermore, the anti-abuse rule of §1.701-2 is applicable to a series or series organization that is classified as a partnership for Federal tax purposes.

5. Applicability to Organizations that Qualify as Insurance Companies

Notice 2008-19 requested comments on proposed guidance setting forth conditions under which a cell of a protected cell company would be treated as an insurance company separate from any other entity for Federal income tax purposes. Those who commented on the notice generally supported the proposed guidance, and further commented that it should extend to non-insurance arrangements as well, including series LLCs. Rather than provide independent guidance for insurance company status setting forth what is essentially the same standard, the proposed regulations define the term series to include a cell, segregated account, or segregated portfolio that is formed under the insurance code of a jurisdiction or is engaged in an insurance business (other than a segregated asset account of a life insurance company).

Although the proposed regulations do not apply to a series organized or established under the laws of a foreign jurisdiction, an exception is provided for certain series conducting an insurance business. Under this exception, a series that is organized or established under the laws of a foreign jurisdiction is treated as an entity if the arrangements and other activities of the series, if conducted by a domestic company, would result in its being classified as an insurance company. Thus, a foreign series would be treated as an entity if more than half of the series' business is the issuing or reinsuring of insurance or annuity contracts. The IRS and the Treasury Department believe it is appropriate to provide this rule even though the proposed regulations otherwise do not apply to a foreign series because an insurance company is classified as a per se corporation under section 7701(a)(3) regardless of how it otherwise would be treated under §§301.7701-1, 301.7701-2, or 301.7701-3.

The IRS and the Treasury Department are aware that insurance-specific guidance may still be needed to address the issues identified in §3.02 of Notice 2008-19 and insurance-specific transition issues that may arise for protected cell companies that previously reported in a manner inconsistent with the regulations. See §601.601(d)(2)(ii)(b).

6. Effect of Local Law Classification on Tax Collection

The IRS and Treasury Department understand that there are differences in local law governing series (for example, rights to hold title to property and to sue and be sued are expressly addressed in some statutes but not in others) that may affect how creditors of series, including state taxing authorities, may enforce obligations of a series. Thus, the proposed regulations provide that, to the extent Federal or local law permits a creditor to collect a liability attributable to a series from the series organization or other series of the series organization, the series organization and other series of the series organization may also be considered the taxpayer from whom the tax assessed against the series may be collected pursuant to administrative or judicial means. Further, when a creditor is permitted to collect a liability attributable to a series organization from any series of the series organization, a tax liability assessed against the series organization may be collected directly from a series of the series organization by administrative or judicial means.

7. Employment Tax and Employee Benefits Issues

A. In general

The domestic statutes authorizing the creation of series contemplate that a series may operate a business. If the operating business has workers, it will be necessary to determine how the business satisfies any employment tax obligations, whether it has the ability to maintain any employee benefit plans and, if so, whether it complies with the rules applicable to those plans. Application of the employment tax requirements will depend principally on whether the workers are employees, and, if so, who is considered the employer for Federal income and employment tax purposes. In general, an employment relationship exists when the person for whom services are performed has the right to control and direct the individual who performs the services, not only as to the result to be accomplished by the work but also as to the details and means by which that result is accomplished. See §§31.3121(d)-1(c)(2), 31.3306(i)-1(b), and 31.3401(c)-1(b).

B. Employment tax

An entity must be a person in order to be an employer for Federal employment tax purposes. See sections 3121(b), 3306(a)(1), 3306(c), and 3401(d) and §31.3121(d)-2(a). However, status as a person, by itself, is not enough to make an entity an employer for Federal employment tax purposes. The entity must also satisfy the criteria to be an employer under Federal employment tax statutes and regulations for purposes of the determination of the proper amount of employment taxes and the party liable for reporting and paying the taxes. Treatment of a series as a separate person for Federal employment tax purposes would create the possibility that the series could be an "employer" for Federal employment tax purposes, which would raise both substantive and administrative issues.

The series structure would make it difficult to determine whether the series or the series organization is the employer under the relevant criteria with respect to the services provided. For example, if workers perform all of their services under the direction and control of individuals who own the interests in a series, but the series has no legal authority to enter into contracts or to sue or be sued, could the series nonetheless be the employer of the workers? If workers perform services under the direction and control of the series, but they are paid by the series organization, would the series organization, as the nominal owner of all the series assets, have control over the payment of wages such that it would be liable as the employer under section 3401(d)?

The structure of a series organization could also affect the type of employment tax liability. For example, if a series were recognized as a distinct person for Federal employment tax purposes, a worker providing services as an employee of one series and as a member of another series or the series organization would be subject to FICA tax on the wages paid for services as an employee and self-employment tax on the member income. Note further that, if a domestic series were classified as a separate entity that is a business entity, then, under §301.7701-3, the series would be classified as either a partnership or a corporation. While a business entity with one owner is generally classified as a corporation or is disregarded for Federal tax purposes, such an entity cannot be disregarded for Federal employment tax purposes. See §301.7701-2(c)(2)(iv).

Once the employer is identified, additional issues arise, including but not limited to the following: How would the wage base be determined for employees, particularly if they work for more than one series in a common line of business? How would the common paymaster rules apply? Who would be authorized to designate an agent under section 3504 for reporting and payment of employment taxes, and how would the authorization be accomplished? How would the statutory exceptions from the definitions of employment and wages apply given that they may be based on the identity of the employer? Which entity would be eligible for tax credits that go to the employer such as the Work Opportunity Tax Credit under section 51 or the tip credit under section 45B? If a series organization handles payroll for a series and is also the nominal owner of the series assets, would the owners or the managers of the series organization be responsible persons for the Trust Fund Recovery Penalty under section 6672?

Special administrative issues might arise if the series were to be treated as the employer for Federal employment tax purposes but not for state law purposes. For example, if the series were the employer for Federal employment tax purposes and filed a Form W-2, "Wage and Tax Statement," reporting wages and employment taxes withheld, but the series were not recognized as a juridical person for state law purposes, then administrative problems might ensue unless separate Forms W-2 were prepared for state and local tax purposes. Similarly, the IRS and the states might encounter challenges in awarding the FUTA credit under section 3302 to the appropriate entity and certifying the amount of state unemployment tax paid.

In light of these issues, the proposed regulations do not currently provide how a series should be treated for Federal employment tax purposes.

C. Employee benefits

Various issues arise with respect to the ability of a series to maintain an employee benefit plan, including issues related to those described above with respect to whether a series may be an employer. The proposed regulations do not address these issues. However, to the extent that a series can maintain an employee benefit plan, the aggregation rules under section 414(b), (c), (m), (o) and (t), as well as the leased employee rules under section 414(n), would apply. In this connection, the IRS and Treasury Department expect to issue regulations under section 414(o) that would prevent the avoidance of any employee benefit plan requirement through the use of the separate entity status of a series.

8. Statement Containing Identifying Information about Series

As the series organization or a series of the series organization may be treated as a separate entity for Federal tax and related reporting purposes but may not be a separate entity under local law, the IRS and Treasury Department believe that a new statement may need to be created and required to be filed annually by the series organization and each series of the series organization to provide the IRS with certain identifying information to ensure the proper assessment and collection of tax. Accordingly, these regulations propose to amend the Procedure and Administration Regulations under section 6011 to include this requirement and a cross-reference to those regulations is included under §301.7701-1. The IRS and Treasury Department are considering what information should be required by these statements. Information tentatively being considered includes (1) the name, address, and taxpayer identification number of the series organization and each of its series and status of each as a series of a series organization or as the series organization; (2) the jurisdiction in which the series organization was formed; and (3) an indication of whether the series holds title to its assets or whether title is held by another series or the series organization and, if held by another series or the series organization, the name, address, and taxpayer identification number of the series organization and each series holding title to any of its assets. The IRS and Treasury Department are also considering the best time to require taxpayers to file the statement. For example, the IRS and Treasury Department are considering whether the statement should be filed when returns, such as income tax returns and excise tax returns, are required to be filed or whether it should be a stand-alone statement filed separately by a set date each year, as with information returns such as Forms 1099. A cross-reference to these regulations was added to the Procedure and Administration regulations under section 6071 for the time to file returns and statements. The proposed regulations under section 6071 provide that the statement will be a stand-alone statement due March 15th of each year. In addition, the IRS and Treasury Department are considering revising Form SS-4, "Application for Employer Identification Number," to include questions regarding series organizations.

Proposed Effective Date

These regulations generally apply on the date final regulations are published in the Federal Register. Generally, when final regulations become effective, taxpayers that are treating series differently for Federal tax purposes than series are treated under the final regulations will be required to change their treatment of series. In this situation, a series organization that previously was treated as one entity with all of its series may be required to begin treating each series as a separate entity for Federal tax purposes. General tax principles will apply to determine the consequences of the conversion from one entity to multiple entities for Federal tax purposes. See, for example, section 708 for rules relating to partnership divisions in the case of a series organization previously treated as a partnership for Federal tax purposes converting into multiple partnerships upon recognition of the series organization's series as separate entities. While a division of a partnership may be tax-free, gain may be recognized in certain situations under section 704(c)(1)(B) or section 737. Sections 355 and 368(a)(1)(D) provide rules that govern certain divisions of a corporation. The division of a series organization into multiple corporations may be tax-free to the corporation and to its shareholders; however, if the corporate division does not satisfy one or more of the requirements in section 355, the division may result in taxable events to the corporation, its shareholders, or both.

The regulations include an exception for series established prior to publication of the proposed regulations that treat all series and the series organization as one entity. If the requirements for this exception are satisfied, after issuance of the final regulations the series may continue to be treated together with the series organization as one entity for Federal tax purposes. Specifically, these requirements are satisfied if (1) The series was established prior to September 14, 2010; (2) The series (independent of the series organization or other series of the series organization) conducted business or investment activity or, in the case of a foreign series, more than half the business of the series was the issuing of insurance or annuity contracts or the reinsuring of risks underwritten by insurance companies, on and prior to September 14, 2010; (3) If the series was established pursuant to a foreign statute, the series' classification was relevant (as defined in §301.7701-3(d)), and more than half the business of the series was the issuing of insurance or annuity contracts or the reinsuring of risks underwritten by insurance companies for all taxable years beginning with the taxable year that includes September 14, 2010; (4) No owner of the series treats the series as an entity separate from any other series of the series organization or from the series organization for purposes of filing any Federal income tax returns, information returns, or withholding documents for any taxable year; (5) The series and series organization had a reasonable basis (within the meaning of section 6662) for their claimed classification; and (6) Neither the series nor any owner of the series nor the series organization was notified in writing on or before the date final regulations are published in the Federal Register that classification of the series was under examination (in which case the series' classification will be determined in the examination).

This exception will cease to apply on the date any person or persons who were not owners of the series organization (or series) prior to September 14, 2010 own, in the aggregate, a 50 percent or greater interest in the series organization (or series). For this purpose, the term interest means (i) in the case of a partnership, a capital or profits interest and (ii) in the case of a corporation, an equity interest measured by vote or value. This transition rule does not apply to any determination other than the entity status of a series, for example, tax ownership of a series or series organization or qualification of a series or series organization conducting an insurance business as a controlled foreign corporation.

Special Analyses

It has been determined that this notice of proposed rulemaking is not a significant regulatory action as defined in Executive Order 12866. Therefore, a regulatory assessment is not required. It also has been determined that section 553(b) of the Administrative Procedure Act (5 U.S.C. chapter 5) does not apply to these regulations.

Pursuant to the Regulatory Flexibility Act (5.U.S.C. chapter 6), it is hereby certified that the regulations will not have a significant economic impact on a substantial number of small entities. The regulations require that series and series organizations file a statement to provide the IRS with certain identifying information to ensure the proper assessment and collection of tax. The regulations affect domestic series LLCs, domestic cell companies, and foreign series and cells that conduct insurance businesses, and their owners. Based on information available at this time, the IRS and the Treasury Department believe that many series and series organizations are large insurance companies or investment firms and, thus, are not small entities. Although a number of small entities may be subject to the information reporting requirement of the new statement, any economic impact will be minimal. The information that the IRS and the Treasury Department are considering requiring on the proposed statement should be known by or readily available to the series or the series organization. Therefore, it should take minimal time and expense to collect and report this information. For example, the IRS and the Treasury Department are considering requiring the following information: (1) The name, address, and taxpayer identification number of the series organization and each of its series and status of each as a series of a series organization or as the series organization; (2) The jurisdiction in which the series organization was formed; and (3) An indication of whether the series holds title to its assets or whether title is held by another series or the series organization and, if held by another series or the series organization, the name, address, and taxpayer identification number of the series organization and each series holding title to any of its assets. The IRS and the Treasury Department request comments on the accuracy of the statement that the regulations in this document will not have a significant economic impact on a substantial number of small entities. Pursuant to section 7805(f) of the Code, this notice of proposed rulemaking has been submitted to the Chief Counsel for Advocacy of the Small Business Administration for comment on its impact on small businesses.

Comments and Requests for a Public Hearing

Before these proposed regulations are adopted as final regulations, consideration will be given to any written comments (a signed original and eight (8) copies) that are submitted timely to the IRS. Alternatively, taxpayers may submit comments electronically directly to the Federal eRulemaking portal at www.regulations.gov.

The IRS and the Treasury Department request comments on the proposed regulations. In addition, the IRS and the Treasury Department request comments on the following issues:

(1) Whether a series organization should be recognized as a separate entity for Federal tax purposes if it has no assets and engages in no activities independent of its series;

(2) The appropriate treatment of a series that does not terminate for local law purposes when it has no members associated with it;

(3) The entity status for Federal tax purposes of foreign cells that do not conduct insurance businesses and other tax consequences of establishing, operating, and terminating all foreign cells;

(4) How the Federal employment tax issues discussed and similar technical issues should be resolved;

(5) How series and series organizations will be treated for state employment tax purposes and other state employment-related purposes and how that treatment should affect the Federal employment tax treatment of series and series organizations (comments from the states would be particularly helpful);

(6) What issues could arise with respect to the provision of employee benefits by a series organization or series; and

(7) The requirement for the series organization and each series of the series organization to file a statement and what information should be included on the statement.

All comments will be available for public inspection and copying. A public hearing may be scheduled if requested in writing by a person who timely submits comments. If a public hearing is scheduled, notice of the date, time and place for the hearing will be published in the Federal Register.

Drafting Information

The principal author of these proposed regulations is Joy Spies, IRS Office of the Associate Chief Counsel (Passthroughs and Special Industries). However, other personnel from the IRS and the Treasury Department participated in their development.

List of Subjects in 26 CFR Part 301

Employment taxes, Estate taxes, Excise taxes, Gift taxes, Income taxes, Penalties, Reporting and Recordkeeping requirements.

Proposed Amendments to the Regulations

Accordingly, 26 CFR part 301 is proposed to be amended as follows: PART 301—PROCEDURE AND ADMINISTRATION

Paragraph 1. The authority citation for part 301 is amended by adding entries in numerical order to read in part as follows:

Authority: 26 U.S.C. 7805 * * *

Section 301.6011-6 also issued under 26 U.S.C. 6011(a). * * *

Section 301.6071-2 also issued under 26 U.S.C. 6071(a). * * *

Par. 2. Section 301.6011-6 is added to read as follows:

§301.6011-6 Statements of series and series organizations.

(a) Statement required. Each series and series organization (as defined in paragraph (b) of this section) shall file a statement for each taxable year containing the identifying information with respect to the series or series organization as prescribed by the Internal Revenue Service for this purpose and shall include the information required by the statement and its instructions.

(b) Definitions—(1) Series. The term series has the same meaning as in §301.7701-1(a)(5)(viii)(C).

(2) Series organization. The term series organization has the same meaning as in §301.7701-1(a)(5)(viii)(A).

(c) Effective/applicability date. This section applies to taxable years beginning after the date of publication of the Treasury decision adopting these rules as final regulations in the Federal Register.

Par. 3. Section 301.6071-2 is added to read as follows:

§301.6071-2 Time for filing statements of series and series organizations.

(a) In general. Statements required by §301.6011-6 must be filed on or before March 15 of the year following the period for which the return is made.

(b) Effective/applicability date. This section applies to taxable years beginning after the date of publication of the Treasury decision adopting these rules as final regulations in the Federal Register.

Par. 4. Section 301.7701-1 is amended by:

1. Adding paragraph (a)(5).

2. Revising paragraphs (e) and (f).

The additions and revisions read as follows:

§301.7701-1 Classification of organizations for Federal tax purposes.

(a) * * *

(5) Series and series organizations—

(i) Entity status of a domestic series. For Federal tax purposes, except as provided in paragraph (a)(5)(ix) of this section, a series (as defined in paragraph (a)(5)(viii)(C) of this section) organized or established under the laws of the United States or of any State, whether or not a juridical person for local law purposes, is treated as an entity formed under local law.

(ii) Certain foreign series conducting an insurance business. For Federal tax purposes, except as provided in paragraph (a)(5)(ix) of this section, a series organized or established under the laws of a foreign jurisdiction is treated as an entity formed under local law if the arrangements and other activities of the series, if conducted by a domestic company, would result in classification as an insurance company within the meaning of section 816(a) or section 831(c).

(iii) Recognition of entity status. Whether a series that is treated as a local law entity under paragraph (a)(5)(i) or (ii) of this section is recognized as a separate entity for Federal tax purposes is determined under this section and general tax principles.

(iv) Classification of series. The classification of a series that is recognized as a separate entity for Federal tax purposes is determined under paragraph (b) of this section.

(v) Jurisdiction in which series is organized or established. A series is treated as created or organized under the laws of a State or foreign jurisdiction if the series is established under the laws of such jurisdiction. See §301.7701-5 for rules that determine whether a business entity is domestic or foreign.

(vi) Ownership of series and the assets of series. For Federal tax purposes, the ownership of interests in a series and of the assets associated with a series is determined under general tax principles. A series organization is not treated as the owner for Federal tax purposes of a series or of the assets associated with a series merely because the series organization holds legal title to the assets associated with the series.

(vii) Effect of Federal and local law treatment. To the extent that, pursuant to the provisions of this paragraph (a)(5), a series is a taxpayer against whom tax may be assessed under Chapter 63 of Title 26, then any tax assessed against the series may be collected by the Internal Revenue Service from the series in the same manner the assessment could be collected by the Internal Revenue Service from any other taxpayer. In addition, to the extent Federal or local law permits a debt attributable to the series to be collected from the series organization or other series of the series organization, then, notwithstanding any other provision of this paragraph (a)(5), and consistent with the provisions of Federal or local law, the series organization and other series of the series organization may also be considered the taxpayer from whom the tax assessed against the series may be administratively or judicially collected. Further, when a creditor is permitted to collect a liability attributable to a series organization from any series of the series organization, a tax liability assessed against the series organization may be collected directly from a series of the series organization by administrative or judicial means.

(viii) Definitions—

(A) Series organization. A series organization is a juridical entity that establishes and maintains, or under which is established and maintained, a series (as defined in paragraph (a)(5)(viii)(C) of this section). A series organization includes a series limited liability company, series partnership, series trust, protected cell company, segregated cell company, segregated portfolio company, or segregated account company.

(B) Series statute. A series statute is a statute of a State or foreign jurisdiction that explicitly provides for the organization or establishment of a series of a juridical person and explicitly permits—

(1) Members or participants of a series organization to have rights, powers, or duties with respect to the series;

(2) A series to have separate rights, powers, or duties with respect to specified property or obligations; and

(3) The segregation of assets and liabilities such that none of the debts and liabilities of the series organization (other than liabilities to the State or foreign jurisdiction related

to the organization or operation of the series organization, such as franchise fees or administrative costs) or of any other series of the series organization are enforceable against the assets of a particular series of the series organization.

(C) Series. A series is a segregated group of assets and liabilities that is established pursuant to a series statute (as defined in paragraph (a)(5)(viii)(B) of this section) by agreement of a series organization (as defined in paragraph (a)(5)(viii)(A) of this section). A series includes a series, cell, segregated account, or segregated portfolio, including a cell, segregated account, or segregated portfolio that is formed under the insurance code of a jurisdiction or is engaged in an insurance business. However, the term series does not include a segregated asset account of a life insurance company. See section 817(d)(1); §1.817-5(e). An election, agreement, or other arrangement that permits debts and liabilities of other series or the series organization to be enforceable against the assets of a particular series, or a failure to comply with the record keeping requirements for the limitation on liability available under the relevant series statute, will be disregarded for purposes of this paragraph (a)(5)(viii)(C).

(ix) Treatment of series and series organizations under Subtitle C – Employment Taxes and Collection of Income Tax (Chapters 21, 22, 23, 23A, 24 and 25 of the Internal Revenue Code).

[Reserved.]

(x) Examples. The following examples illustrate the principles of this paragraph (a)(5):

Example 1. Domestic Series LLC.

(i) Facts. Series LLC is a series organization (within the meaning of paragraph (a)(5)(viii)(A) of this section). Series LLC has three members (1, 2, and 3). Series LLC establishes two series (A and B) pursuant to the LLC statute of state Y, a series statute within the meaning of paragraph (a)(5)(viii)(B) of this section. Under general tax principles, Members 1 and 2 are the owners of Series A, and Member 3 is the owner of Series B. Series A and B are not described in §301.7701-2(b) or paragraph (a)(3) of this section and are not trusts within the meaning of §301.7701-4.

(ii) Analysis. Under paragraph (a)(5)(i) of this section, Series A and Series B are each treated as an entity formed under local law. The classification of Series A and Series B is determined under paragraph (b) of this section. The default classification under §301.7701-3 of Series A is a partnership and of Series B is a disregarded entity.

Example 2. Foreign Insurance Cell.

(i) Facts. Insurance CellCo is a series organization (within the meaning of paragraph (a)(5)(viii)(A) of this section) organized under the laws of foreign Country X. Insurance CellCo has established one cell, Cell A, pursuant to a Country X law that is a series statute (within the meaning of paragraph (a)(5)(viii)(B) of this section). More than half the business of Cell A during the taxable year is the issuing of insurance or annuity contracts or the reinsuring of risks underwritten by insurance companies. If the activities of Cell A were conducted by a domestic company, that company would qualify as an insurance company within the meaning of sections 816(a) and 831(c).

(ii) Analysis. Under paragraph (a)(5)(ii) of this section, Cell A is treated as an entity formed under local law. Because Cell A is an insurance company, it is classified as a corporation under §301.7701-2(b)(4).

* * * * *

(e) State. For purposes of this section and §§301.7701-2 and 301.7701-4, the term State includes the District of Columbia.

(f) Effective/applicability dates—

(1) In general. Except as provided in paragraphs (f)(2) and (f)(3) of this section, the rules of this section are applicable as of January 1, 1997.

(2) Cost sharing arrangements. The rules of paragraph (c) of this section are applicable on January 5, 2009.

(3) Series and series organizations—

(i) In general. Except as otherwise provided in this paragraph (f)(3), paragraph (a)(5) of this section applies on and after the date final regulations are published in the Federal Register.

(ii) Transition rule—

(A) In general. Except as provided in paragraph (f)(3)(ii)(B) of this section, a taxpayer's treatment of a series in a manner inconsistent with the final regulations will be respected on and after the date final regulations are published in the Federal Register, provided that—

(1) The series was established prior to September 14, 2010;

(2) The series (independent of the series organization or other series of the series organization) conducted business or investment activity, or, in the case of a series established pursuant to a foreign statute, more than half the business of the series was the issuing of insurance or annuity contracts or the reinsuring

of risks underwritten by insurance companies, on and prior to September 14, 2010;

(3) If the series was established pursuant to a foreign statute, the series' classification was relevant (as defined in §301.7701-3(d)), and more than half the business of the series was the issuing of insurance or annuity contracts or the reinsuring of risks underwritten by insurance companies for all taxable years beginning with the taxable year that includes September 14, 2010;

(4) No owner of the series treats the series as an entity separate from any other series of the series organization or from the series organization for purposes of filing any Federal income tax returns, information returns, or withholding documents in any taxable year;

(5) The series and series organization had a reasonable basis (within the meaning of section 6662)

for their claimed classification; and

(6) Neither the series nor any owner of the series nor the series organization was notified in writing on or before the date final regulations are published in the Federal Register that classification of the series was under examination (in which case the series' classification will be determined in the examination).

(B) Exception to transition rule. Paragraph (f)(3)(ii)(A) of this section will not apply on and after the date any person or persons who were not owners of the series organization (or series) prior to September 14, 2010 own, in the aggregate, a fifty percent or greater interest in the series organization (or series). For purposes of the preceding sentence, the term interest means—

(1) In the case of a partnership, a capital or profits interest; and

(2) In the case of a corporation, an equity interest measured by vote or value.

Steven T. Miller,

Deputy Commissioner for Services and Enforcement.

PRIVATE LETTER RULING 200402001

Private Letter Ruling 200402001, October 01, 2003

This is in reply to your letter of June 3, 2003, requesting rulings that the contracts issued by Taxpayer's wholly owned subsidiary qualify as insurance contracts for federal income tax purposes and that the subsidiary is taxable under §831 of the Internal Revenue Code as an insurance company other than a life insurance company.

FACTS

Based on the representations made by Taxpayer, the relevant facts are as follows. Taxpayer is a corporation chartered under the laws of State. Taxpayer uses the calendar year as its taxable year and uses the accrual method of accounting for both its financial records and for federal income tax purposes. Pursuant to §1362(a), Taxpayer has elected to be an S corporation.

Taxpayer produces Equipment A and Equipment B. Taxpayer provides Equipment A and Equipment B to dealers in automobiles. These dealers install Equipment A and Equipment B on automobiles they sell to retail customers. Taxpayer has caused to be formed Subsidiary in State. The purpose of Subsidiary is to offer extended service protection plans to customers purchasing Equipment A and B, as well as offering an extended service protection plan covering Equipment C, which is not produced by Taxpayer.

With respect to Equipment A, Subsidiary will offer Plan D. If, while Plan D is in force, Equipment A fails in the manner described in Plan D, Subsidiary will pay the contract holder either Amount 1 or Amount 2, depending upon the result of the failure. Subsidiary will reimburse the contract holder for expenses incurred by the contract holder for travel (meals and lodging; airfare; car rental) and for notification to family, business associates, and insurance companies necessitated by the failure. Plan D also provides for a credit of Amount 2 with the retail dealer who sold the contract holder the affected automobile to be used by the contract holder towards the purchase of a replacement automobile from that dealer.

With respect to Equipment B, Subsidiary will offer Plan E. If, while Plan E is in force, Equipment B fails in the manner described in Plan E, Subsidiary will cause to have the resulting damage done to the automobile repaired; however, Subsidiary's liability for damage done to the exterior of the automobile is limited to the current value of the automobile as reflected in the National Automobile Dealers Association Official Used Car Guide.

With respect to Equipment C, Subsidiary will offer Plan F. If, while Plan F is in force, Equipment C fails in the manner described in Plan F, Subsidiary will cause to have Equipment C repaired or replaced, including installation. In connection with this, Subsidiary will also provide, if appropriate, immediate "roadside" assistance in an amount not to exceed Amount 3. Plan F excludes coverage for more than one event during a seven day period.

For all of the plans, the customer/contract holder pays only the consideration agreed to at the time the plan is issued, and the consideration is not returned to the customer/contract holder if no claim is made. Plan D is non-cancelable and non-refundable. Plan F may be cancelled and if it is cancelled a portion of the consideration will be returned to the contract holder with the amount depending on how long the plan had been in force. Plan E is silent regarding cancellation. None of the plans cover any consequential or other damages suffered by the contract holder, except to the extent stated. The coverage provided by the plans is not a substitute for any warranty made by the manufacturer or seller of the equipment. Subsidiary will not perform any of the repair work contemplated by the plans.

All of the plans are administered and marketed by Taxpayer. Through representatives of Taxpayer, Subsidiary will enter into arrangements with automobile dealers under which the dealers offer for sale Plans D, E, and F. Regardless of the price charged the contract holder for the plan, the dealer must remit to Taxpayer a predetermined amount for each plan sold. Taxpayer will retain a fee as compensation for its services and will remit the balance to Subsidiary. Taxpayer will investigate and process all claims made under the plans. When a claim under Plan E or F is approved by Taxpayer, Subsidiary will reimburse the dealer or other authorized service provider for the parts and labor required to perform the appropriate repair or replacement. When a claim under Plan D is approved by Taxpayer, Subsidiary will pay the appropriate benefit to the contract holder.

In order to comply with applicable state regulation, and to facilitate the conduct of its business, Subsidiary has entered into an agreement with Company, a licensed insurance company, by which Company indemnifies Subsidiary in the event Subsidiary is unable to perform its obligation(s) under the plans.

Subsidiary will generate almost all of its revenue from the sale of the plans since issuing the plans is its primary and predominant business activity.

LAW AND ANALYSIS

Section 831(a) provides that taxes, as computed under §11, will be imposed on the taxable income (as defined by §832) of each insurance company other than a life insurance company.

Section 1.831-3(a) of the Income Tax Regulations provides that, for purposes of §§831 and 832, the term "insurance companies" means only those companies that qualify as insurance companies under the definition in §1.801-3(a)(1).

Section 1.801-3(a)(1) provides that the term "insurance

company" means a company whose primary and predominant business activity during the taxable year is the issuing of insurance or annuity contracts or the reinsuring of risks underwritten by insurance companies. Section 1.801-3(a)(1) further provides that though the company's name, charter powers, and subjection to state insurance laws are significant in determining the business that a company is authorized and intends to carry on, it is the character of the business actually done in the taxable year that determines whether the company is taxable as an insurance company under the Code. Seealso, Bowers v. Lawyers Mortgage Co., 285 U.S. 182, 188 (1932) (to the same effect as the regulation); Rev. Rul. 83-172, 1983-2 C.B. 107 (holding taxpayer was an insurance company as defined in §1.801-3(a)(1), notwithstanding that taxpayer was not recognized as an insurance company for state law purposes).

Neither the Code nor the Regulations thereunder define the terms "insurance" or "insurance contract". The accepted definition of "insurance" for federal income tax purposes relates back to Helvering v. LeGierse, 312 U.S. 531, 539 (1941), in which the Court stated that "[h]istorically and commonly insurance involves risk-shifting and risk-distributing." Case law has defined "insurance" as "involve[ing] a contract, whereby, for an adequate consideration, one party undertakes to indemnify another against loss arising from certain specified contingencies or perils... It is contractual security against possible anticipated loss." Epmeier v. United States, 199 F.2d 508, 509-10 (7\th/ Cir. 1952). In addition, the risk transferred must be risk of economic loss. Allied Fidelity Corp. v. Commissioner, 572 F.2d 1190, 1193 (7th/ Cir.), cert. denied, 439 U.S. 835 (1978).

Risk shifting occurs when a party facing the possibility of an economic loss transfers some or all of the financial consequences of the potential loss to the insurer. See Rev. Rul. 92-93, 1992-2 C.B. 45 (while parent corporation purchased a group-term life insurance policy from its wholly owned insurance subsidiary, the arrangement was not held to be "self-insurance" because the economic risk of loss was not that of the parent) modified on other grounds, Rev. Rul. 2001-31, 2001-1 C.B. 1348. If the insured has shifted its risk to the insurer, then a loss by the insured does not affect the insured because the loss is offset by the insurance payment. SeeClougherty Packing Co. v. Commissioner, 811 F.2d 1297, 1300 (9th Cir. 1987).

Risk distribution incorporates the statistical phenomenon known as the law of large numbers. Distributing risk allows the insurer to reduce the possibility that a single costly claim will exceed the amount taken in as a premium and set aside for the payment of such a claim. Insuring many independent risks in return for numerous premiums serves to distribute risk. By assuming numerous relatively small, independent risks that occur randomly over time, the insurer smoothes out losses to match more closely its receipt of premiums. See Clougherty Packing Co., 811 F.2d at 1300.

Based on the representations concerning Plans D, E, and F, we conclude that, for federal income taxes, Plans D, E, and F are insurance contracts. The plans are aleatory contracts under which Subsidiary is obligated to indemnify the contract holders for economic loss arising from the mechanical breakdown of a piece of equipment that is not covered by the manufacturer's warranty. The plans are not prepaid service contracts because Subsidiary does not perform any repair services. By accepting a large number of risks, Subsidiary has distributed the risk of loss under the contracts so as to make the average loss more predictable.

Based on the representations concerning its business activities, we conclude that Subsidiary will qualify for purposes of §831 as an insurance company other than a life insurance company so long as its primary and predominant business activity is issuing the plans.

CONCLUSIONS

1. Plans D, E, and F are insurance contracts for federal income tax purposes.

2. Subsidiary will qualify as an insurance company for purposes of §831 so long as issuing Plans D, E, and F is its primary and predominant business activity.

CAVEATS

1. Except as expressly provided herein, no opinion is expressed or implied concerning the tax consequences of any aspect of any transaction or item discussed or referenced in this letter.

2. No ruling has been requested, and no opinion is expressed, concerning whether Subsidiary's gross premiums written include the entire amount the purchasers of Plans D, E, and F pay to the Taxpayer for the contracts.

3. No opinion is expressed concerning the purpose and motive of the transaction or the application of §§482 or 845 to the transaction.

Section 6110(k)(3) of the Code provides that this letter may not be used or cited as precedent. A copy of this letter must be attached to any income tax return to which it is relevant.

PRIVATE LETTER RULING 200907006

Private Letter Ruling 200907006, February 13, 2009

This is in response to the letter submitted by Company dated May 12, 2008, primarily requesting a ruling under § 831 relating to Company's status as an insurance company for federal income tax purposes.

FACTS

Company was incorporated in Foreign Country M on Date A. Company has been licensed by the Insurance Regulators of Foreign County M as a Class 2 Association Insurance Company effective for Year C. Also effective for Year C, Company has made an election under § 953(d) to be taxed as a domestic corporation. All of the stock of Company is owned by Individual A.

Insured Corporation 1 is a domestic corporation engaged the E extraction business. The stock of Insured Corporation is Number m % owned by Trusts for the benefit of Individual B and Number m % owned by Trusts for the benefit of Individual C.

Insured Corporation 2 is a domestic corporation engaged in the E transportation and processing business. All of the stock of Insured Corporation 2 is owned by Insured Corporation 1.

Insured Partnership 1 is a limited partnership, which is engaged in the E transportation business. Corporation Q is the general partner of Insured Partnership 1 and has a Number d % ownership interest in Insured Partnership 1. Partnership R, Individual D, Corporation S, Partnership T and Partnership U, own, respectively, a Number a %, Number b %, Number h %,

Number k %, and a Number f % interest in Insured Partnership 1.

Insured Partnership 2 is a limited partnership, which is engaged in a business, in part, related to E extraction activities. Partnership V is the general partner of Insured Partnership 2 and it has a Number a % interest in Insured Partnership 2. The remaining ownership in Insured Partnership 2 is in the hands of Partnership T with a Number n % interest and Partnership U with a Number i % interest.

Insured Partnership 3 is a limited partnership engaged in the business of the extraction of F. Corporation V is the general partner of Operating Partnership 3 with a Number a % ownership interest. The remaining ownership in Insured Partnership 3 is held Number l % each by Partnership T and Partnership U.

Insured Partnership 4 is a limited partnership engaged in the business of E extraction and processing. Corporation X is the general partner of Operating Partnership 4 with a Number a % ownership interest. The remaining ownership in Insured Partnership 4 is Number l % each owned by Partnership T and Partnership Y.

Insured Partnership 5 is a limited partnership, which is engaged in the business of E waste disposal. Partnership Y, (a partnership) is the general partner of Insured Partnership with a Number a % interest, the remaining interests are owned by Individual D with a Number e % interest and Partnership T and Partnership U each with a Number j % interest.

Neither Individual B nor Individual C own or control more than 50% percent of any of the Company's direct insureds (Insured Corporations 1 and 2, and the Insured Partnerships 1 through 5). Further, Individual C, the 100% owner of Company, also does not possess a 50% ownership or control of any of Company's insureds.

Company offers to its direct insureds (Insured Corporations 1 and 2 and Insured Partnerships 1 through 5) policies which comprise the following four types of contracts: (1) Z policy, (2) employment related practices liability policy, (3) executive liability policy, and (4) commercial crime policy.

The most significant policy is the Z policy. This policy is a package policy that contains coverage for buildings, business personal property, business income and extra expense, legal defense and other business related coverages. The employment-related practices liability policy provides coverage for liability arising out of claims for injury to an employee because of an employment-related offence, as well as a duty to defend. The executive liability coverage policy provides two coverages: one applies to liability arising out of claims for wrongful acts or interrelated wrongful acts committed by the named company's directors or officers, the other is a corporate reimbursement coverage that applies to claims for which the named company is legally obligated to indemnify its directors or officers when such claims involve wrongful acts or interrelated wrongful acts committed by them. The commercial crime policy covers business losses due to employee theft of money, securities, other property of the insured, including client's property on the client's premises.

In order to increase its overall risk distribution, Company participates in a reinsurance pool operated by Lead Company, an insurance company incorporated in Foreign Country M, consisting of Number c independent insurers in addition to Company. These other insurers and their insureds are unrelated to Company and Company's insureds (i.e., Insured Corporations 1 and 2 and Insured Partnerships 1 through 5).[1] Thus, while Company, as a direct writer, receives premiums from its insureds under Coinsurance Agreement A (an automatic pro rata indemnity reinsurance treaty) it cedes 100% of these directly written premiums on each line it insures to the reinsurance pool. Further, using Coinsurance Agreement B (another automatic pro rata indemnity reinsurance agreement), Company will then assume a quota share of the premiums from the reinsurance pool which is equivalent in dollar terms to the amount it ceded on each line of insurance.

The following applies to all of the insurers participating in the reinsurance pool:/1/

All insurers issue insurance contracts and charge premiums for the insurance coverage provided under their respective insurance contracts. All insureds use recognized actuarial techniques, based, in part, on commercial rates for similar coverage, to determine the premiums charged to an individual insured./2/

Each of the insurers pools all the premiums it receives in its general funds and pays claims out of those funds. Each insurer investigates any claim made by any of the more than 12 independent policyholders to determine the validity of the claim prior to making any payment on such claim. Each insurer conducts no business other than the issuing and administering of insurance contracts.

No insured has any obligation to pay any insurer additional premiums if that insured's actual losses during any period of coverage exceed the premiums paid by that insured. Premiums paid by any insured may be used to satisfy claims of the other insureds. No insured that terminates its insurance coverage is required to make additional premium or capital payments to that insurer to cover losses in excess of its premiums paid. Company, Lead Company, or any of the other insurer members of the pool participating in the reinsurance pool are not related.

As a result of Company's participation in the reinsurance pool, the written premiums of Company will, generally, have the following characteristics on each line of coverage it insures: (1) Company will assume (in total) risks from the more than 12 independent policyholders with respect to insured businesses of these policyholders, and (2) no single insured will account for more than 15 % of the total risks assumed by Company through the reinsurance pool regardless of whether Insured Corporation 2 is counted as an insured separate from Insured Corporation 1.

Also, it is represented that there are no guarantees of Company's obligations by Individuals A, B, C or any other related person. In addition, Company states that it is well capitalized.

LAW AND ANALYSIS

Section 831(a) of the Internal Revenue Code provides that taxes, computed as provided in § 11, are imposed for each taxable year on the taxable income of each insurance company other than a life insurance company. Section 831(c) provides that, for purposes of § 831, the term "insurance company" has the meaning given to such term by § 816(a). Under § 816(a), the term "insurance company" means "any company more than half of the business of which during the taxable year is the issuing of insurance or annuity contracts or the reinsuring of risks underwritten by insurance companies."

Neither the Code nor the regulations define the terms "insurance" or "insurance contract" in the context of property and casualty insurance. The Supreme Court of the United States has explained that in order for an arrangement to constitute insurance for federal income tax purposes, both risk shifting and risk distribution must be present. Helvering v. LeGierse, 312 U.S. 531 (1941). The risk transferred must be risk of economic loss. Allied Fidelity Corp. v. Commissioner, 572 F.2d 1190, 1193 (7th Cir. 1978). The risk must contemplate the fortuitous occurrence of a stated contingency, Commissioner v. Treganowan, 183 F.2d 288, 290-291 (2d Cir. 1950), and must not be merely an investment or business risk. Rev. Rul. 2007-47, 2007-2 C.B. 127. In addition, the arrangement must constitute insurance in the commonly accepted sense. See, e.g., Ocean Drilling & Exploration Co. v. United States, 988 F.2d 1135, 1153 (Fed. Cir. 1993); AMERCO, Inc. v. Commissioner, 979 F.2d 162 (9th Cir. 1992).

Risk shifting occurs if a person facing the possibility of an economic loss transfers some or all of the financial consequences of the potential loss to the insurer such that a loss by the insured does not affect the insured because the loss is offset by a payment from the insurer. Risk distribution incorporates the statistical phenomenon known as the law of large numbers. Distributing risk allows the insurer to reduce the possibility that a single costly claim will exceed the amount taken in as premiums and set aside for the payment of such as claim. By assuming numerous relatively small, independent risks that occur randomly over time, the insurer smooths out losses to match more closely its receipt of premiums. Clougherty Packing Co. v. Commissioner, 811 F.2d 1297, 1300 (9th Cir. 1987).

Courts have recognized that risk distribution necessarily entails a pooling of premiums, so that a potential insured is not in significant part paying for its own risks. Humana, Inc. v. Commissioner, 881 F.2d 247, 257 (6th Cir. 1989). See also Ocean Drilling and Exploration Co., 988 F.2d at 1153 ("Risk distribution involves spreading the risk of loss among policyholders."); Beech Aircraft Corp. v United States, 797 F.2d 920, 922 (10th Cir. 1986) ("[R]isk distributing means that the party assuming the risk distributes his potential liability, in part, among others.")

In Rev. Rul. 2002-91, 2002-2 C.B. 991, the Internal Revenue Service considered a situation where a group of unrelated businesses in a concentrated industry that faced a significant liability hazard formed a group captive. No member of the group owned more than 15% of the group captive or had more than 15% of the vote on any corporate governance issue. In addition, no members' individual risk insured by the group captive exceeded 15% of the total risk insured by the group captive. Thus, no one member controls the group captive. The group captive was adequately capitalized and it used recognized actuarial techniques, based, in part, on commercial rates for similar coverage, to determine premiums to be charged to an individual member. Based upon all of the facts and circumstances described in the revenue ruling the Service concluded that the arrangement between the member/insured and the group captive constitutes insurance for federal income tax purposes and that the amounts paid as insurance premiums to the group captive are insurance premiums deductible as ordinary and necessary expenses. The revenue ruling also concluded that the group captive was in the business of insurance and was treated as an insurance company taxable under § 831.

The present situation presented by Company has aspects to it that make it similar to Rev. Rul. 2002-91 at the directly written policy level. There are multiple insureds none of whom control Company and Company provides those insureds with coverage. The bulk of the insureds have a connection with the E industry and generally each has been issued identical policy forms. Thus, a sufficient level of risk distribution of homogeneous risks units has been achieved at the direct written policy level. In addition, as a matter of insurance practice and theory, Company's entry into the reinsurance pool allows it to assume a share of numerous relatively small, independent risks that occur randomly over time allowing it to smooth out losses to more closely match its receipt of premiums. Clougherty Packing Co. 811 F.2d at 1300. Accordingly, Company is functioning as an insurance company both as a direct writer and as a reinsurer. Thus, under the facts as presented Company is functioning as an insurance company in the traditional sense.

Section 162(a) of the Internal Revenue Code provides, in part, that there shall be allowed as a deduction all of the ordinary and necessary expenses paid or incurred during the taxable year in carrying on any trade or business.

Section 1.162-1(a) of the Income Tax Regulations provides, in part, that among the items included in business expenses are insurance premiums against fire, storms, theft, accident, or other similar losses in the case of a business.

CONCLUSION

Based solely on the information submitted and the representations made, and provided that Company is adequately capitalized, we conclude that the arrangement between the insureds and Company constitutes insurance for federal income tax purposes. This means that Company is in the business of issuing insurance and reinsurance contracts and will be treated as an insurance company taxable under § 831 so long as it meets the definition of § 831(c); and that the consideration made by the insureds to Company is eligible to meet the definition of insurance premiums as described in § 1.162-1(a) of the Regulations.

Except as expressly provided herein, no opinion is expressed in this letter ruling under the provisions of any other section of the Code or Regulations. No opinion is expressed as to whether or not the amount of premiums charged by Company has been calculated correctly or whether other requirements under § 162 have been met. See e.g., Rev. Rul. 2007-3, 2007-4 I.R B. 350. Further, no opinion has been requested and none has been expressed as to whether the reinsurance pool is an entity for federal income tax purposes. This ruling letter is directed only to the taxpayer who requested it. Section 6110(k)(3) of the Code provides that it may not be used or cited as precedent.

/1

In addition to Company and Lead Company, the other pool members include Independent Insurers 1 through 5.

/2/

More specifically, the pricing of the policies is based on an actuarial model that is published by the Insurance Services Office and the results of that model are compared with available market based pricing from other insurance companies.

PRIVATE LETTER RULING 200950016

Private Letter Ruling 200950016, December 11, 2009

This is in response to the letter submitted on behalf of Company dated April 9, 2009, primarily requesting a ruling under section 831 relating to Company's status as an insurance company for federal income tax purposes. Specifically, the Company has requested rulings that (1) the reinsurance arrangement involving Company is insurance for federal income tax purposes, and (2) Company is an insurance company for federal income tax purposes.

FACTS

Company was incorporated in State on Date A. Company became licensed by State as a captive insurance company on Date B. All of the stock of Company is owned by a group of Number a individuals. These individuals also own Number b entities, which in turn own Number c franchises in a single industry.

Each of the Number b entities entered into two separate contracts with Insurer, an entity unrelated to Company, in an effort to secure insurance covering workers' compensation, general liability, property, automobile, and crime risks. For purposes of this letter ruling, it is assumed that Insurer is an insurance company as defined in section 816(a). One contract covers workers' compensation risks, while the other contract covers general liability, property, automobile, and crime risks. Pursuant to these contracts, Insurer would reimburse each of the entities up to a specified dollar amount for its losses associated with the types of risks set forth above in exchange for a premium. Company represents that Insurer performs the underwriting on all contracts issued to the Number b entities. Company represents that Number d other entities in the same industry entered into contracts that are identical in all material respects to the contracts entered into between Insurer and the Number b entities.

Insurer retains the exposure for all specified losses in excess of Number e dollars (up to limits specified in each contract) per occurrence for all risks except losses related to crime. For crime risks, Insurer retains exposure for all specified losses in excess of Number f dollars (up to a stated maximum amount set forth in the contract). The remaining risks for all types of coverage covered by the policies issued by Insurer to the Number b entities as well as the Number d entities are ceded by Insurer to Reinsurer A. Reinsurer A, which is unrelated to Company, is assumed for purposes of this letter ruling to be an insurance company as defined in section 816(a).

Reinsurer A retains the first Number g dollars of risk exposure for all risks covered by the contracts issued by Insurer to each of the Number b entities as well as the Number d entities. Through a retrocession agreement, Reinsurer A cedes Number f dollars in excess of the first Number g dollars to Reinsurer B.

Reinsurer B is a foreign segregated cell insurance company that provides quota share reinsurance to Company and Number h other entities unrelated to Company covering the entire layer of risks ceded by Reinsurer A. In exchange for a portion of the overall premium pursuant to the quota share reinsurance arrangement, Company reimburses Reinsurer B for a proportional share of its losses that are covered by the contracts underwritten by Insurer. For purposes of this ruling, it is assumed that Reinsurer B is an insurance company as defined in section 816(a).

Company has represented that its sole business is the reinsuring of risks pursuant to the quota share agreement.

Company further represents that it complies with the minimum capital and surplus requirements mandated by the laws of State, files annual statements with the insurance regulatory agency of State, and complies with State's requirements for filing premium tax returns. In addition, Company represents that none of its owners guarantee its performance under the quota share reinsurance arrangement.

LAW AND ANALYSIS

Requested Ruling #1

Neither the Code nor the regulations define the terms "insurance" or "insurance contract" in the context of property and casualty insurance. The Supreme Court of the United States has explained that in order for an arrangement to constitute insurance for federal income tax purposes, both risk shifting and risk distribution must be present. Helvering v. LeGierse, 312 U.S. 531 (1941). The risk transferred must be risk of economic loss. Allied Fidelity Corp. v. Commissioner, 572 F.2d 1190, 1193 (7th Cir. 1978). The risk must contemplate the fortuitous occurrence of a stated contingency, Commissioner v. Treganowan, 183 F.2d 288, 290-91 (2d Cir. 1950), and must not be merely an investment or business risk. Rev. Rul. 2007-47, 2007-2 C.B. 127. In addition, the arrangement must constitute insurance in the commonly accepted sense. See, e.g., Ocean Drilling & Exploration Co. v. United States, 988 F.2d 1135, 1153 (Fed. Cir. 1993); AMERCO, Inc. v. Commissioner, 979 F.2d 162 (9th Cir. 1992).

Risk shifting occurs if a person facing the possibility of an economic loss transfers some or all of the financial consequences of the potential loss to the insurer such that a loss by the insured does not affect the insured because the loss is offset by a payment from the insurer. Risk distribution incorporates the statistical phenomenon known as the law of large numbers. Distributing risk allows the insurer to reduce the possibility that a single costly claim will exceed the amount taken in as premiums and set aside for the payment of such as claim. By assuming numerous relatively small, independent risks that occur randomly over time, the insurer smoothes out losses to match more closely its receipt of premiums. Clougherty Packing Co. v. Commissioner, 811 F.2d 1297, 1300 (9th Cir. 1987).

Courts have recognized that risk distribution necessarily entails a pooling of premiums, so that a potential insured is not in significant part paying for its own risks. Humana, Inc. v. Commissioner, 881 F.2d 247, 257 (6th Cir. 1989). See also Ocean Drilling and Exploration Co., 988 F.2d at 1153 ("Risk distribution involves spreading the risk of loss among policyholders."); Beech Aircraft Corp. v. United States, 797 F.2d 920, 922 (10th Cir. 1986) ("[R]isk distributing means that the party assuming the risk distributes his potential liability, in part, among others.")

The "commonly accepted sense" of insurance derives from all the facts surrounding each case, with emphasis on comparing the implementation of the arrangement with that known to be insurance. Court opinions identify several nonexclusive factors bearing on this, such as the treatment of an arrangement under the applicable state law, AMERCO, 96 T.C. at 41; the adequacy of the insurer's capitalization and utilization of premiums priced at arm's length, The Harper Group v. Commissioner, 96 T.C. 45, 55 (1991), aff'd 979 F.2d 1341 (9th Cir. 1992); separately maintained funds to pay claims, Ocean Drilling & Exploration Co. v. United States, 24 Cl. Ct. 714, 728 (1991), aff'd per curiam, 988 F.2d 1135 (Fed. Cir. 1993); and the language of the operative agreements and the method of resolving claims, Kidde Indus. Inc. v. Commissioner, 49 Fed. Cl. 42, 51-52 (1997).

In the present situation, there is risk shifting and risk distribution. Risk of loss for various property and casualty risks faced by the Number b entities and the Number d entities was shifted to Insurer when each entered into the contracts with Insurer. Pursuant to these contracts, Insurer would reimburse each of the entities up to a specified dollar amount for its losses associated with the types of risks set forth above in exchange for a premium. Thus, each of the Number b entities' and the Number d entities' risk of loss was shifted to Insurer.

Moreover, there is risk distribution in the arrangement described above. There are multiple insureds, none of whom control Company and Company provides those insureds with coverage. The insureds are in the same industry and each has been issued policy forms that are identical in all material respects. In addition, there are a sufficient number of unrelated insureds such that no one insured is paying for a significant portion of its own risks. Thus, a sufficient level of risk distribution of homogenous risks has been achieved through this arrangement.

As stated above, Company is solely in the business of reinsuring of risks pursuant to the quota share reinsurance arrangement. Reinsurance is commonly thought of as a contract whereby one insurer transfers or 'cedes' to another insurer all or part of the risk it has assumed under a separate or distinct policy or group of policies in exchange for a portion of the premium. In essence, reinsurance is insurance for insurance companies. COUCH ON INSURANCE § 9:1 (2008). And this view of reinsurance has been shared in the context of litigation concerning federal income taxes. See, e.g., Colonial Am. Life Ins. Co. v. Commissioner, 491 U.S. 244, 246-47 (1989).

Here, the quota share arrangement between Reinsurer B and Company has all the hallmarks of reinsurance. As such, the arrangement between Company and Reinsurer B constitutes insurance for federal income tax purposes.

Requested Ruling #2

Section 831(a) of the Internal Revenue Code provides that taxes, computed as provided in section 11, are imposed for each taxable year on the taxable income of each insurance company other than a life insurance company. Section 831(c) provides that, for purposes of section 831, the term "insurance company" has the meaning given to such term by section 816(a). Under section 816(a), the term "insurance company" means "any company more than half of the business of which during the taxable year is the issuing of insurance or annuity contracts or the reinsuring of risks underwritten by insurance companies."

As stated above, it is assumed for purposes of this letter ruling that Insurer, Reinsurer A, and Reinsurer B are insurance companies as defined in section 816(a). Furthermore, Company has represented that its sole business is the reinsuring of risks pursuant to the quota share arrangement with Reinsurer B. Therefore, because Company's only business is the reinsuring of risks underwritten by insurance companies, it is an insurance company for federal income tax purposes.

CONCLUSION

Based solely on the information submitted and the representations made, we conclude that the arrangement between Company and Reinsurer B is insurance for federal income tax purposes. In addition, based on the information submitted and the representations made, and based on the assumptions that Insurer, Reinsurer A, and Reinsurer B are insurance companies within the meaning of section 816(a), we conclude that Company is in the business of reinsuring risks underwritten by insurance companies and will be treated as an insurance company taxable under section 831.

Except as expressly provided herein, no opinion is expressed or implied concerning the tax consequences of any aspect of any transaction or item discussed or referenced in this letter. Specifically, no opinion has been requested and none has been expressed as to whether Insurer, Reinsurer A, and Reinsurer B are insurance companies within the meaning of section 816(a). Furthermore, no opinion has been requested and none has been expressed as to whether Reinsurer B is an entity for federal income tax purposes.

The rulings contained in this letter are based upon information and representations submitted by the taxpayer and accompanied by a penalty of perjury statement executed by an appropriate party. While this office has not verified any of the material submitted in support of the request for rulings, it is subject to verification on examination.

This ruling is directed only to the taxpayer requesting it. Section 6110(k)(3) of the Code provides that it may not be used or cited as precedent.

PRIVATE LETTER RULING 201030014

Private Letter Ruling 201030014, July 30, 2010

This is in response to the letter submitted by Company dated May 12, 2008, primarily requesting a ruling under § 831 relating to Company's status as an insurance company for federal income tax purposes.

FACTS

Company was incorporated in Foreign Country M on Date A. Company has been licensed by the Insurance Regulators of Foreign County M as a Class 2 Association Insurance Company effective for Year C. Also effective for Year C, Company has made an election under § 953(d) to be taxed as a domestic corporation. All of the stock of Company is owned by Trust; in turn, Individual A and Individual B are each Number a % beneficial owners of Trust. Individual B is the spouse of Individual A.

Sole Proprietorship is the Y professional practice of Individual A, the income and expenses of which are reported on the joint federal income tax return of Individual A and B.

Company issues to Sole Proprietorship contracts which cover insurance risks: (1) capital asset (output) coverage,/1/ (2) employment related practices liability coverage, (3) executive liability coverage, and (4) commercial crime coverage. Company is responsible for the issuance of contracts, billing premiums and claims processing with respect to its insured.

Company participates in a pool operated by Lead Company, incorporated and licensed as an insurance company in Foreign

Country M. The pool consists of Number b independent entities in addition to Company. All participants in the pool issue contracts by which for consideration they provide coverage for certain insurance risks.

They use recognized actuarial techniques, based, in part, on commercial rates for similar coverage, to determine the consideration to be charged./2/ The aggregate number of other entities which are covered by the participants on a per line of business basis is at least Number d and as many a Number e. Each participant conducts no business other than the issuing and administering the contracts described herein.

Company receives consideration for the coverage it provides to Sole Proprietorship. Under "Coinsurance Agreement A" (an automatic pro rata indemnity reinsurance treaty) it contributes all of this consideration on each line it insures to the pool. Further, using "Coinsurance Agreement B" (another automatic pro rata indemnity reinsurance agreement) Company will then receive a quota share of the aggregate consideration contributed to the pool which is equivalent in dollar terms to Number f % of the amount it contributed to the pool for each line of coverage. Under Coinsurance Agreement B, Company (in its role as a reinsurer) is liable for its pro rata share of the claims which are incurred and reported during the accounting period./3/

No entity covered by a participant has any obligation to pay any additional consideration if that entity's actual losses during any period of coverage exceed the consideration paid. Consideration paid by any covered entity may be used to satisfy claims of the other covered entities. No entity that terminates its coverage is required to make additional contributions to a participant to cover losses in excess of the consideration paid. Company, Lead Company, or any of the other participants in the pool are not related.

As a result of Company's participation in the pool, the net consideration received by Company will, generally, have the following characteristics on each line of coverage it provides: (1)

through the other participants, Company will, thus, assume (in total) risks from no less than Number d and as many as Number f independent entities in any line of coverage, and (2) through operation of the pool, all of the covered entities, including Sole Proprietorship, will account for no more than 15% of the total risks assumed by Company. Also, it is represented that there are no guarantees of Company's obligations by Trust, Individuals A or B, or any other related person. In addition, Company represents that that it is well capitalized and does not provide any shareholder loans.

LAW AND ANALYSIS

Section 831(a) of the Internal Revenue Code provides that taxes, computed as provided in § 11, are imposed for each taxable year on the taxable income of each insurance company other than a life insurance company. Section 831(c) provides that, for purposes of § 831, the term "insurance company" has the meaning given to such term by § 816(a). Under § 816(a), the term "insurance company" means "any company more than half of the business of which during the taxable year is the issuing of insurance or annuity contracts or the reinsuring of risks underwritten by insurance companies."

Neither the Code nor the regulations define the terms "insurance" or "insurance contract" in the context of property and casualty insurance. The Supreme Court of the United States has explained that in order for an arrangement to constitute insurance for federal income tax purposes, both risk shifting and risk distribution must be present. Helvering v. Le Gierse, 312 U.S. 531 (1941). The risk transferred must be risk of economic loss. Allied Fidelity Corp. v. Commissioner, 572 F.2d 1190, 1193 (7th Cir. 1978). The risk must contemplate the fortuitous occurrence of a stated contingency, Commissioner v. Treganowan, 183 F.2d 288, 290-291 (2d Cir. 1950), and must not be merely an investment or business risk. Rev. Rul. 2007-47, 2007-2 C.B. 127. In addition, the arrangement must constitute insurance in the commonly accepted sense. See, e.g., Ocean

Drilling & Exploration Co. v. United States, 988 F.2d 1135, 1153 (Fed. Cir. 1993); AMERCO, Inc. v. Commissioner, 979 F.2d 162 (9th Cir. 1992).

Risk shifting occurs if a person facing the possibility of an economic loss transfers some or all of the financial consequences of the potential loss to the insurer, such that a loss by the insured does not affect the insured because the loss is offset by a payment from the insurer. Risk distribution incorporates the statistical phenomenon known as the law of large numbers. Distributing risk allows the insurer to reduce the possibility that a single costly claim will exceed the amount taken in as premiums and set aside for the payment of such a claim. By assuming numerous relatively small, independent risks that occur randomly over time, the insurer smooths out losses to match more closely its receipt of premiums. Clougherty Packing Co. v. Commissioner, 811 F.2d 1297, 1300 (9th Cir. 1987).

Courts have recognized that risk distribution necessarily entails a pooling of premiums, so that a potential insured is not in significant part paying for its own risks. Humana, Inc. v. Commissioner, 881 F.2d 247, 257 (6th Cir. 1989). See also Ocean Drilling and Exploration Co., 988 F.2d at 1153 ("Risk distribution involves spreading the risk of loss among policyholders."); Beech Aircraft Corp. v. United States, 797 F.2d 920, 922 (10th Cir. 1986) ("[R]isk distributing means that the party assuming the risk distributes his potential liability, in part, among others.") On the other hand, a purported insurance arrangement where an issuer who contracts with only one policyholder and retains the risk under such contract does not qualify as an insurance contract for federal income tax purposes. See Rev. Rul. 2005-40, 2005-2 C.B. 4.

Rev. Rul. 2002-89, 2002-2 C.B. 984, set forth circumstances under which arrangements between a domestic parent corporation and its wholly owned subsidiary constitute insurance and explained that a parent/wholly owned subsidiary arrangement does not constitute insurance if the parent accounts for 90% of the risk, but does if other insureds constitute more than 50% of the risk.

Rev. Rul. 2002-90, 2002-2 C.B. 985, holds that an arrangement between a licensed insurance subsidiary of parent, and each of 12 of parent's operating subsidiaries where, inter alia, no one subsidiary accounts for less than 5% nor more than 15% of the total risk insured by the insurance subsidiary constitutes insurance.

Rev. Rul. 2002-91, 2002-2 C.B. 991, holds that an arrangement involving a group of unrelated businesses of which, inter alia, none accounted for more than 15% of the total insured risk constitutes insurance.

Rev. Rul. 2005-40, applies the principles of Rev. Ruls. 2002-89 and 2002-90 to situations involving corporations and single-member limited liability companies.

As pointed out in the law background of Rev. Rul. 2009-26, 2009-38 I.R.B. 366, the Internal Revenue Code of 1986 and administrative guidance treat reinsurance in a manner similar to direct insurance for many purposes; for example, both direct insurance and reinsurance business may qualify a taxpayer as an insurance company under section 816(a) or 831(c), as applicable./4/

In Alinco Life Insurance Co. v. United States, 373 F.2d 336 (Ct Cl. 1967), a large finance company formed a wholly-owned subsidiary corporation (Alinco), which qualified as a life insurance company under the laws of Indiana. Customers of the finance company (borrowers) purchased credit life insurance from an unrelated insurance company, which in turn reinsured a fixed proportion of those contracts with Alinco.

Even through Alinco reinsured risks underwritten by only one insurance company, those risks aggregated nearly one billion dollars of business, with a large number of customers, for which Alinco was required by the state insurance department to maintain reserves. Interpreting regulatory language that was identical to what now appears in § 816(a), the court concluded that Alinco was in the business of "reinsuring risks" underwritten by insurance companies.

Section 162(a) of the Code provides, in part, that there shall be allowed as a deduction all of the ordinary and necessary expenses paid or incurred during the taxable year in carrying on a trade or business.

Section 1.162-1(a) of the Income Tax Regulations provides, in part, that among the items included in business expenses are insurance premiums against fire, storms, theft, accident, or other similar losses in the case of a business.

In the present situation, under Coinsurance Agreement A Company contributes all of its direct consideration and associated risks to the pool and, under Coinsurance Agreement B, Company receives a quota share of the consideration and associated risks from the pool equal in dollar terms to Number f % of the amount Company ceded to the pool on each line of coverage. The result is that there are a sufficient number of unrelated covered entities such that none is paying for a significant portion of its own risks. Accordingly, given that insurance risks are covered, the arrangement achieves adequate risk shifting and risk distribution such that the contracts issued by Company constitute insurance for federal income tax purposes. For the year for which the predicate facts were represented, this appears to be more than half of Company's business.

CONCLUSION

Based solely on the information submitted and the representations made, and provided that Company is adequately capitalized and continues to operate as a participant in the pool (in the manner described above), we conclude that the arrangement between the Sole Proprietorship and Company constitutes insurance for federal income tax purposes, such that consideration paid by Sole Proprietorship to Company is an insurance premium under § 1.162-1(a) of the Income Tax Regulations, and Company would qualify under part II of subchapter L for the taxable year if it were a domestic corporation.

Except as expressly provided herein, no opinion is expressed in this letter ruling under the provisions of any other section of the Code or Regulation. No opinion is expressed as to whether or not the amount of premiums charged by Company has been calculated correctly or whether other requirements under § 162 have been met. See e.g., Rev. Rul. 2007-3, 2007-1 C.B. 350. Further, no opinion has been requested and none has been expressed as to whether the pool is an entity for federal income tax purposes, or as to the classification of any other participant or the treatment of any arrangement involving any other participant. This ruling letter is directed only to the taxpayer who requested it. Section 6110(k)(3) of the Code provides that it may not be used or cited as precedent.

/1/

This contract is a package policy that contains coverage for buildings, business personal property, business income and extra expense, legal defense and other business related coverage. Further, the capital asset (output) policy issued to Sole Proprietorship contained a number of additional endorsements including professional liability business interruption and excess professional liability legal claim expenses.

/2/

More specifically, the pricing of the contracts is based on an actuarial model that is published by the Insurance Services Office and the results of that model are compared with available market based pricing from other insurance companies.

/3/

Incurred Claims means (a) paid claims, plus, (b) ceded outstanding claim reserves and (including present value reserves on continuing, unreported and reported but unpaid claims, and a claim liability for claims in course of settlement and for incurred but not reported claims), less (c) ceded outstanding claims and liabilities as of the end of the previous accounting period.

/4/

On the other hand, section 845 which grants to the Secretary explicit authority to reallocate, recharacterize, or make other adjustments with respect to certain reinsurance arrangements does not refer to direct insurance.

PRIVATE LETTER RULING 201126036

Private Letter Ruling 201126036, April 6, 2011

This is our final determination that you do not qualify for exemption from Federal income tax under Internal Revenue Code section 501(a) as an organization described in Code section 501(c)(15).

We made this determination for the following reason(s):

There is an insufficient number of insureds to provide for an adequate premium-pooling base. In addition, your risk is too heavily concentrated in just a few insureds. As a result, your business lacks one of the principal elements of insurance, risk distribution. Thus, because you do not qualify as an insurance company, you do not meet the statutory requirement for exemption under section 501(c)(15) of the Code.

You must file Federal income tax returns on the form and for the years listed above within 30 days of this letter, unless you request an extension of time to file. File the returns in accordance with their instructions, and do not send them to this office. Failure to file the returns timely may result in a penalty.

We will make this letter and our proposed adverse determination letter available for public inspection under Code section 6110, after deleting certain identifying information. Please read the enclosed Notice 437, Notice of Intention to Disclose, and review the two attached letters that show our proposed deletions. If you disagree with our proposed deletions, follow the instructions in Notice 437. If you agree with our deletions, you do not need to take any further action.

If you have any questions about this letter, please contact the person whose name and telephone number are shown in the heading of this letter. If you have any questions about your Federal income tax status and responsibilities, please contact IRS Customer Service at 1-800-829-1040 or the IRS Customer Service number for businesses, 1-800-829-4933. The IRS Customer Service number for people with hearing impairments is 1-800-829-4059.

Sincerely, *****, Director, Exempt Organizations.

We have considered your application for recognition of exemption from Federal Income tax under Internal Revenue Code section 501(a). Based on the information provided, we have concluded that you do not qualify for exemption under section 501(c)(15) of the Code.

FACTS:

You were incorporated on Date A in Offshore B. You are in the business of providing certain commercial casualty and property insurance-type services. You also "reinsure" certain contracts as described below. You filed an election under section 953(d) of the Code which allows an election by a foreign insurance company to be treated as a domestic corporation.

You are wholly owned by D. You have only one class of stock composed of E shares of no par value stock. Out of these E shares, you issued F shares to D. The consideration paid for these shares was G. H and I serve as your only corporate officers and directors. H serves as your director, chief executive officer, president, secretary and assistant treasurer. I serves as your director, vice president, treasurer and assistant secretary. Neither H nor I holds financial interests in any other insurance companies. Moreover, neither H nor I has any agreement or relationship with any of the shareholders of the insurance companies with which you conduct business.

You have employed J as your resident manager for an annual compensation estimated to be less than K.

You operate primarily to provide casualty and property "insurance" coverage to M. M is made up of ff entities. There is only a description of one entity provided in your application. This entity is gg, which is not the precise name of any one of the ff entities. It is described as one of the largest privately owned structural steel service centers in hh. The application indicates that the ff entities are related or affiliated businesses. By "related" or "affiliated" is meant persons related to H for which you may provide direct written coverages. H owns jj% of the common stock of each of the ff entities that compose M. N also owns jj% of the common stock of each of the ff entities that compose M.

In year C, you wrote direct-written "insurance" contracts to M titled: (1) Special Risk – Product Recall Insurance Policy, (2) Special Risk – Regulatory Changes Insurance Policy, (3) Special Risk – Expense Reimbursement Insurance Policy, (4) Special Risk – Punitive Wrap Liability Insurance Policy, (5) Excess Pollution Liability Insurance Policy, (6) Special Risk – Tax Liability Insurance Policy for C, (7) Special Risk – Tax Liability Insurance Policy for ii, (8) Special Risk – Tax Liability Insurance Policy for kk, (9) Special Risk – Deductible/Self Insured Retention Expense Reimbursement Insurance Policy, (10) Special Risk – Product Pricing Insurance Policy, (11) Special Risk – Loss of Major Supplier(s) Insurance Policy and (12) Special Risk – Loss of Services Insurance Policy.

In addition to the L direct-written "insurance" contracts issued by you to M, you and MM entered into an agreement titled "Joint Underwriting Stop Loss Endorsement." MM is not related to you, D, M, H, I, N or O, the other lead insurer on the "insurance" contracts with M. You represent that MM is a regulated insurer. It appears that under this agreement, you are responsible for payment of claims up to certain specified thresholds. If the thresholds are met, then MM becomes liable for payment of claims up to certain specified limits. If the specified limits for

MM's payment of claims are exceeded, then you again become liable. It also appears that for each of the above-referenced contracts, you receive Q% of the total premiums and O receives Q% of the total premiums. MM receives R% of the total premiums.

During year C, you entered into two types of reinsurance arrangements. In the first arrangement, you assumed reinsurance contracts from MM. The primary issuers on these contracts are unaffiliated insurance companies that underwrite credit-type policies (credit property, credit disability, and/or credit life) and policies for vehicle service contracts. For year C, you received $S in "premium" income from this arrangement.

The second arrangement is referred to by you as a "reinsurance risk pooling program." In this arrangement, you participate in a "reinsurance risk pool" with several other unrelated insurance companies ("pool participants"). The risk pool is operated by MM. Each pool participant has one or more affiliated operating entities for which it underwrites insurance coverage (generally casualty type coverage). MM insures a portion of the direct insurance underwritten by the pool participants using a so-called "stop loss" endorsement. MM currently participates in over T insurance policies with more than U insureds. MM blends together its direct-written insurance and then reinsures the entire book on a quota-share basis with each of the pool participants. During year C, you received $V in "premiums" with respect to this second arrangement.

Your gross income totaled $W for year C which is $X of direct written premiums and $Y of reinsurance assumed and pooled premiums.

Of your total premium income for year C, Z% is from M (assuming you receive Q% of the contract premiums as previously discussed), aa% is from the first reinsurance arrangement, and bb% is from the "reinsurance risk pooling program." You have decided to reserve conservatively during the policy period at cc% of its direct written premiums.

For year C, your assets totaled $dd, and total capital equaled $G.

LAW:

Section 501(c)(15) of the Code recognizes as exempt insurance companies or associations other than life (including interinsurers and reciprocal underwriters) if the net written premium (or, if greater, direct written premiums) for the taxable year do not exceed $350,000. For years after December 31, 2003, the law has been amended stating gross receipts can total $600,000 and premium income must be at least 50% of total gross receipts.

Section 1.801-3(a)(1) of the Income Tax regulations defines the term "insurance company" to mean a company whose primary and predominant business activity during the taxable year is the issuing of insurance or annuity contracts or the reinsuring of risks underwritten by insurance companies. Thus, though its name, charter powers, and subjection to State insurance laws are significant in determining the business which a company is authorized and intends to carry on, it is the character of the business actually done in the taxable year which determines whether a company is taxable as an insurance company under the Internal Revenue Code.

Neither the Code nor the regulations define the terms "insurance" or "insurance contract." The standard for evaluating whether an arrangement constitutes insurance is Helvering v. LeGierse, 312 U.S. 531 (1941), in which the Court stated that "historically and commonly insurance involves risk-shifting and risk-distributing in a transaction which involve[s] an actual 'insurance risk' at the time the transaction was executed." Insurance has been described as "involv[ing] a contract, whereby, for adequate consideration, one party agrees to indemnify another against loss arising from certain specified contingencies or perils. Epmeier v. United States, 199 F.2d 508, 509-10 (7th Cir. 1952). Insurance is contractual security against possible anticipated loss. Id. Cases analyzing "captive insurance" arrangements have distilled the concept of "insurance" for federal income tax purposes to three elements applied consistently with principles of federal income taxation: (1) involvement of an insurance risk; (2) shifting and distribution of that risk; and (3) insurance in its commonly accepted sense. See e.g., AMERCO, Inc. v. Commissioner, 979 F.2d 162, 164-65 (9th Cir. 1992), aff'g. 96 T.C. 18 (1991).

The risk transferred must be risk of economic loss. Allied Fidelity Corp. v. Commissioner, 572 F.2d 1190, 1193 (7th Cir. 1978). The risk must contemplate the fortuitous occurrence of a stated contingency, Commissioner v. Treganowan, 183 F.2d 288, 290-91 (2d Cir. 1950), and must not be merely an investment or business risk. LeGierse, 312 U.S. at 542; Rev. Rul. 89-96, 1989-2 C.B. 114.

Rev. Rul. 2007-47, 2007-30 I.R.B. 127, provides that an arrangement that provides for the reimbursement of inevitable future costs does not involve the requisite insurance risk for purposes of determining (1) whether the amount paid for the arrangement is deductible as an insurance premium and (2) whether the assuming entity may account for the arrangement as an "insurance contract" for purposes of subchapter L of the Code. In Rev. Rul. 2007-47, a domestic corporation engaged in a business process that was inherently harmful to people and property. Applicable government regulations require the corporation to take action to remediate the harm and, therefore, the domestic corporation will incur future cost to restore its business location. There is no uncertainty that future costs will be incurred. The domestic corporation entered into a contract with a domestic insurance company to be reimbursed for its future costs. The arrangement had no limits on its duration. Citing and amplifying Rev. Rul. 89-96, 1989-2 C.B. 114, Rev. Rul. 2007-47 holds that this was not an insurance arrangement. Arrangements that are entered into to manage losses that are at least substantially certain to occur, or that are not the result of fortuitous events, do not constitute insurance. The fortuity principle is central to the notion of what constitutes insurance. Rev. Rul. 2007-47 holds that an arrangement that purports to be an insurance contract that lacks the requisite insurance risk, or fortuity, may instead be characterized as a deposit arrangement, a loan or a contribution to capital, an option or indemnity contract based on the substance of the arrangement between the parties.

Risk shifting occurs if a person facing the possibility of an economic loss transfers some or all of the financial consequences of the potential loss to the insurer such that a loss by the insured does not affect the insured because the loss is offset by a payment from the insurer. See Rev. Rul. 60-275, 1960-2 C.B. 43 (risk shifting not present where subscribers, all subject to the same flood risk, agreed to coverage under a reciprocal flood insurance exchange).

Risk distribution incorporates the statistical phenomenon known as the law of large numbers. The concept of risk distribution "emphasizes the pooling aspect of insurance: that it is the nature of an insurance contract to be part of a larger collection of coverages, combined to distribute risks between insureds." AMERCO and Subsidiaries v. Commissioner, 96 T.C. 18, 41 (1991), aff'd, 979 F.2d 162 (9th Cir. 1992). In Treganowan, 183 F.2d at 291, the court quoting Note, The New York Stock Exchange Gratuity Fund: Insurance That Isn't Insurance, 59 Yale L.J. 780, 784 (1950), explained that "[b]y diffusing the risks through a mass of separate risk shifting contracts, the insurer casts his lot with the law of averages. The process of risk distribution, therefore, is the very essence of insurance." See also Beech Aircraft Corp. v. United States, 797 F.2d 920, 922 (10th Cir. 1986), (risk distribution "means that the party assuming the risk distributes his potential liability, in part, among others"); Ocean Drilling & Exploration Co. v. United States, 988 F.2d 1135, 1153 (Fed. Cir. 1993) ("[r]isk distribution involves spreading the risk of loss among policyholders").

Distributing risk allows the insurer to reduce the possibility that a single costly claim will exceed the amount taken in as premiums and set aside for the payment of such a claim. By assuming numerous relatively small, independent risks that occur over time, the insurer smoothes out losses to match more closely its receipt of premiums. Clougherty Packing Co. v. Commissioner, 811 F.2d 1297, 1300 (9th Cir. 1987). Risk distribution necessarily entails a pooling of premiums, so that a potential insured is not in significant part paying for its own risks. See Humana, Inc. v. Commissioner, 881 F.2d 247, 257 (6th Cir. 1989).

In Situation 1 of Rev. Rul. 2002-89, 2002-2 C.B. 984, S, a wholly owned subsidiary of P, a domestic parent corporation, entered into an annual arrangement with P whereby S provided coverage for P's professional liability risks. The liability coverage S provided to P accounted for 90% of the total risks borne by S. Under the facts of Situation 1 the Service concluded that insurance did not exist for federal income tax purposes. On the other hand, in Situation 2 of Rev. Rul. 2002-89, the premiums that S received from the arrangement with P constituted less than 50% of S's total premiums for the year. Under the facts of Situation 2, the Service reasoned that the premiums and risks of P were pooled with those of unrelated insureds and thus the requisite risk shifting and risk distribution were present. Accordingly, under Situation 2, the arrangement between P and S constituted insurance for federal income tax purposes.

In Rev. Rul. 2002-90, 2002-2 C.B. 985, S, a wholly owned insurance subsidiary of P, directly insured the professional liability risks of 12 operating subsidiaries of its parent. S was adequately capitalized and there were no related guarantees of any kind in favor of S. Most importantly, S and the insured operating subsidiaries conducted themselves in a manner consistent with the standards applicable to an insurance arrangement between unrelated parties. Together, the 12 operating subsidiaries had a significant volume of independent, homogeneous risks. Under the facts presented, the ruling concludes the arrangement between S and each of the 12 operating subsidiaries of S's parent constitutes insurance for federal income tax purposes.

Situation 1 of Rev. Rul. 2005-40, 2005-40 I.R.B. 4, describes a scenario where a domestic corporation operated a large fleet of automotive vehicles in its courier transport business covering a large portion of the United States. This represented a significant volume of independent, homogeneous risks. For valid non-tax business purposes, the transport company entered into an insurance arrangement with an unrelated domestic corporation, whereby in exchange for an agreed amount of "premiums," the domestic carrier "insured" the transport company against the risk of loss arising out of the operation of its fleet in the conduct of its courier business. The unrelated carrier received arm's length premiums, was adequately capitalized, received no guarantees from the courier transport company and was not involved in any loans of funds back to the transport company. The transport company was the carrier's only "insured." While the requisite risk-shifting was seemingly present, the risks assumed by the carrier were not distributed among other insureds or policyholders. Therefore, the arrangement between the carrier and the transport company did not constitute insurance for federal income tax purposes.

The facts in Situation 2 of Rev. Rul. 2005-40 mirror the facts of Situation 1 except that in addition to its arrangement with the transport company, the carrier entered into a second arrangement with another unrelated domestic company. In the second arrangement, the carrier agreed that in exchange for "premiums," it would "insure" the second company against its risk of loss associated with the operation of its own transport fleet. The amount that the carrier received from the second agreement constituted 10% of the total amounts it received during the tax year on a gross and net basis. Thus, 90% of the carrier's business remained with one insured. The revenue ruling concluded that the first arrangement still lacked the requisite risk distribution to constitute insurance even though the scenario involved multiple insureds.

In Situation 4 of Rev. Rul. 2005-40, 12 LLCs elected classification as associations, each contributing between five and 15% of the insurer's total risks. The Service concluded that this transaction constituted insurance for federal income tax purposes.

ANALYSIS:

The principal concern with regard to your activities is whether there is sufficient risk distribution. As discussed above, the idea of risk distribution involves some mathematical concepts. For example, risk distribution is said to incorporate the statistical phenomenon known as the "law of large numbers" whereby distributing risks allows the insurer to reduce the possibility that a single costly claim will exceed the amount taken in as premiums. The concept hinges on the assumption of "numerous relatively small" and "independent risks" that "occur randomly over time." Clougherty Packing Co., supra.

As discussed, in Rev. Rul. 2002-90, the Service concluded that insurance existed where 12 insureds each contributed between five and 15% to the insured's total risks. Similarly, in Situation 4 of Rev. Rul. 2005-40, the Service concluded that insurance existed where 12 LLCs, electing classification as associations, each contributed between five and 15% of the insurer's total risks. Moreover, in Situation 2 of Rev. Rul. 2002-89, supra, the Service concluded that insurance existed where a wholly owned subsidiary insured its parent, but the arrangement represented less than 50% of the insurer's total risk for the year.

The present facts are similar to those under Situation 1 of Rev. Rul. 2002-89, supra, and Situation 2 of Rev. Rul. 2005-40, supra. In Situation 1 of Rev. Rul. 2002-89, supra, the liability coverage provided to the parent corporation by its wholly owned subsidiary accounted for 90% of the total risks borne by the subsidiary. Similarly, in Situation 2 of Rev. Rul. 2005-40, supra, a second insured contributing 10% of the insurer's risks was added to the single-insured scenario of Situation 1. The Service concluded in both of the above scenarios that insurance did not exist because there lacked a sufficient number of insureds to provide for an adequate premium pooling base.

Assuming that all of your contracts do constitute insurable risks, Z% of your total risks for the C tax year are with the ee insureds that compose M. In your case, the fact pattern for the year in question presents a heavy concentration of risks in just a few insureds. In our view, such concentration of risk does not allow the insurer to reduce the possibility that a single costly claim will not exceed the amount of premiums taken in from such a limited number of insureds. Therefore, there is not sufficient risk distribution to conclude that insurance exists. Consequently, you do not qualify as an insurance company.

You appear to rely on Harper Group & Subsidiaries v. Commissioner, 96 T.C. 45 (1991), to support your argument that you qualify as an insurance company. You believe that the court in Harper Group holds that where a single-insured paid 71% of the total premium, risk distribution was sufficient to qualify the arrangement as insurance. Because less than 70% of your risk is from M, you assert that the arrangement should qualify as insurance under Harper Group. This is a misunderstanding of Harper Group. In Harper Group, 67% to 71% of the total premiums received for the years at issue were not related to a single policyholder. Rather, the 67% to 71% were the total percentages received from all related policyholders, including brother-sister corporations (a total of 13 entities). The court's analysis in Harper Group must be read in its entirety and all the facts and circumstances must be considered, i.e. that there are 13 entities making up the nearly two thirds risk concentration in all the years at issue. The Service took a similar position in Rev. Rul. 2002-90, concluding that insurance existed in an arrangement involving 12 insureds, each contributing between five and 15% of the insurer's total risks. Moreover, in situation 4 of Rev. Rul. 2005-40, the Service concluded that insurance existed where

12 LLCs, electing classification as associations, each contributed between five and 15% of the insurer's total risks. Also, in situation 2 of Rev. Rul. 2002-89, the Service concluded that insurance existed where a wholly owned subsidiary insured its parent, but the arrangement represented less than 50% of the insurer's total risk for the year.

Based on the above discussion of the facts of Harper Group and the cited revenue rulings, the court's analysis in Harper Group supports the Service's position that you do not qualify as an insurance company.

CONCLUSION:

Because you do not qualify as an insurance company for federal income tax purposes, you fail to meet the requirement of section 501(c)(15) of the Code. Therefore, you do not qualify for exemption under section 501(c)(15) and must file federal income tax returns.

You have the right to file a protest if you believe this determination is incorrect. To protest, you must submit a statement of your views and fully explain your reasoning. You must submit the statement, signed by one of your officers, within 30 days from the date of this letter. We will consider your statement and decide if the information affects our determination.

Your protest statement should be accompanied by the following declaration:

> Under penalties of perjury, I declare that I have examined this protest statement, including accompanying documents, and, to the best of my knowledge and belief, the statement contains all the relevant facts, and such facts are true, correct, and complete.

You also have a right to request a conference to discuss your protest. This request should be made when you file your protest statement. An attorney, certified public accountant, or an individual enrolled to practice before the Internal Revenue

Service may represent you. If you want representation during the conference procedures, you must file a proper power of attorney, Form 2848, Power of Attorney and Declaration of Representative, if you have not already done so. For more information about representation, see Publication 947, Practice before the IRS and Power of Attorney. All forms and publications mentioned in this letter can be found at www.irs.gov, Forms and Publications.

If you do not intend to protest this determination, you do not need to take any further action. If we do not hear from you within 30 days, we will issue a final adverse determination letter. That letter will provide information about filing tax returns and other matters. Please send your protest statement, Form 2848 and any supporting documents to this address:

Internal Revenue Service
SE:T:EO:RA:T:3, PE-3L7
Attn: *****
1111 Constitution Ave, N.W.
Washington, DC 20224

You may also fax your statement using the fax number shown in the heading of this letter. If you fax your statement, please call the person identified in the heading of this letter to confirm that he or she received your fax. If you have any questions, please contact the person whose name and telephone number are shown in the heading of this letter.

Sincerely, *****, Director, Exempt Organizations, Rulings & Agreements.

PRIVATE LETTER RULING 201219009

Private Letter Ruling 201219009, February 3, 2012

This is in response to the letter submitted by Company dated September 12, 2011, primarily requesting a ruling under § 831 relating to Company's status as an insurance company for federal income tax purposes.

FACTS

Company was incorporated in Foreign Country M and started insurance operations on Date A. Company has been issued a Class 2 Association License by the Insurance Regulator of Foreign County effective for Year B. Also effective for Year B, Company has made an election under § 953(d) to be taxed as a domestic corporation. All of the stock of Company is owned one-half by Individual A and one-half percent by Individual B.

Insured Partnership specializes in O surgery and utilizes a variety of specialized and sophisticated medical equipment and lasers in order to perform their surgical procedures. Individuals A, B and C each own a one third ownership interest in the Insured Partnership.

Company offers the Insured Partnership insurance coverage which comprise the following four types of contracts: (1) P policy, (2) employment related practices liability policy, (3) executive liability policy, and (4) commercial crime policy.

The most significant policy is the P policy. This policy is a package policy that contains coverage for buildings, business personal property, business income and extra expense, legal defense and other business related coverages. The employment-related practices liability policy provides coverage for liability arising out of claims for injury to an employee because of an employment-related offence, as well as a duty to defend. The executive liability coverage policy provides two coverages: one applies to liability arising out of claims for wrongful acts or interrelated wrongful acts committed by the named company's directors or officers, the other is a corporate reimbursement coverage that applies to claims for which the named company is legally obligated to indemnify its directors or officers when such claims involve wrongful acts or interrelated wrongful acts committed by them. The commercial crime policy covers business losses due to employee theft of money, securities, other property of the insured, including client's property on the client's premises.

In order to achieve its overall risk distribution, Company participates in a reinsurance pool consisting of Number Q independent insurers (Independent Insurers 1 to 14) in addition to Company. These other insurers and their insureds are unrelated to Company and Company's insured (Insured Partnership). Thus, while Company, as a direct writer, receives premiums from its insured under Coinsurance Agreement A (a pro rata indemnity reinsurance treaty) it cedes Number R percent of these directly written premiums on each line it insures to the reinsurance pool. Further, using Coinsurance Agreement B (another pro rata indemnity reinsurance agreement), Company will then assume a quota share of the premiums from the reinsurance pool which is roughly equivalent in dollar terms to the amount it ceded on each line of insurance.

The following applies to all of the insurers participating in the reinsurance pool:

All insurers issue insurance contracts and charge premiums for the insurance coverage provided under their respective insurance contracts. All insureds use recognized actuarial techniques, based, in part, on commercial rates for similar coverage, in order to determine the premiums charged to an individual insured.

Each of the insurers pools all the premiums it receives in its general funds and pays claims out of those funds. Each insurer investigates any claim made by an insured to determine the validity of the claim prior to making payment on that claim. Each insurer conducts no business other than the issuing and administering of insurance contracts.

No insured has any obligation to pay any insurer additional premiums if that insured's actual losses during any period of coverage exceed the premiums paid by that insured. Premiums paid by any insured may be used to satisfy claims of the other insureds. No insured that terminates its insurance coverage is required to make additional premium or capital payments to that insurer to cover losses in excess of its premiums paid.

There is a real possibility that an insurer will sustain a loss in excess of the premiums it has received from its insureds. Finally, Company is not related to any other of the Number Q insurers participating in the reinsurance pool, nor is Company related to any of the Number S independent insureds who are directly insured by any of the Number Q other insurers participating in the reinsurance pool.

As a result of Company's participation in the reinsurance pool, the written premiums of Company will, generally, have the following characteristics on each line of coverage it insures: (a) Company will assume (in total) risks from the more than 12 independent policyholders with respect to insured businesses of these policyholders, and (b) no single insured will account for more than 15 percent of the total risks assumed by Company. Also, it is represented that there are no guarantees of Company's obligations by Individuals A, B, C or any other related person. In addition, Company states that it is well capitalized.

LAW AND ANALYSIS

Section 831(a) of the Internal Revenue Code provides that taxes, computed as provided in § 11, are imposed for each taxable year on the taxable income of each insurance company other than a life insurance company. Section 831(c) provides that, for purposes of § 831, the term "insurance company" has the meaning given to such term by § 816(a). Under § 816(a), the term "insurance company" means "any company more than half of the business of which during the taxable year is the issuing of insurance or annuity contracts or the reinsuring of risks underwritten by insurance companies."

Neither the Code nor the regulations define the terms "insurance" or "insurance contract" in the context of property and casualty insurance. The Supreme Court of the United States has explained that in order for an arrangement to constitute insurance for federal income tax purposes, both risk shifting and risk distribution must be present. Helvering v. LeGierse, 312 U.S. 531 (1941). The risk transferred must be risk of economic loss. Allied Fidelity Corp. v. Commissioner, 572 F.2d 1190, 1193 (7th Cir. 1978). The risk must contemplate the fortuitous occurrence of a stated contingency, Commissioner v. Treganowan, 183 F.2d 288, 290-291 (2d Cir. 1950), and must not be merely an investment or business risk. Rev. Rul. 2007-47, 2007-2 C.B. 127. In addition, the arrangement must constitute insurance in the commonly accepted sense. See, e.g., Ocean Drilling & Exploration Co. v. United States, 988 F.2d 1135, 1153 (Fed. Cir. 1993); AMERCO, Inc. v. Commissioner, 979 F.2d 162 (9th Cir. 1992).

Risk shifting occurs if a person facing the possibility of an economic loss transfers some or all of the financial consequences of the potential loss to the insurer such that a loss by the insured does not affect the insured because the loss is offset by a payment from the insurer. Risk distribution incorporates the statistical phenomenon known as the law of large numbers. Distributing risk allows the insurer to reduce the possibility that a single costly claim will exceed the amount taken in as premiums and set aside for the payment of such a claim. By assuming numerous relatively small, independent risks that occur randomly over time, the insurer smooths out losses to match more closely its receipt of premiums. Clougherty Packing Co. v. Commissioner, 811 F.2d 1297, 1300 (9th Cir. 1987).

Courts have recognized that risk distribution necessarily entails a pooling of premiums, so that a potential insured is not in significant part paying for its own risks. Humana, Inc. v. Commissioner, 881 F.2d 247, 257 (6th Cir. 1989). See also Ocean Drilling and Exploration Co., 988 F.2d at 1153 ("Risk distribution involves spreading the risk of loss among policyholders."); Beech Aircraft Corp. v United States, 797 F.2d 920, 922 (10th Cir. 1986) ("[R]isk distributing means that the party assuming the risk distributes his potential liability, in part, among others.") On the other hand, a purported insurance arrangement where an issuer who contracts with only one policyholder and retains the risk under such contract does not qualify as an insurance contract for federal income tax purposes. See Rev. Rul. 2005-40, 2005-2 C.B. 4.

Rev. Rul. 2002-89, 2002-2 C.B. 984, set forth circumstances under which arrangements between a domestic parent corporation and its wholly owned subsidiary constitute insurance and explained that a parent/wholly owned subsidiary arrangement does not constitute insurance if the parent accounts for 90 percent of the risk, but does if other insureds constititute more than 50 percent of the risk.

Rev. Rul. 2002-90, 2002-2 C.B. 985, holds that an arrangement between a licensed insurance subsidiary of parent, and each of the 12 of parent's operating subsidiaries where, inter alia, no one subsidiary accounts for less than 5 percent nor more than 15 percent of the total risk insured by the insurance subsidiary constitutes insurance.

In Rev. Rul. 2002-91, 2002-2 C.B. 991, holds than an arrangement involving a group of unrelated businesses of which, inter alia, none accounted for more than 15 percent of the total insured risk constitutes insurance.

Rev. Rul. 2005-40, applies the principles of Rev. Ruls. 2002-89 and 2002-90 to situations involving corporations and single member limited liability companies.

As pointed out in the law background of Rev. Rul. 2009-26, 2009-38 I.R.B. 366, the Internal Revenue Code of 1986 and administrative guidance treat reinsurance in an manner similar to direct insurance for many purposes: for example, both direct insurance and reinsurance business may qualify a taxpayer as an insurance company under § 816(a) or 831(c), as applicable./1/

In Alinco Life Insurance Co. v. United States, 373 F.2d 336 (Ct. Cl. 1967) a large finance company formed a wholly-owned subsidiary corporation (Alinco), which qualified as a life insurance company under the laws of Indiana. Customers of the finance company (borrowers) purchased credit life insurance from an unrelated insurance company, which in turn reinsured a fixed proportion of those contracts with Alinco.

Even though Alinco reinsured risks underwritten by only one insurance company, those risks aggregated nearly one billion dollars of business, with a large number of customers, for which Alinco was required by the state insurance department to maintain reserves. Interpreting regulatory language that was identical to what now appears in § 816(a), the court concluded that Alinco was in the business of "reinsuring risks" underwritten by insurance companies.

Section 162(a) of the Internal Revenue Code provides, in part, that there shall be allowed as a deduction all of the ordinary and necessary expenses paid or incurred during the taxable year in carrying on any trade or business.

Section 1.162-1(a) of the Income Tax Regulations provides, in part, that among the items included in business expenses are insurance premiums against fire, storms, theft, accident, or other similar losses in the case of a business.

In the present situation, under Coinsurance Agreement A, Company contributes a substantial amount of its direct consideration (received from its insureds) and associated risks to the pool, and under Coinsurance Agreement B, receives a quota share of the consideration and associated risks from the pool roughly equal in dollar terms to Number R percent of the amount Company ceded to the pool on each line of coverage. The result is that there are a significant number of unrelated covered entities such that none is paying for a significant portion of its own risk. Accordingly, given that insurance risks are covered, the arrangement achieves adequate risk shifting and risk distribution such that the contracts issued by Company to its insureds constitute insurance for federal income tax purposes. For the year for which the predicate facts were represented, this appears to be more than half of Company's business.

CONCLUSION

Based solely on the information submitted and the representations made, and provided that Company is adequately capitalized and continues to operate as a participant in the pool (in the manner described above), we conclude that the arrangement between Insured Partnership and Company constitutes insurance for federal income tax purposes, such that the consideration paid by the insured to Company is eligible to meet the definition of insurance premiums under § 1.162-1(a) of the Income Tax Regulations, and Company would qualify under Part II of subchapter L for the taxable year if it were a domestic corporation.

CAVEATS

Except as expressly provided herein, no opinion is expressed in this letter ruling under the provisions of any other section of the Code or Regulations. Further, no opinion is expressed as to the federal income tax consequences of the transaction described above if Company makes any loans to its affiliated insureds or parties related thereto. No opinion is expressed as to whether or not the amount of premiums charged by Company has been calculated correctly or whether other requirements under § 162 have been met. See e.g., Rev. Rul. 2007-3, 2007-1 C.B. 350. Further, no opinion has been requested and none has been expressed as to whether the reinsurance pool is an entity for federal income tax purposes. This ruling letter is directed only to the taxpayer who requested it. Section 6110(k)(3) of the Code provides that it may not be used or cited as precedent.

/1/

On the other hand, § 845 which grants to the Secretary explicit authority to reallocate, recharacterize, or make other adjustments with respect to certain reinsurance arrangements does not refer to direct insurance.

PRIVATE LETTER RULING 201350008

Private Letter Ruling 201350008, December 13, 2013

Pursuant to section 7.07(2)(a) of Rev. Proc. 2012-1, 2012-1 I.R.B. 1, 30, this is to notify you that we were unable to rule on a letter ruling request submitted by Company regarding section 831 of the Internal Revenue Code (the "Code").

Company was incorporated in Foreign Jurisdiction on Date and is licensed as an insurance company by the insurance regulators of Foreign Jurisdiction. Company made a permanent election under section 953(d) of the Code to be taxed as a domestic corporation for federal tax purposes and it annually files a Form 1120-PC tax return. Company's U.S. address is Address.

Company directly issued purported insurance contracts with a one year coverage period to Insured Affiliate 1 and Insured Affiliate 2 (collectively, the "Insured Affiliates"). Company joined a reinsurance pool (the "Pool") consisting of several other unrelated purported insurance companies. Under the reinsurance agreements Company ceded to the Pool a substantial portion of its direct written premiums and risks and assumed from the Pool a roughly equal amount of premiums and risks. The agreements contained language providing for experience refunds and experience loss carryforwards, which were to be paid back with interest.

Company sought two rulings:

1. That Company would be treated as an insurance

company under section 831of the Code for federal tax purposes.

2. That the purported insurance premiums paid to Company by Insured Affiliates would be deductible as "insurance premiums" under section 162 of the Code for federal tax purposes.

LAW AND ANALYSIS

Section 831(a) of the Code provides that taxes, computed as provided in section 11, are imposed for each taxable year on the taxable income of each insurance company other than a life insurance company. Section 831(c) provides that, for purposes of section 831, the term "insurance company" has the meaning given to such term by section 816(a). Under section 816(a), the term "insurance company" means "any company more than half of the business of which during the taxable year is the issuing of insurance or annuity contracts or the reinsuring of risks underwritten by insurance companies."

Neither the Code nor the Income Tax Regulations define the terms "insurance" or "insurance contract" in the context of property and casualty insurance. The Supreme Court of the United States has explained that in order for an arrangement to constitute insurance for federal tax purposes, both risk shifting and risk distribution must be present. Helvering v. Le Gierse, 312 U.S. 531 (1941). The risk transferred must be risk of economic loss. Allied Fidelity Corp. v. Commissioner, 572 F.2d 1190, 1193 (7th Cir. 1978). The risk must contemplate the fortuitous occurrence of a stated contingency, Commissioner v. Treganowan, 183 F.2d 288, 290-291 (2d Cir. 1950), and must not be merely an investment or business risk. Rev. Rul. 2007-47, 2007-2 C.B. 127. In addition, the arrangement must constitute insurance in the commonly accepted sense. See, e.g., Ocean Drilling & Exploration Co. v. United States, 988 F.2d 1135, 1153 (Fed. Cir. 1993); AMERCO, Inc. v. Commissioner, 979 F.2d 162 (9th Cir. 1992).

Our review of the materials that Company submitted in

connection with its letter ruling request led us to identify three areas of concern:

1. Whether the pooling arrangement actually provided risk shifting and risk distribution. In particular, we were concerned that the reinsurance agreements between Company and the Pool contained provisions whose net effect might be to negate risk shifting and risk distribution.

2. Whether some or all of the purported insurance contracts were insurance for federal tax purposes, as opposed to, for example, contracts covering investment or business risks.

3. Whether the premiums paid by Insured Affiliates to Company reflected an arms- length transaction between the parties.

The Company did not provide sufficient information for us to address these concerns. Accordingly, we are unable to rule pursuant to sections 10.06 and 15.10(1)(c) of Rev. Proc. 2012-1.

Had we been able to rule, the letter ruling would have been controlling for only the year specified in the letter ruling because section 831(c) imposes an annual test and the specific contracts involved covered risks for only a one year period.

This writing may contain privileged information. Any unauthorized disclosure of this writing may undermine our ability to protect the privileged information. If disclosure is determined to be necessary, please contact this office for our views.

Lightning Source UK Ltd.
Milton Keynes UK
UKHW050424151019
351327UK00015B/125/P